Among the Indians

HENRY A. BOLLER IN INDIAN COSTUME

AMONG THE INDIANS

Four Years on the Upper Missouri, 1858-1862

Henry A. Boller

Edited by Milo Milton Quaife

A
BISON
BOOK

UNIVERSITY OF NEBRASKA PRESS

LINCOLN AND LONDON

This volume reproduces the text and footnotes of chapters one through thirty-three of *Among the Indians: Eight Years in the Far West, 1858–1866,* through the courtesy of The Lakeside Classics, published by R. R. Donnelley & Sons Co., who are the sole proprietors of the special contents. The subtitle of this edition has been changed to: *Four Years on the Upper Missouri, 1858–1862.*

International Standard Book Number 0–8032–5714–7

Library of Congress Catalog Card Number 76–100810

First Bison Book printing: October 1972

Most recent printing shown by first digit below:

3   4   5   6   7   8   9   10

Manufactured in the United States of America

CONTENTS

v

INTRODUCTION

[*This Introduction has been condensed from the "Historical Introduction" by Milo Milton Quaife in the Lakeside Classics edition of* Among the Indians. *All quotations are from this source.*]

HENRY A. BOLLER was born in Philadelphia on August 17, 1836, the son of a prosperous importer. As a boy he was entranced by narratives of Indian life and adventure. The walls of his playroom were ornamented with drawings of Indians he had made, guided by one of George Catlin's books, and he recruited his own band of Indians from among the boys in the neighborhood. In 1852 he enrolled in the University of Pennsylvania, but his thoughts were "afar upon the open boundless prairies of the West," and he dropped out of college in his senior year. In a letter to his father, dated March 23, 1857, Boller speaks of his interest in travel and the Indians, and asks approval for making a voyage to China or India. Permission was not forthcoming, but a few weeks later he and his father traveled to St. Louis. Subsequent events show that the purpose of the trip probably was to explore the possibilities of entering into the fur trade. In the spring of the following year, young Boller returned to St. Louis where he enrolled as a clerk in the "Opposition" trading firm of Clark, Primeau and Company.

For a generation or more prior to the conclusion of its operations in 1866 the American Fur Company dominated the trade of the Upper Missouri area. Rival firms and partnerships, commonly known as the "Opposition," flourished and failed with bewildering rapidity, and it is frequently difficult to determine who their members were, or when they began or concluded their operations. In 1858 the firm of Clark, Primeau and Company was operating two posts, one among the Blackfeet high up the Missouri and the other at the Mandan—Gros Ventre village site which is better known by the name of Fort Berthold. The "Company" in the firm name was evidently a trader named Atkinson, concerning whom almost no information has been found. He was important enough, however, to have the "fort" to which Boller was assigned named in his honor. The other partners were Charles Primeau and Malcolm Clark, both of whom were veteran traders.

Boller departed upriver on May 23, 1858, and remained at Fort Atkinson until the spring of 1860. At that time the firm of Clark, Primeau and Company was absorbed by the American Fur Company, and Boller returned to St. Louis, expecting to go back to his home in the East. But

> while awaiting the closing of his accounts in the office of Robert Campbell he encountered Charles Larpenteur, another derelict trader. . . . Larpenteur wished to continue in the fur trade and from the ensuing discussions the new firm of Larpenteur, Smith and Company was evolved.[1] Members of the Company in

[1] The editor notes that "both Larpenteur and Boller have recorded the history of the company somewhat fully, although Boller's account was left unfinished. The two accounts are so contradictory in numerous material respects that it seems hopeless to attempt to reconcile them. . . . I chiefly follow Boller's narrative. The reader may find Larpenteur's side of the story in his *Forty Years a Fur Trader on the Upper Missouri, 1833–1872* [Elliott Coues, ed., New York, 1898; Milo Milton Quaife, ed., Chicago, The Lakeside Classics, 1933]. According to him, Smith was able to put $4000 into the firm and Boller agreed to obtain 'by telegraph' $2000 from his father. Larpenteur expected to obtain his share of the capital from Robert Campbell, while Lemon's contribution remains unrecorded. Boller states, however, that Larpenteur contributed no capital, his knowledge of Indians and the fur trade being accepted as his contribution."

addition to Larpenteur and Boller were "Old Jeff" Smith, a veteran trader, who more recently had been employed by the American Fur Company at Fort Berthold, and Robert Lemon, a clerk of Robert Campbell at St. Louis, who seems to have had no prior experience as a trader.

Seldom has a more unfortunate partnership existed. Larpenteur, a veteran of twenty-five years in the fur trade, entertained delusions of grandeur and throughout a long lifetime exhibited an unusual facility for quarreling with his associates. In particular, he resented the advice of Smith, like himself a veteran of the fur trade, and Boller, whom he characterized as "a young blatherskite." The two partners in their turn suspected Larpenteur of dishonesty (quite probably unjustly) and unknown to him intrigued with Lemon to undermine him.

Because there was no longer an Opposition steamboat operating on the Missouri, the partners were forced to send their goods by steamboat up the Mississippi to St. Paul, whence they would be conveyed overland by wagon to their Upper Missouri destination. It was mid-August before the Company was fairly organized, and while Smith and Lemon stayed in St. Louis to complete buying supplies, Boller and Larpenteur went to St. Paul to make arrangement for the overland journey.

. . . In due time Smith and Lemon arrived from St. Louis with the goods and all three partners pushed the work of loading the wagons. While thus enagaged, with coats off and "working like beavers," Larpenteur [who had been visiting relatives] appeared resplendent in gloves and polished boots, and politely inquired how his "young men" were getting along. This was too much for "Old Jeff" Smith, who responded with a torrent of curses, at which Larpenteur visibly paled, and removing his gloves went dazedly to work. . . . Although Boller endeavored to patch up the quarrel, Smith and Larpenteur remained enemies from this time onward.

At length all was in readiness and the wagons were driven a mile from the levee where a temporary camp was made. The train comprising seven wagons (eight according to Larpenteur), fourteen yokes of cattle, three horses, and fourteen men, proceeded without special incident to the point beyond Pembina where the caravan was to separate into two parties. Here Boller and Smith digressed southward to their old station at Fort Berthold, while Larpenteur and Lemon continued westward to their intended post among the Assiniboines above the mouth of the Yellowstone.

At Fort Berthold Boller and Smith established themselves in one of the native earthen
dwellings, which they improved to suit the
purposes of a trading house, in which they
operated throughout the winter. Larpenteur
represents that he had a highly successful
season, while Smith and Boller secretly intrigued with Lemon to counteract his assumed
design to rob them of their share of the furs.
In March (1861) Boller journeyed to Fort
Stuart (Larpenteur's post) to learn the state
of affairs there. The end of the season was now
close at hand and Boller urged that the winter's harvest of furs be taken to St. Louis by
way of the overland route to St. Paul which
had been followed on the outward journey
the preceeding summer. He was outvoted by
Larpenteur and Lemon, however, and early
in July (Smith and Boller having gone in
advance) Larpenteur departed with the furs
for St. Louis in a 65-foot Mackinaw boat
which he had constructed for this purpose.

In St. Louis that summer the firm was re-
organized. According to Larpenteur's account,
he and Lemon remained the dominant partners, Smith was dropped, and Boller was
permitted to retain a small share in the
Company on condition that he remain away
from the Upper Missouri. However, in a
chronological outline which Boller made

when revising *Among the Indians,* he recorded: "1862: Dissolved the fur company after a prosperous trade and returned in the fall from the Upper Missouri."

In any event, Boller returned to Philadelphia, where, in March of 1863, he became secretly engaged to Mary Parsons. From May, 1863, until the spring of 1864, he was again in the West at the newly discovered Montana gold field and Salt Lake. He returned briefly to Philadelphia and then again left for Montana, this time staying more than two years. In 1866 Boller went to California to procure a herd of horses for the Montana market, and in July of that year returned to the East. On November 15, he was married to Mary Parsons.

Mrs. Boller frequently contributed to *Lippincott's Magazine* and *Harper's Bazaar,* and it is probable that she encouraged her husband to write the story of his adventures.

At any rate the book was written, its contents following closely the daily "Journals" or diaries which Boller had kept during his stay in the Indian country. The signed preface which it included is dated "Philadelphia, July, 1867," and the book was published, apparently, later in the same year. [The title page gives the date

as 1868, but a long critical review of the book
was published in the *Nation* on November
28, 1867.] For some unexplained reason it
supplied the reader with no information concerning the Author's background, nor any
hint of his two-year's experience as a partner
in Larpenteur, Smith, and Company. Left
unexplained also were Boller's several removals
during the eight-year western sojourn. In fact,
the title (quite possibly provided by the publisher) *Among the Indians: Eight Years in the
Far West, 1858–1862* tends to confuse the
reader, for only the four years from 1858 to
1862 were actually passed "among the Indians."

From 1868 until 1878, Boller and his family lived in Junction City, Kansas, where he
was in the cattle business. They then moved
to Denver, where Boller was employed first as
an insurance agent and subsequently was con-
nected with various real estate firms. In 1898
he was urged by Elliott Coues to revise his
book, but he died on November 1, 1902, with
the revision incomplete.

A Note on the Text

This edition of *Among the Indians* omits
the final ten chapters of the original work
(pages 357-436 in The Lakeside Classics edition), which sketched Boller's experiences in

Montana, described Salt Lake and the Mormon community, and gave his views on the "Indian question." As the editor pointed out, only the four years that Boller was a fur trader were actually spent among the Indians, and it is his narrative of these years that has unique value and interest today. "From the viewpoint of Boller's future readers," wrote Dr. Quaife, "his entrance upon the fur trade occurred at an opportune moment. The Indian tribes of the area were in a state of transition and his four-year sojourn at Fort Atkinson afforded almost the last opportunity to observe the red man's primitive way of life. Through the magic of Boller's sympathetic pages his readers are afforded a remarkably realistic picture of the ideals and the daily life of the Indian as he existed a century ago."

Among the Indians

PREFACE

THE following pages have been written from a journal and notes kept during my residence of eight years in the Far West. I have endeavored to narrate truthfully and without exaggeration only such incidents as fell under my personal observation, and also to portray faithfully Indian life in its home aspect.

At the present time, when the Indian is being held up before the world as an incarnate fiend, it is but fair that his redeeming qualities should likewise be recorded.

I shall ever look back upon the years spent in the Indian country as among the pleasantest of my life, and if in all my dealings with white men I had found the same sense of honor that characterized my savage friends, my appreciation of human nature would be much higher.

Philadelphia, July, 1867

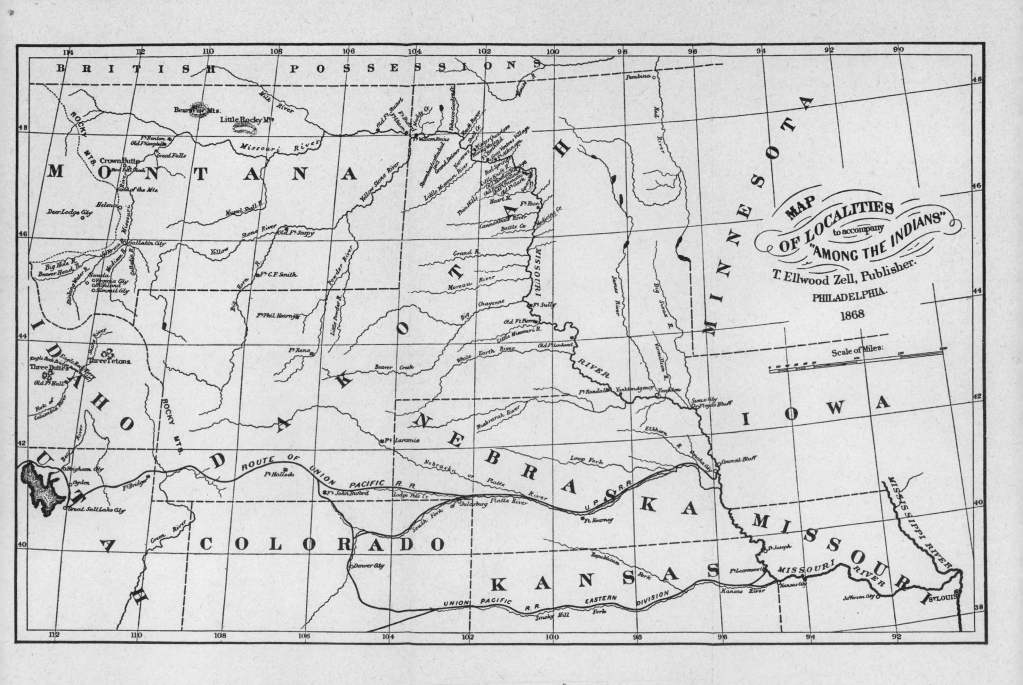

MAP
OF LOCALITIES
to accompany
"AMONG THE INDIANS"
T. Ellwood Zell, Publisher.
PHILADELPHIA.
1868

Scale of Miles:

BRITISH POSSESSIONS

MONTANA

IDAHO

DAKOTA

MINNESOTA

IOWA

NEBRASKA

UTAH

COLORADO

KANSAS

MISSOURI

ROUTE OF UNION PACIFIC R.R.

UNION PACIFIC R.R. EASTERN DIVISION

Missouri River

MISSISSIPPI RIVER

St. Louis

Among the Indians

Chapter I

Fur Trade and Navigation on the Upper Missouri

AT no period in its history has the Great West attracted such universal interest as the present. From the discovery of gold on the Pacific Coast to the magnificent enterprises which are now being inaugurated, the changes have succeeded each other with wonderful rapidity. The daring of the pioneers who first explored the fastnesses of the Rocky Mountains, the toilsome emigration to Oregon and California, the constantly increasing commerce of the Plains, the telegraph, the daily mail stage, and now, last and greatest, the Pacific Railroad—all these changes in an ordinary lifetime![1]

[1]Completion of the Pacific Railroad in 1869 signalized the attainment of a quarter-century-old dream. At Promontory, Utah on May 10, 1869 the Central Pacific, building eastward from California, and the Union Pacific, building westward from Omaha, were formally united in a picturesque ceremony. Prayers were recited, "grandiloquent" speeches delivered, the last golden spike was driven with a silver hammer by President Leland Stanford of the Central Pacific, and its final strokes were broadcast

Of the various great fur companies that formerly thrived and flourished, with their wild array of retainers, the Hudson's Bay alone remains, and is every year becoming more and more circumscribed in its sphere of action. It is also the oldest, having been chartered in 1670 by Charles the Second, and granted almost unlimited powers. The North West Company, established in 1783, was for a time a most formidable rival. Next came the Mackinac Company, which claimed the trade of the country watered by the Mississippi and its tributary streams; the Rocky Mountain Fur Company in 1808, with its headquarters at St. Louis; and the American Fur Company in 1809, under the auspices of John Jacob Astor. Besides these, there were minor associations and numerous individual traders.[2]

throughout the land by telegraphic connections. To complete the ceremony two facing locomotives moved forward until their noses touched and a one-word telegram "Done" was broadcast. In subsequent decades additional transcontinental lines were constructed, the most recent one the "Milwaukee" road, begun in 1847 as the Milwaukee and Waukesha, and completed in 1909 as the Chicago, St. Paul, and Pacific.

[2] For a more comprehensive sketch of these early companies see the Introduction to Charles Larpenteur, *Forty Years a Fur Trader on the Upper Missouri,* the Lakeside Classics volume for 1933. The Hudson's Bay Company still flourishes throughout western Canada, having adapted itself to changing conditions by maintaining

department stores in various cities. The North West Company, for almost half a century the vigorous competitor of the Hudson's Bay Company for the fur-trade of interior America, came into existence during the opening years of the American Revolution when several Montreal traders pooled their interests for mutual advantage. Unlike its great rival, the North West Company was never a corporation, and its component interests changed from time to time.

One such change was marked by the reorganization which occurred in 1783. Barred from access to the interior by way of Hudson Bay, the North-Westers utilized canoes and mackinaw boats to develop the Ottawa River route to the Upper Great Lakes and beyond to the distant reaches of the Far Northwest. In 1821 the long rivalry of the two companies was terminated by their amalgamation under the name of the older organization. The North-Westers, writes Historian Grace Lee Nute, "had had nearly fifty years of valorous exploration and trail-blazing; they had forced the Hudson's Bay Company to build forts in the interior; they had developed the voyageur to the acme of his unique service ability; they had discovered a way to maintain a canoe route to the Pacific through the use of pemmican, a concentrate of buffalo meat and grease; and they had contributed an éclat to the fur trade that gives it a charm forever in American and Canadian annals." Sketch in *Dict. Am. Hist.*

The Mackinac Company was organized toward the close of the eighteenth century by a group of traders who maintained their headquarters on Mackinac Island and operated westward and southward in the Mississippi River area. Following the return of Lewis and Clark from their exploring expedition to the Pacific in 1804–1806, St. Louis merchants dispatched trading outfits to the Upper Missouri and presently organized the Missouri Fur Company. At this juncture John Jacob Astor sought admission to the Company and being rebuffed organized the American Fur Company in 1808 with a design for expansion of imperial scope. Boller, who had no personal knowledge of

St. Louis, formerly a frontier village, inhabited principally by French Creoles, and a general rendezvous for traders and trappers, whence they started on their long and perilous journeys, is now the leading city in the Mississippi Valley. The Mackinaw boat has given place to the steamboat; the cordelle, or towing-line, has been superseded by the steam engine.[3]

this earlier period, misstates the date and, more seriously, seems to confuse the Company with the subsequent Rocky Mountain Fur Company, organized by William H. Ashley and William Henry in 1822. Until its voluntary dissolution in 1834, the latter Company operated vigorously in the upper Missouri River area and beyond to the Pacific. Meanwhile Astor, the greatest figure in the history of the American fur trade, established a Western Department of the American Fur Company at St. Louis. For a few years it confined its activities to the Lower Missouri. Following its absorption of the Columbia Fur Company in 1827, however, it extended its operations to the Upper Missouri, where it remained the dominant figure for forty years. Astor retired from the organization in 1834, selling his interest in the Western Department to Pratte, Chouteau and Company of St. Louis. Until 1866 this organization and its successors continued to operate on the Upper Missouri under the name of the American Fur Company. In 1858 Boller, young and inexperienced, appeared upon the scene as a member of one of the "Opposition" companies to begin the career to which his narrative is devoted.

[3] Like the gay-colored Mackinaw blanket coat, the Mackinaw boat celebrates the fame of the ancient fur-trade center on Mackinac Island. Evolved from the birch-bark canoe of the Indian, it was first used by the Montreal traders and others in the Upper Great Lakes area. With the

There are yet voyageurs living who have been
on the cordelle from Independence, Missouri to
Fort Benton, a distance of nearly three thousand
miles. The most incessant and persevering toil
was necessary to stem the turbulent current,
and the hardy voyageurs never hesitated for a
moment to plunge into the water, reckless of
heat or cold, when the shifting channel made it

extension of the fur trade to the Missouri River it became
the indispensable vehicle of navigation upon that river
and its principal tributaries. Perhaps the best description
of it as it was developed on the Great Lakes is found in
Henry R. Schoolcraft's *Narrative Journal of Travels
through the Northwestern Regions of the United States* . . . .
in the Year 1820 (Albany, 1821) 67–70. For another description see Mrs. John H. Kinzie, *Wau-Bun. The "Early
Day" in the Northwest*, the Lakeside Classics volume for
1932, pp. 42–43.

On the Missouri, with different sources of supply and
different navigational conditions, the Mackinaw boat underwent considerable changes from its Great Lakes proto-
type. In particular, much larger boats were built. The
Great Lakes vehicle might be 30 or more feet long and 6 or
7 wide, with a cargo-carrying capacity of four tons, in
addition to the crew of several men. Charles Larpenteur,
however, on one occasion built a boat 65 feet long and 11
feet beam. On another down-river voyage he had a fleet of
eight boats, each carrying 250 packs of buffalo robes,
weighing probably 12 tons or more, exclusive of crew and
supplies. For descriptions of the Missouri River Mackinaw
boat see Hiram M. Chittenden. *Early Steamboat Navigation on the Missouri River* . . . . (2 vols., New York, 1903),
I, 94–96; Philippe Régis De Trobriand, *Army Life in
Dakota*, the Lakeside Classics volume for 1941, pp.
98–100.

necessary to cross from point to point.[4] In 1832 the American Fur Company ascended with a steamboat as high as Fort Union, six miles above the mouth of the Yellowstone. This was the second grand link in the chain of events. The cordelle was now reduced to seven hundred miles, that being the distance between Fort Union and the Blackfoot post. For a number of years the Fur Company's steamboat regularly made its annual trip, and the subject of navigating the upper river was as often talked of.

In 1850 the *El Paso* ascended without difficulty as high as the Round Butte, a distance of perhaps three hundred miles. In the summer of 1859 the Fur Company sent up, in addition to their annual steamer, a small stern-wheel boat, called the *Chippewa,* drawing very little water, expressly to make the attempt, which was entirely successful; and to Mr. Charles P. Chouteau[5] of the American Fur Company and Captain John B. La Barge[6] of

[4] Charles Larpenteur has recorded a vivid description of the difficulties of cordelling on the Missouri. In 1846 he required seventy days of arduous toil to ascend from Fort Union to Fort Benton, proceeding much of the time at the rate of one and one-half miles per hour. *Forty Years a Fur Trader,* Chap. *13.*

[5] The son of Pierre Chouteau, Jr., long the leading figure in the affairs of the Western Department of the American Fur Company.

[6] Younger brother of Captain Joseph M. La Barge (for whom see *post*, p. 357) and a veteran navigator of the

the *Chippewa,* belongs the credit of proving
that the Missouri River was navigable by steam
to within a few miles of the Great Falls.[7]

Upper Missouri. To him vitriol-tongued Charles Larpenteur awarded the distinction of being the meanest man
he ever knew. La Barge dropped dead at the wheel of his
vessel while making a landing at Bismarck in 1885.

[7] Boller's resumé of early-day steamboating progress on
the Upper Missouri is not entirely accurate. In May, 1819
the *Independence*, the first steamboat to enter the Missouri,
ascended the river for some 200 or 300 miles. In 1832 the
American Fur Company's steamer, *Yellowstone*, succeeded, after failing in two prior attempts, in reaching
Fort Union, a few miles above the mouth of the Yellowstone. On the return voyage to St. Louis the vessel paused
at Fort Tecumseh long enough to rename the place Fort
Pierre, in honor of Pierre Chouteau, Jr., present on the
voyage, who had been one of the most active promoters of
the *Yellowstone*'s activities. Born in St. Louis in 1789, his
entire life (he died in 1865) centered in that city. He
manifested a decided talent for business, engaging in
numerous and widely-extended activities and accumulat-
ing a fortune of several million dollars. In 1834 the Fur
Company's *Assiniboine* ascended to the vicinity of the
Poplar River, about 80 miles above the mouth of the
Yellowstone. This record stood until 1853 when the *El
Paso* ascended the river some 125 miles farther to a point
about five miles above the mouth of Milk River, called for
more than half a century El Paso Point. In 1859 the Fur
Company's *Chippewa*, a light draft vessel captained by
John B. La Barge, ascended to the site of former Fort
McKenzie, within 15 miles of Fort Benton. A year later the
Chippewa and the *Keystone* reached the latter place,
practically the head of steam navigation on the Missouri,
although in 1866 the steamer *Peter Belen* ascended to
within six miles of Great Falls.

In June, 1861 the *Chippewa* blew up and burned at a

The cordelle was a memory of the past. A new era in the history of the Great West had been inaugurated, whose effects were not apparent, however, until several years later.

The American Fur Company (Upper Missouri Outfit) held their sway for many years. During most of the time they had more or less opposition, principally from traders who had been at some time or other in their employ. These traders were usually well sustained by the Indians, who fully appreciated the advantages to be gained from competition. In 1860 this competing interest was bought out by the American Fur Company, with the expectation of monopolizing the entire trade of the Missouri, as in the early days.

In 1866 they retired from the field they had so long occupied and in which such striking changes were going on. Up to 1864 the Fur Company's steamers were the only ones that ascended the river. In that year Montana became the grand center of attraction, and a number of steamboats

point long known as Disaster Bend, a little below the mouth of Poplar River, Montana. Loaded with fur-trade goods, her cargo included large quantities of alcohol and gunpowder. At supper-time a deck-hand went into the hold equipped with a lighted candle to purloin some liquor. In the process he set fire to the vessel and the explosion of the gunpowder completed her destruction.
    Data abstracted from Chittenden, *Hist. of Early Steamboat Navigation on the Missouri River*, I, 220–21; Charles Larpenteur, *Forty Years a Fur Trader*, 276–78.

went up under individual auspices, loaded with passengers and freight. Each succeeding year this number increased until in 1867 over forty steamboats ascended the Missouri.

Military posts have been established at various points on the river. The Indian tribes are in a state of anarchy, the quiet seclusion of the Indian country is forever destroyed, and the reign of the fur trader is virtually at an end.[8]

When the toils and sufferings of the pioneer explorers of the Missouri River and the trackless wilderness are compared with the steady progress of improvement, sometimes scarcely perceptible at first but increasing with giant strides as the years roll round, who will not unhesitatingly admit that "Westward the star of empire takes its way"?

[8] The discovery of gold at Virginia City (1862) and other points induced a rush to the mines which led to the creation of Montana Territory in 1864. Capt. John Mullan in 1863 described a feasible overland route from Fort Benton to the mining camps, and about the same time (1863–65) John M. Bozeman traced the route of the Bozeman Trail, running from Julesburg, Colorado on the South Platte to Virginia City and bisecting the choicest hunting grounds of the Sioux. These several developments led to the Red Cloud War of 1866–67 to which Mrs. Margaret I. Carrington's thrilling narrative, *Absaraka Home of the Crows*, the Lakeside Classics volume for 1950, is devoted. For a recent account of early gold mining activities in Montana see Merrill G. Burlingame and K. Ross Toole, *A History of Montana* (2 vols. New York, 1957), Vol. I.

CHAPTER II

From St. Louis to Fort Clark

THE annual departure of the Fur Company's steamboat from St. Louis, with supplies for the various trading-posts on the Upper Missouri and its tributaries was an event that formerly excited great interest. Crowds thronged the levee watching the bustle to and fro and the last hurried preparations for starting. Black volumes of smoke pour from the tall chimneys, the waste steam escapes with a hoarse roar, and a few preliminary turns of the wheels add to the fast increasing excitement. Curiosity-seekers crowd the cabin, peering into every nook and corner as if they expected to discover some phantom of the wilderness, and listen eagerly to the conversation between the members of the Fur Company and their friends.

Here is the well-known Col. Robert Campbell,[9] himself a mountaineer in the early days of the

[9] Robert Campbell was born in Ireland in 1804. He migrated to the United States prior to October, 1825, when he joined at St. Louis William H. Ashley's second trading expedition to the Rocky Mountains. Afflicted with lung trouble, he enlisted in the venture in the hope of regaining his health. He succeeded, and for a decade remained active in the Upper Missouri and Rocky Mountain fur trade. Retiring to St. Louis in 1835, he engaged in

fur trade, and although he has not taken an active part for many years he still feels that interest in seeing the expedition off which is natural to any one who has shared in the perils and excitement of frontier life. The Colonel is talking to Indian Agent Vaughan[10] and Malcolm Clark, the

varied activities by which he accumulated a great fortune. Until his death over forty years later he remained prominent in business and civic affairs. In an era of cut-throat competition in the fur trade he maintained a reputation for fairness and honesty in all his dealings. He succumbed at last to his old enemy, tuberculosis, dying in 1878 at the age of seventy-five. *Dict. Am. Biog.*

[10] Charles Larpenteur, who had a poor opinion of all Indian agents, characterized Vaughan as "a jovial old fellow who had a very fine paunch for brandy, and when he could not get brandy would take almost anything which would make drunk come. He was one [agent] who remained most of his time with his Indians, but what accounts for that is the fact that he had a pretty young squaw for a wife; and as he received many favors from the [American Fur] Company he must have been in their favor." Vaughan had an encounter in 1855 with Sir George Gore, the British sportsman and "dude" traveler, from which he emerged second-best. When Sir George arrived at the mouth of the Yellowstone Vaughan called upon him to demand what his business was in the Indian country, to which Sir George replied that it was none of his business. Vaughan then demanded to see his authority for his presence in the country and was shown the passport of the Superintendent of Indian Affairs at St. Louis. Disgruntled by his reception by Sir George, Vaughan subsequently wrote several complaining letters to his superior concerning him. Charles Larpenteur, *Forty Years a Fur Trader*, 346; *Montana Hist. Soc. Contributions*, IX, 248-49.

latter a veteran of over twenty years' experience, and thoroughly versed in all the wiles and mysteries of Indian trading. Clark wears a blue blanket capote, and displays a tobacco-sack of scarlet cloth beautifully garnished with beads, the handiwork of his Blackfoot wife.[11]

[11] Malcolm Clark, for many years a prominent figure on the Upper Missouri, was the son of Captain Nathan Clark of the Fifth U. S. Infantry, who for some years was stationed at Fort Snelling (near present-day St. Paul). Throughout his active life Malcolm Clark's career was a stormy one. Admitted to West Point, he was expelled in consequence of a quarrel during which he whipped his opponent with a rawhide. He participated in the Texan struggle for independence and subsequently found his way to the Upper Missouri where he married a Blackfoot woman and devoted his time and energies to the fur trade. In the summer of 1863 he killed Owen McKenzie the half-breed son of Kenneth McKenzie, in a personal quarrel, and was himself murdered by Indians in August, 1869. Charles Larpenteur, who disliked McKenzie, tended to exculpate Clark for this killing. Indian Agent Reed, however, reported to the Government that Charles Chouteau, an eye-witness of the affair, stated to him that Clark "coolly" killed McKenzie "under the most aggravating circumstances." Talented relatives of Clark have defended his character with more or less success. Perhaps an unbiased judgment would be that in a rude and violent era Clark distinguished himself for aggressiveness and violence. In 1858 he was a member of the opposition firm of Clark, Primeau and Company, Boller's employer. Subsequent to the merger of the companies in 1860 both Primeau and Clark joined the American Fur Company. For his career see Charlotte Ouisconsin Van Cleve, *Three Score years and Ten* (Minneapolis, 1895); articles by the same author and by a daughter of Clark in *Montana Hist.*

At length the order is given in sharp, decided tones to clear the boat. The rush and confusion are at their height. Farewells are heartily exchanged, and the deck-hands haul in the heavy stages. On the hurricane deck the Captain is calling the roll of his voyageurs, who are singing, or rather shouting, their Canadian boat-songs with greater energy than music. Some few stragglers hurry aboard at the last moment, fearful of being left, carrying a shooting-iron in one hand, and a mysterious black bottle in the other. Much amusement is created among the voyageurs by the fruitless attempts of a couple of landlords to find delinquent boarders who have been snugly hid away by their comrades, and intend to remain so until under weigh, leaving their too confiding hosts to mourn over hopes departed.

The last hawser is at length cast loose and the last plank drawn in, thereby compelling the luckless Bonifaces to leap ashore, up to their knees in water, to the delight and amusement of the lookers-on, and after slowly swinging out into the stream, on the morning of May 23d, 1858, the good steamboat *Twilight,* Captain John Shaw, commenced her long mountain trip.

The voyage up the river was unmarked by any incident worthy of notice until we had passed be-

Society Contributions, I, 90–98 and II, 255–68; Charles Larpenteur, *Forty Years a Fur Trader,* 298.

yond the confines of civilization and entered the borders of the Sioux country, more than twelve hundred miles above St. Louis. Here we met the first large body of Indians, a band of Yanktons, who were encamped awaiting the arrival of their annuities, which were on board the *Twilight* in charge of the Agent, Col. Redfield.

This band of Yanktons had recently, through a delegation sent to Washington, sold a portion of their beautiful country, Dacota, to the United States, reserving a tract on which the Government bound itself to establish a farm and a school for their benefit.[12]

The white skin lodges scattered over the broad green prairie, the horses feeding in all directions, and the gay dresses of the Indians on the river's bank formed a wild and picturesque scene. As we neared the camp, firing salutes meanwhile from the cannon on board, men, women, and children

[12] The Yanktons comprised one of the three major divisions of the Sioux Confederacy. They occupied the area of eastern South Dakota, living midway between the Santees to the eastward and the Tetons on the west. By the treaty concluded at Washington on April 19, 1858, they ceded all of their country save for a reservation of some 400,000 acres, to the United States. The cession comprised the country lying between the Big Sioux and the Missouri rivers and south of a line running from Pierre to Watertown. The treaty is printed in *South Dakota Hist. Colls.*, I, 445–56. By a prior treaty concluded in 1851 the Sioux had surrendered all of Dakota lying eastward of the Big Sioux River.

flocked down to the water's edge to witness the landing of the "Fire Canoe."

The squaws, however, generally remained in the background, although the young and pretty ones, with their cheeks tinged with vermilion, were, like their sisters of a lighter hue, by no means averse to displaying their charms or displeased with the attention they excited. The old ones on the contrary, their scant leathern dresses blackened and greasy with age and dirt, remained completely in the rear, scolding almost incessantly at the dogs and children.

None of the squaws with this band would have stood for types of that female beauty which has its existence only in the imagination of the novelist. Some of the old ones, worn out by age and hard work, were surely fit living representations of Egyptian mummies. The boys and dogs ran about, and like boys and dogs everywhere else contrived to be constantly in the way. The urchins were mostly naked, or at best wore a breech-cloth only, and carried small bows with blunt arrows. As soon as the landing was effected Col. Redfield stepped ashore, when the chiefs and principal men hastened to grasp him by the hand, uttering the universal salutation, "How!" The cabin having been previously arranged by removing the tables and placing a semicircle of chairs, the chiefs were at once formally invited on board. The council made slow progress, like most Indian "talks," during which the pipe was industriously circulated. The Agent, through his interpreter, addressed them at length, urging them to love their enemies and obey the wishes of their Great Father, the President; and this advice, though well meant, would doubtless be more honored in the breach than the observance. It was difficult to satisfy the Indians about their presents, and they would not consent to receive them until they had gone on shore and counted the bales and boxes. Then, finding that the number agreed with what their Agent had told them, they returned to continue the council.

The cabin of the *Twilight* presented an unusual appearance. The group of Indians comprised the dignitaries of the band, dressed and painted after their own wild fashion. A handsome pipe of red stone, filled with chash-hash-ash, or inner bark of the red willow, passed from one to another almost without interruption, and its fragrant odor pervaded the entire apartment. During the council a few visitors were permitted to come on board. They peered into every nook and corner, and nothing seemed to escape their prying glances. Those on shore indulged freely in remarks upon the deliberations of their chiefs, and among other pleasant suggestions one fellow coolly proposed a general scalping of the whites!

Although this humane project seemed to meet with universal favor, it was deemed inexpedient for the present. At the close of the council the Agent presented the two principal chiefs with large silver medals bearing the likeness of their Great Father, President Buchanan, saying, as he did so, "This is made of the real stuff," which information was doubtless highly gratifying to two such profound judges of the purity of metals in general, and silver in particular, as He-who-strikes-the-Rees and the Little Crow. Afterwards he presented the head chief (Strike-the-Rees) with a spy-glass of inferior quality and a box of India-rubber balls; the latter "for his boys," said the Agent, bouncing one. The expression on the Indian's countenance when he received these munificent gifts was one of mingled amusement and contempt.[13]

[13] Strike-the-Rees was born near Yankton about Sept. 1, 1804. Lewis and Clark, who were then in the vicinity, made an American citizen of him with appropriate ceremony. Throughout his life he took pride in the tradition of his christening, and remained loyal to the U.S. Government, rendering special service in keeping the Yanktons friendly following the Sioux uprising of 1862 in Minnesota. Of him, Governor Andrew J. Faulk said: "This venerable chief never quarreled with the whites, never stole from them, but lived and died at peace with them. He was really a great man. . . ." He died at the Yankton Agency in 1887 and a permanent monument to his memory, surmounted by a statue, has been built by the Indians. Doane Robinson, *Encyclopedia of South*

The council concluded with a feast, consisting of "black medicine" (coffee) and hard bread. The decks were then cleared and the expedition once more proceeded on its way.

The next excitement was caused a few days later by a party of twenty-five or thirty mounted Sioux on the Dakota side, who ordered us to stop and land. Their commands not being complied with, they began firing, but without effect, as the distance was too great. Another party now showed themselves on the Nebraska side, and as the boat kept steadily on her way, they, too, fired, but with like result. Our Dakota friends, finding their efforts to stop us unavailing, rode furiously off, with gleaming weapons and fluttering pennons, forming a striking picture as their outlines became sharply defined against the clear, blue sky, while cresting the hills in their wild gallop.

A few miles farther on, where the channel ran close in shore, a crackling of branches was heard and the Indians appeared on the bank, demanding a talk with the Agent. Making a merit of necessity the boat landed, and Col. Redfield, with Zephyr, his interpreter, went ashore.[14] The

Dakota (Pierre, 1925), 713; *South Dakota Hist. Colls.*, I, 51–52.

[14]Zephyr Recontre, a veteran servant of the Government as Indian interpreter. Captain Joseph La Barge

Indians seemed greatly excited by their chase after the boat, and Medicine Cow, the chief, gave the Agent the comforting assurance that he would get——(as the interpreter expressed it) at Fort Pierre, where several thousand of the different bands of the great Sioux nation were encamped, impatiently awaiting their annuities. After a present of tobacco and provisions the boat was permitted to move on.

The Indians in this party were splendid-looking men, well armed and equipped.

It was at the close of a beautiful day in June when we laid up in sight of Fort Pierre, the first trading-post on the river.[15] All that night our ears

credited Zephyr with saving his life in the winter of 1840–41, when menaced by hostile Indians. Chittenden, *Hist. of Early Steamboat Navigation on the Missouri River,* I, 67; II, 400–402.

[15] Fort Pierre, about three miles above the mouth of Bad or Teton River, developed through a series of changes from a small trading post established here by Joseph La Framboise in October, 1817. In 1828 the American Fur Company bought the establishment and during the next few years erected a new post (completed in 1834). Under its regime Fort Pierre (named in honor of Pierre Chouteau Jr.) became the largest and best-equipped post on the Upper Missouri, saving only Fort Union. In 1855 the U.S. Government bought the property and two years later dismantled it, rebuilding in its stead Fort Randall near the point where the South Dakota-Nebraska boundary intersects the Missouri.

Despite the commercial importance of Fort Pierre it was not popular with the doughboys of the fifties. One

were greeted with the unaccustomed sound of the
wolves howling in every direction. Fort Pierre was
one of the largest posts in the Indian country,
and some years ago was the center of a flourishing
trade with the Sioux, which has since greatly
fallen off, many of them trading on the Platte and
at the posts on the Upper Missouri with the Rees
and Gros Ventres, having patched up a very convenient treaty with their old enemies. The
Indians here assembled belonged principally to
the Minneconjou, Two Kettle, and Yanc-toh-wah
bands of the Sioux. Hundreds of lodges were
pitched in the vicinity of the fort, and bands of
horses were feeding over the prairie.[16]

army legend affirmed that it had been founded by Peter
the Hermit, who selected the site because of its indescribable dreariness and desolation. Another contemporary
version, however, ascribed its founding to a more celebrated character.

"They say old Shoto built it
But we know it is not so
For the man who built this bloody ranch
Is reigning down below."
South Dakota Hist. Colls., I, 262–64 and 278–87.

[16] The Two Kettle band was one subdivision of the
Teton Sioux (other bands included the Hunkpapas,
Ogalalas, Blackfeet, etc.). Lewis and Clark in September,
1805 encountered them at the mouth of the Teton (or
Bad) River (vicinity of Pierre, South Dakota) whose valley
they occupied. At a subsequent date the band became
much scattered. Lt. G. K. Warren in 1855–57 estimated
their number at 100 warriors and 800 total population.
South Dakota Hist. Colls. I, 101–102 and 341–42.

Some of the squaws, especially those belonging to the Two Kettle band, were quite prepossessing in their appearance. One in particular excited universal admiration: she wore a dress made from the skin of the big-horn, tanned soft and white and lavishly embroidered with beads, and managed the spirited American horse upon which she was mounted with a dashing grace worthy of a Di Vernon.

The presents for each band were placed in separate piles, and immediately upon the termination of the council most of the Indians hurried off to their respective camps, whence they quickly returned leading horses harnessed to travées, and upon these primitive vehicles the goods were speedily dragged away to be distributed by the chiefs at their leisure.

These travées are of the simplest possible construction, being merely two poles tied together at one end and fastened to the pack-saddle, the remaining ends being left to trail on either side. A couple of stretchers are lashed behind the horse at suitable distances, to which is secured a network of raw hide and it is then ready for use. A horse will draw from two hundred and fifty to three hundred pounds weight upon one of them, and the lodge, household utensils, dried meat, children, and puppies are usually transported in this way. Smaller ones are made for the benefit of the dogs, who are thus unwillingly compelled to make themselves useful.

After leaving Fort Pierre no incident occurred worthy of notice until the afternoon of the fourth day when several horsemen appeared on a high bluff, close under which the boat would have to pass. Warrior after warrior came dashing up at full speed until fifteen or twenty dark forms stood out against the sky.

Preparations were made to land, seeing which, the Indians turned their ponies loose and remained quiet and impassive. This was a portion of Big Head's band of Yanc-toh-wahs. The camp itself was out of sight beyond a distant range of hills. A long, dark line of warriors, riding abreast, emerged from an intervening roll of the prairie and with full pomp and panoply advanced to meet us, headed by the famous chieftain, Big Head, in person. All were dressed in shirts of deerskin profusely decorated with scalp-locks, stained horsehair, and devices worked in porcupine quills and beads. War eagle feathers were fastened in their hair and pennons of scarlet cloth fluttered from the lances. They were armed *cap-à-pie* with shields, bows and arrows, and firearms, while the tomahawk and scalping-knife were indispensable accompaniments. Some wore necklaces formed of the claws of the grizzly bear, highly prized as trophies and ornaments.

Onward they came, firing their guns into the air with whoops and yells, and finally halted about fifty yards from where the Agent and his interpreter stood. Then dismounting, they seated themselves in a line, holding their horses behind them by their lariats. Big Head and his principal chiefs, advancing, shook hands haughtily with the Agent and conducted themselves in an insolent and overbearing manner.

In reply to the question why they had fired off their guns as they approached, the chief said that when they met friends on the prairie they met them with empty guns. As they had carefully reloaded, the only inference to be drawn from this remark was that they considered us in the light of possible foes. We all breathed more freely when the good *Twilight* was once more breasting the swift current of the Missouri and we had left Big Head and his grim warriors far in our rear. None of the old mountaineers went ashore on this occasion, but had their rifles ready for instant use, well knowing the treacherous nature of this band. Malcolm Clark remarked to me that we were very fortunate in getting off without a difficulty, as they were evidently ripe for mischief.

Early in the morning of the 19th of June we arrived at the village of the Riccarees.[17] Unlike

[17] The Arikara tribe, more frequently called by the shortened name "Rees." They were the most northerly

the Sioux, who are always roaming, the Rees have a permanent settlement which they occupy during the spring and summer, moving away in the fall to some well timbered point where there are good indications of game and an abundance of grass for their horses. Here, securely sheltered from the fierce wintry winds, they devote themselves to the chase, dressing furs, and drying meat to serve them when hunting becomes dangerous and difficult from the breaking up of the rivers and the forays of their enemies. They cultivate large fields of corn and also pumpkins

extension of the Caddoan stock, which ranged the Plains from Texas northward. In Dakota they became allies of the Mandan and Hidatsa tribes and inveterate enemies of the Sioux.

Although they welcomed the whites upon their first appearance in the country they subsequently became decidedly hostile. In 1823 they defeated William H. Ashley's trading expedition with severe loss, whereupon a combined force of traders and the United States Army, led by Colonel Henry Leavenworth, returned to the scene and laid siege to the Arikara village, then at the mouth of Grand River. After several removals, about the year 1862 they joined the Mandans and Hidatsas or Gros Ventres, who in 1845 had settled at Fort Berthold. In 1858, when Boller first encountered them, they seem to have been located at Fort Clark. Following the abandonment of that place by the American Fur Company in 1860 the Arikaras removed to Fort Berthold, where for the sake of mutual protection from the Sioux they settled beside the Mandan and Gros Ventre villages. Descendants of the three allied tribes still occupy the extensive Fort Berthold Indian Reservation.

and squashes, which agreeably vary their diet of buffalo meat. These summer lodges are large and covered with dirt, forming a great contrast to the white conical ones of the Sioux.[18]

Both the trading-posts presented rather a dilapidated appearance, owing to the great scarcity of timber and the danger of sending their men to secure a supply from a distance. Fort Clark (so named after the renowned explorer of the Missouri), the post of the American Fur Company, was built on the lower side of the village, and about three hundred yards from it Fort Primeau, the post of the Opposition Company.[19]

[18]Four tribes formerly living in North Dakota built earth lodges, lived in permanent villages, and cultivated crops of corn, squashes, and other vegetables. These conditions of sedentary life placed them at a great disadvantage when waging war with the Sioux and other roving tribes. For a detailed description of the earth lodges see article by Russell Reid in *North Dak. Hist. Quarterly*, IV, 174–85 (April, 1930). For illustrations of the Mandan and other earth lodges see plates reproduced from drawings by Sitting Rabbit, a young Mandan Indian, in *North Dak. Hist. Colls.*, I, preceding p. 434. One recent historical romancer professes to perceive in the Mandan earth lodges evidences of mediaeval Norse architecture, supposedly derived from an imaginary amalgamation with the tribe of a handful of Norsemen who paid an equally imaginary visit to western Minnesota in 1362. H. R. Holand, *Westward from Vinland*, (New York, 1940), 263–86.

[19]Fort Clark was established in 1831 among the Mandans about eight miles below the mouth of Knife River. The site was two miles north of the present-day village of

This fort took its name from Mr. Charles Primeau, one of the oldest and best of the mountain traders.[20]

Both the forts as well as the village itself were completely infested with rats, to the discomfort and annoyance of all the inhabitants, both white and red. These pests had been an importation from one of the Company's steamboats years before, and had multiplied to such an alarming extent that the Indians, who at first felt themselves particularly favored above their neighbors

Fort Clark and less than a mile below and on the opposite side of the river from former Fort Mandan, Lewis and Clark's 1804–05 winter-quarters. Lewis F. Crawford, *Hist. of North Dakota* (Chicago, 1931), I, 95. No description remains of Fort Primeau, the headquarters of the rival fur-trade establishment at this point. Under the American Fur Company regime Fort Clark became one of the leading trading centers of the Upper Missouri, ranking after Fort Union and Fort Pierre. It was abandoned following the amalgamation of the fur-trade companies in 1860.

[20] Despite Boller's characterization, but little has been learned concerning Primeau. Boller's manuscript memoranda state that he was a native of St. Louis and that he joined the American Fur Company as a clerk. Subsequently at various times he was a member of several Opposition companies. In 1858 he was a member of the firm of Clark Primeau and Company, Boller's employer. He evidently rejoined the American Fur Company following the merger of 1860, and in 1862 was serving it at Fort Pierre. In 1896 Boller reports him as living near Fort Yates and serving as a Government interpreter. Larpenteur, *Forty Years a Fur Trader*, index entries under Primeau and Alexander Harvey.

by the acquisition, had abundant reason to change their opinion.

The Riccarees were savage-looking Indians and more sullen and insolent than any we had yet met. The men had villainous countenances, which in many cases were disfigured by the loss of an eye, either from accident or disease. Sore and inflamed eyes are very common among them, owing to their filthy habits and smoky lodges.

Out on the prairie beyond the village were circles of human skulls, with two medicine poles in the center of each, bearing propitiatory offerings to the Great Spirit. The dead, dressed in their best garments, are laid on scaffolds in the open air, and after they decay and fall to pieces the skulls are arranged in circles, the bones collected and buried, and the mounds surmounted with a buffalo skull.

While strolling about with several of the party we heard shooting in the direction of the boat and rapidly retraced our steps. We found, upon reaching the landing, that the Indians had attempted to come on board in numbers and upon being repulsed fired their guns into the air in token of their anger and sullenly retired to the village, where they held an excited talk among themselves. The Agent, having some business at Fort Clark, was proceeding thither alone and unarmed when a well-known rascal—the Whiteface Bear—ran up to him and discharged his gun into the ground close by his feet. The only notice taken of this outrage was an involuntary jump, and the Agent continued his walk without further molestation.

After a tedious delay the council finally came off. The chief, White Parflesh, was the principal speaker, and for a long time refused, in the name of his tribe, to take the annuities. The necessities of his people, however, and the tempting display of presents overcame his scruples. The goods were soon put ashore, and speedily transported by the Indians to their village.

Quite an addition was here made to our party in the shape of some eighteen Mandans, men, women, and children, who were desirous of rejoining their people at the Gros Ventres' village some sixty miles higher up.

The various delays had consumed so much time that it was noon before we were ready to continue our voyage. As the boat would have to pass close under the high promontory upon which the village was built, some apprehension was felt as to the probability of our being attacked, for an armed band of Riccarees was gathered there. The pilot-house had been protected by heavy planks before starting, but, happily, the precaution was unnecessary. The *Twilight* swept majestically through the bend, and all thoughts of danger passed away.

Chapter III

To the Yellowstone and Back

NINE miles above the Riccarees, at the mouth of Little Knife River, was a small village of Mandans.[21] Most of the survivors of this nearly extinct tribe live with the Rees and Gros Ventres, but a few families still remained here to cultivate their old cornfields, which from present appearances promised an abundant yield.

At sundown, when we stopped to cut wood as usual, our Indians went out to look for game, but hastily returned, saying that they had discovered Sioux on horseback. This intelligence caused considerable alarm among them and the whole party ascended to the hurricane deck and were soon in battle-array. I was greatly amused at watching one of the Indians load his

[21] Here we encounter a geographical confusion. The Knife River is approximately nine miles above Fort Clark, the site of the Arikara village. On earlier maps (for example, the 1856 map accompanying Lt. G. K. Warren's survey) this was called the Big Knife River. On the same map the Little Knife River is a stream emptying into the Missouri from the north, at the upper end of the Grand Detour (in present-day Mountrail County). A second Little Knife River is shown on modern maps as a minor tributary of the Knife in present-day Dunn County, some seventy miles west of the mouth of the Knife. Apparently Boller's Little Knife is intended for the Knife (Big Knife) River.

fusee.[22] After a double handful of powder, he put in nine half-ounce balls one upon another, with a large wad of red flannel between each. The gun was literally loaded halfway up to the muzzle, and it seemed to me as if the safest place when fired off would have been directly in front. While the warriors kept watch on deck the squaws voluntarily assisted the voyageurs in carrying heavy logs of wood on board, which had been previously chopped down and cut into convenient lengths for transportation.

The following morning witnessed our arrival at the village of the Minnetarees, or as they are commonly called, but without the slightest reason, Gros Ventres.[23] The lodges were precisely like those of the Rees, and the village was similarly

[22] The fusee was a flintlock musket which was long current in the Indian trade. Uncle Dick Wootton describes it as "a fire-lock musket with a bore half as big as that of a small cannon." *Uncle Dick Wootton*, the Lakeside Classics volume for 1957, p. 27.

[23] The Gros Ventres (Big Bellies) or Minitari belonged to the Hidatsa tribe. They are not to be confused with the entirely distinct Gros Ventres of the Prairie, a northerly off-shoot of the Arapahoe tribe. The latter were of Algonquin origin, while the former were Siouxan. The name Big Bellies was bestowed upon them by the Canadian French for some problematical reason ("I do not know why, for their bellies are no larger than those of the others, and to the contrary, like all Indians they are spare and generally of sinewy, slender build." De Trobriand, *Army Life in Dakota*, 39).

built upon a commanding bluff, surrounded by a fine expanse of prairie, while the windings of the river could be traced for many miles. One side of the village was protected by the swift current of the Missouri and the remainder by pickets, which made it perfectly secure against attack.

Fort Atkinson, on the lower side, and Fort Berthold, on the upper, were the rival trading establishments. As it was at the former of these that I made my home for several years, a full description will be reserved for another chapter.[24]

[24] Fort Atkinson, maintained by Opposition traders, was located on the north side of the Missouri in present-day McLean County, on a site now covered by the water impounded by the Garrison Dam. According to Boller the fort must have been established some years prior to 1858, whose rebuilding at this time he describes (*post*, Chap. 6). The site was about 45 miles by water above the mouth of Knife River. Here Boller resided for four years following his arrival in 1858.

Close by was Fort Berthold, the American Fur Company post, which was established in 1845, following the removal of the Mandan and Hidatsa (Gros Ventre, Minitari) Indians to this point. It was named Fort Berthold in honor of Bartholomew Berthold of St. Louis, brother-in-law and former partner in trade of Pierre Chouteau, Jr. Apparently the Indian village was located between the rival trading posts. Following the merger of the fur companies in 1860 the Arikaras settled at the site and this same year the American Fur Company acquired Fort Atkinson and transferred the name and equipment of Fort Berthold to it, abandoning the original structure. On December 25, 1863 the Sioux in overwhelming numbers attacked the fort, whose seventeen white inmates made a

We found but very few Indians here, in fact, scarcely any but the old people and children, the rest being away hunting, under the lead of Noc-pitts-ee-top-pish, or Four Bears, their principal chief. To land the supplies and give Col. Redfield an opportunity to hold the inevitable council with his red children detained us several hours, but by afternoon we were again en route and about dusk passed the mouth of the Little Missouri, at this season a stream of considerable magnitude.

The next day we entered upon the Grand Detour, or Big Bend of the Missouri. This bend is nearly seventy miles around and not more than eighteen across at the narrowest part. It commences at Shell Creek and terminates at Knife River.[25] Buffaloes are usually found in great numbers in this region, but as the running

determined and successful defense. The following season (1864) General Sully placed a small garrison of soldiers at Fort Berthold, one of whose subsequent commanders was General Philippe Regis De Trobriand, whose *Army Life in Dakota* was published as the Lakeside Classics volume for 1941. Another interesting description of the place is provided by Luther S. Kelly in his *Yellowstone Kelly* (New Haven, 1926). In 1870 the Fort Berthold Reservation for the Mandan, Arikara, and Hidatsa (Gros Ventre) tribes, comprising over 2,000,000 acres, was established in the area adjacent to Fort Berthold. Subsequently reduced to about 625,000 acres, in 1947 it was occupied by 1720 Indians.

[25] That is, the southward-flowing Little Knife, in Mountrail County, North Dakota.

season had not yet commenced none of the vast herds were on the river, and up to this time we had only seen a few bulls. The scenery from this point grows bolder and more imposing. Ranges of towering clay bluffs of the most fantastic shapes, often resembling gigantic ruins, meet the eye. All colors are here depicted, from the darkest blue to a bright vermilion, and when the rays of the sun light up their walls and towers the effect is picturesque in the extreme, reminding one of castles in the Old World. Many of these bluffs are hundreds of feet high, and so steep as to be inaccessible save to the Big Horn or Rocky Mountain goat.

About the middle of the bend we met the hunting-band of Gros Ventres, who had not found any buffaloes yet, and were in a starving condition, their main subsistence being upon roots and berries. The same evening we stopped a few minutes with a party of Assiniboines. Their village of a hundred and fifty lodges was encamped close at hand. They were on their way to the Yellowstone to meet the rest of the nation and receive their annuities.

These Assiniboines seemed to be very poor, having but few horses and depending almost entirely upon their dogs, which were very numerous, as their beasts of burden. Of course we had to stop with them a short time, after which we continued on, and as it was a bright clear night kept running until the moon went down. We gained here an accession to our party in the persons of an Indian and his squaw, evidently on their bridal trip and most devoted in their attentions to each other, to the great amusement of the spectators.

The following morning a gang of elk was discovered crossing the river ahead of the boat, but before we neared them they had disappeared in the forest, with the exception of a doe, which came trotting along utterly regardless of our proximity. The cause of her apparent boldness was soon explained by the fact that a fawn was seen swimming rapidly down stream, unable to climb the steep bank with the rest, and its mother was keeping up with it and guiding it until they should come to a place low enough for it to scramble out. The boat's course was altered so as to bring her close in shore, and our Indian, fitting an arrow to his bow, crouched down on the guards watching his opportunity. The elk, in its anxiety for its young one, had lost its usual timidity and instead of fleeing to the forest, came hesitatingly within a few yards of us. The Indian's shaft now struck it deep in the shoulder, too far back, however, to take immediate effect, and the stricken animal, giving two or three convulsive bounds, dashed through the underbrush and was lost to view. The yawl in the meantime had been sent in pursuit of the fawn, and shortly returning with the little captive, comfortable quarters were provided for it on board. After this exciting little incident a band of buffaloes, the first we had seen on the trip, was discovered, barely distinguishable in the dim distance.

Our Indian, who rejoiced in the title of the Son of the Pipe, was unremitting in his attentions to his little squaw, and never was lover more devoted to his fair mistress than was this dusky warrior to his prairie bird. Their favorite haunt was in the shade of the pilot-house. Here they enjoyed themselves to their heart's content, and derived inexhaustible amusement from painting their swarthy countenances with vermilion in all the variations their vivid imaginations could devise. After one coat of paint had been laid on, they would mutually admire each other, then, upon due deliberation, would rub it off and try another fashion.

A delightfully refreshing shower at the close of the hot and sultry day drove the lovers from their trysting-place, and soon after the boat stopped to wood. Could a painter have transferred that scene to canvas he would have made a glorious picture. The storm had passed over behind the forest, the heavy clouds formed a background, as if a sable curtain had been drawn across, while the golden beams of the setting sun threw into strong relief the figures of the men cutting down trees, forming a magnificent contrast of light and shade.

We were now on the confines of the Assiniboine country and our expectations of meeting some of that nation were soon realized.[26] A party of five Indians was discovered scrambling over the bluffs, evidently with the intention of intercepting the boat. When taken on board they proved to be Assiniboines on the war-path against the Onc-pa-pas.[27] Each one carried a bundle of dry meat slung on his back, so as to obviate the dangerous necessity of hunting in an enemy's country. All were armed with fusees and bows and arrows, and carried, in addition, lariats to bring back the horses they expected to steal.

The Missouri had now become very narrow and remarkably crooked, curving repeatedly upon itself, but the channel was better and more easily navigated than in the lower river. In the afternoon we came in sight of Fort William, three miles be-

[26] The Assiniboines were an offshoot of the Sioux family, who were settled on the Upper Missouri and northward in present-day Canada. The Fort Laramie Treaty of 1851 assigned them a reservation between the Missouri and the Yellowstone and in the seventies they were removed to the Fort Peck and Fort Belnap reservations. James Truslow Adams (Ed.), *Dictionary of American History* (5 vols., New York, 1940).

[27] The Hunkpapas, a division of the Sioux Confederacy.

low the mouth of the Yellowstone, where we landed.[28] Many Assiniboines were encamped around the fort, awaiting their annuities. While discharging the supplies for this post it was determined by Major Clark, the principal Bourgeois of the Company, to abandon it and establish a new one some eighty miles up the river. No sooner said than done. All the materiel of the fort was in an incredibly short time shipped aboard the *Twilight*, leaving the robes and peltries to be taken on the return voyage.

For several years past the country around the Yellowstone had been completely overrun by strong war parties of Sioux bound against the Crows and Assiniboines, who, if they fell in with white men, did not hesitate to rob and often kill. So daring had they become of late that it was almost impossible for the hunters to go out after game. The horses were run off in broad daylight under the very guns of the fort and during certain seasons of the year the most untiring vigilance

[28] Fort William, named in honor of William T. Sublette, was located on the northeast side of the Missouri about two miles by land and six by water below Fort Union. Subsequently Fort Buford, a U.S. Army post was located on practically the same site. Fort William was begun August 29, 1833 as an Opposition post to Fort Union. Charles Larpenteur, who participated in the work, has described it in Chap. 13 of his *Forty Years a Fur Trader*. For a comprehensive sketch of Fort William see *South Dak. Hist. Colls.*, I, 354-55.

was necessary to avoid surprise. In consequence, the Assiniboines were afraid to come down to trade, and under these circumstances the removal of Fort William to the heart of their hunting-grounds could hardly fail to be advantageous in every point of view.

Everything having been received on board, we left for Fort Union, the post of the American Fur Company, distant by water nine miles though by land only three.[29] On the way we passed the mouth of the far-famed Yellowstone, the largest tributary of the Missouri River, whose waters flow through the finest hunting-grounds of the West. We remained at Fort Union all night to land Col. Redfield and the government annuities. The fort presented a very imposing appearance,

[29]Fort Union was established on the northerly side of the Missouri some three miles above the mouth of the Yellowstone in 1829, although the work of construction was not completed until 1834. Meanwhile, in 1832 the fort was practically burned down. It became the headquarters of the American Fur Company on the Upper Missouri, and as such the best-equipped and most important trading post in the area. In 1867 the property was purchased by the U.S. Government, which utilized the material in the construction of the new Fort Buford on the Missouri some two or two and one-half miles (by land) below Fort Union. In the spring of 1869 youthful Yellowstone Kelly visited the site of Fort Union and "amid the ruins of the burned stockade and blackened chimneys" mused upon the scenes of daily activity currently enacted at Fort Peck, higher up the river. For a comprehensive sketch of Fort Union see *Dict. Am. Hist.*

and being one of the oldest of the American Fur Company's posts, was admirably equipped in every respect. From here were annually dispatched the outfits for the Crow Indians on the Yellowstone and the Blackfeet on the headwaters of the Missouri. Captain James Kipp, the Bourgeois in charge, welcomed us with true mountain hospitality.[30] We remained there all night, and by the next evening had arrived at the proposed site for the new fort and the terminus of our

[30] James Kipp was born near Montreal, Canada in 1788. He entered upon the fur trade in early manhood and in or prior to 1822 migrated to the Upper Missouri area, where for several decades he was an active and well-known trader. Upon the founding of the Columbia Fur Company he became Kenneth Mackenzie's trusted assistant, and upon the absorption of the Company by the American Fur Company he followed Mackenzie into that organization. He commanded Fort Clark for several years, established Fort Piegan among the Blackfeet for the Company in 1831, and a year later (Fort Piegan having been burned) established Fort Mackenzie a few miles up river to replace it. Prince Maximilian of Wied spent two months here in 1833 as a guest of the Company and his book of *Travels* supplies much contemporary information about the place. Kipp left the Indian country in or prior to 1865, presumably by reason of old age. He settled on a farm in Clay County, Missouri, where he died near Barry on July 2, 1880, aged 92 years. Boller characterized him as an educated man who was reported to be the only white man who mastered the Mandan language. For sketches of his career, differing in some details, see Larpenteur, *Forty Years a Fur Trader,* 97; *North Dak. Hist. Colls.,* I, 368; *South Dak. Hist. Colls.,* I, 352–53: *Report* of Smithsonian Institution, 1885, pt. 2, p.381

voyage, more than twenty-three hundred miles from St. Louis.

Very beautiful in its primeval solitude was the spot whose tranquillity was soon to be rudely broken by the echoing axe of the woodsman, the rifle of the mountaineer, and the varied bustle of the trading-post. The startled deer sped away over the hills, the antelope halted afar off, and the gaunt gray wolf sneaked from the presence of man. Timber was abundant and close at hand, the Missouri's waters rolled at our feet, and the grassy prairies were literally stocked with game. With all these natural advantages, and the greatly diminished danger of incursions from the Sioux, the new post seemed established under the most favorable auspices.[31]

[31] It seems impossible to reconcile the varying statements concerning the location and date of construction of this fort. Boller (p. 39) places it eighty miles up river from Fort William and fixes the early summer of 1858 as the date of its establishment. This would be in the approximate vicinity of the mouth of Poplar River, in present-day Roosevelt County, Montana. A year later, in 1859, he reports the return of the steamer from Fort Stuart "eighty miles above the mouth of the Yellowstone" (p. 344). Captain Joseph La Barge places Fort Stuart at the mouth of Poplar River as of the early summer of 1861. Chittenden, *Hist. of Early Steamboat Navigation on the Missouri*, II, 293. Yet Charles Larpenteur, who took command of Fort Stuart in the summer of 1859, fixes its then location as thirty-five miles above Fort Union, states that it had been built by the firm of Frost, Todd and Co. who, being too extravagant, had lost it, that he found it

By early dawn the work of discharging freight was commenced. The goods were piled into a "baggage" and covered with tarpaulins to protect them from the weather until suitable storehouses could be erected. Besides these, Mackinaw boats must also be built to carry the outfit intended for Fort Campbell, the Blackfoot post, a distance by water of not less than seven hundred miles.[32]

in bad condition in 1859, that it stood adjoining Fort Kipp, and that upon his return from St. Louis in the summer of 1860 he found both forts had been burned; whereupon, he removed to Poplar River, a one-day journey of twenty-five miles, where he built "a little fort" and passed a profitable winter (1860–61). At this time Boller and Larpenteur were partners, and the former, who visited the fort, could not conceivably have been ignorant of its location. A probable interpretation of the conflicting statements of Boller and Larpenteur would be that Larpenteur correctly placed the Fort Stuart of 1859 and earlier some thirty-five miles above Fort Union, and that Boller, when writing his narrative several years later, confused this location with the subsequent one at Poplar River. But the difficulty still remains of reconciling Boller's description of the site as a primitive wilderness in which a new fort was about to be built with Larpenteur's statement that the fort had been built at some earlier date and was already (in 1859) in a run-down condition.

[32]Information concerning Fort Campbell is chiefly lacking. The most recent (two-volume) history of Montana, by Burlingame and Toole does not mention it. Charles E. De Land, former South Dakota historian, states that the fort "seems to be but imperfectly known in the annals of the fur trade, and its precise location is not clear." *South Dak. Hist. Colls.*, I, 362. A tantalizing note

These boats have to be cordelled, or drawn by men the entire distance, and the toils and difficulties of the undertaking can only be appreciated by those who have experienced them. The men chiefly employed by the fur companies were French Canadians—tough, hardy fellows, who assimilate readily to the mode of life they are compelled to adopt in the Indian country. Several of the mountaineers who had come up from Fort William had brought their squaws and families along. These at once proceeded to pitch their lodges, camp-fires were kindled, and a new home in the wilderness, with its few simple comforts, soon established.

By dint of hard work all the freight was discharged by noon and the steamboat was ready to commence her homeward voyage. The voyageurs drank a parting health with each other and the *Twilight* slowly swung out into the stream amid the cheers of those on shore, which were answered by her cannon. A bend of the river soon hid from our view the friends we had left behind, standing on the green prairie's edge to take their last look at us. Nearly twelve moons would wax and wane before they would be greeted by the ar-

by Lt. J. H. Bradley may refer to the fort: "Fort Campbell, built by J. B. S. Todd, Major D. M. Frost, and Atkinson in 1859. Afterwards sold to the American Fur Company. Malcolm Clarke, Matthew Carroll, Clarke." *Montana Hist. Soc. Contributions* IX, 351.

rival of another steamboat, and in that time what changes might not occur, subjected as they would be to the crafty hostility of the Indians and the numberless perils of mountain life.

Swiftly down stream sped the good *Twilight*, past headland and prairie, until, as the setting sun was casting its lengthening rays on the white-washed bastions of Fort Union, she rounded to under the bluff. A short stay and we were off again, passing the mouth of the Yellowstone to Fort William, where a huge beacon-fire was blazing on the bank, surrounded by a group of wild-looking mountaineers eagerly awaiting our return. Morning at length dawned upon the dismantled fort, where but a short time before all had been life and animation. It now had a deserted and forlorn appearance, and in a little while the crumbling adobe walls would be all that remained of what had once been a bustling post. We took on board the proceeds of the last year's trade, consisting of over a thousand packs of robes and peltries, and with a farewell salute, our prow was again turned toward the settlements.

While passing through the Big Bend we ran into a small band of buffaloes crossing the river, and Captain Shaw, going out in his yawl, succeeded in killing three, which were towed alongside and hoisted on board to be butchered. The following afternoon we came in sight of the dirt-covered lodges of the Minnetarees, and soon after the *Twilight* landed in the eddy below the village. The robes and peltries in Fort Atkinson were shipped aboard, and after my personal baggage had been carried on shore I bade farewell to my late associates and walked up to the fort in company with my friend McBride.[33] Before entering the stockade I looked back in time to catch a

[33]This was John C. McBride concerning whose earlier career but little information has been found. Evidently he was a veteran fur trader, and a member of the Opposition Company in whose service Boller had enlisted as a clerk. Louis Sears' recollections place him in command of Fort Atkinson in 1855–56, when he aided the English traveler, Sir George Gore with supplies after he had been plundered by the Sioux. *N. Dak. Hist. Colls.*, I, 349. Although Boller was a much younger man than McBride a warm friendship between the two developed. In the spring of 1859 McBride left Fort Atkinson (Boller, *post,* pp. 344, 347–48), and may have retired from the fur trade at this time. However this may be, a long letter written to Boller from Big Sioux on Feb. 28, 1863 discloses that he had been living at Sioux City at least since the summer of 1862, where he had been busy in starting a ferry boat, with which he had since been doing a good business. For further concerning his Indian family see *post,* note 34. On May 3, 1894 Ab Nash, postmaster at Wheeler, South Dakota, replying to Boller's inquiry, stated that he formerly knew McBride very well but had lost sight of him in recent years. Upon inquiring he learns that he had died at the Yankton Agency about four years ago (i.e., 1890). He had obtained a tract of land there and was farming at the time of his death. His wife and children were still living there.

parting glimpse of the tall chimneys of the *Twilight* disappearing behind the forest that skirted the southern bend of the river, and realized for the first time how completely I was isolated from civilization and thrown upon my own resources.

CHAPTER IV

A Day in an Indian Village

AT length I had arrived at my destination in the Indian country. For years it had been a cherished project to penetrate the heart of the wilderness and see the Indians as they really were, those too far beyond the pale of civilization to have felt the corrupting influences of its overflow. As the steamboat that had brought me here rapidly pursued her course down stream I realized my complete separation from all former associations, placed as I now was among new and strange scenes and dependent upon the uncertain friendship of wild and often treacherous savages. Still it was my own free choice to dwell among them and as my baggage was carted up to the fort the novelty of the situation and speculation as to what would come next gave me no time to feel lonely. A crowd of Indians, chiefly women, followed, darkening the doors and windows and peering into the room, eager, with the usual curiosity of their sex, to behold the *itch-u-manny* or new arrival, and exchanging comments, highly amusing doubtless, judging from the boisterous mirth they elicited, but, happily totally unintelligible to the object thereof.

As evening approached the gates of the fort

were closed and barred to keep out intruders, and supper being announced, we proceeded to the kitchen, or mess-room, where it was served. The appearance of the edibles, it must be confessed, was anything but inviting, but stimulated by a keen appetite I fell to and ate heartily. The meal consisted of bacon, coffee, and bread. Bourgeois McBride apologized for the absence of fresh buffalo meat, for the reason that the Indians, having been much harassed lately by war-parties of the Sioux, were afraid to go any distance to hunt. The repast was, however, greatly enjoyed by the long-haired, wild-looking set that graced the board, all of whom had been on short allowance for several weeks preceding the arrival of the steamboat.

Night coming on, arrangements were made for my sleeping. A rough bunk of cottonwood plank was hastily knocked together, and half a dozen buffalo robes made a comfortable bed. Before turning in, McBride's squaw cooked some dried buffalo meat and *pomme blanche,* which I found, with my improved appetite, very palatable.[34] I was tired enough to wish for a good

[34] This was Susan (Susanne), McBride's first and only Indian woman, concerning whom a separate chapter might be written. Before Boller had been many months at Fort Atkinson she had become "like a sister" to him, washing and mending his apparel, keeping his bed and possibles in order, and the house "as neat as a pin." Thus

he wrote his father in a letter of Dec. 1, 1858, requesting that a pretty dress be sent him to give to Susan (whose physical proportions he described somewhat quaintly) together with presents for the children, "two boys and one girl, all under six." Somewhat earlier (August 7, 1858) in a long letter to his sister, Boller had disclosed much more about Susan and McBride. On a recent summer evening the Burgeois was seated at the door of his quarters, smoking his pipe and talking over with Boller (who stood leaning against the door, swatting mosquitoes) and the courier plans for the coming fall campaign, when suddenly from the direction of the corral a dark figure muffled in a blanket rushed through the doorway, making a thrust at McBride with a butcher knife as it passed. The Burgeois sprang after her (for it was Susan) and wrested the knife from her grasp, whereupon she seized an iron bar utilized as a fire poker and aimed a blow at him with it. McBride jerked it from her, and knocking her down proceeded to administer a good beating, during which she cried out "kill me," "shoot me," and that she did not want to live. The beating ended, she fled from the post, and although the traders pursued her, she was swallowed up in the darkness. Although the men sat up until one o'clock she did not return. Meanwhile McBride related to his companions that she was the only Indian woman he had ever had, and that she would be the last. He had lived with her seven years, with no "flare up" until now and he had hoped to take her below and "make a white woman" of her. But it was no use; an Indian would be an Indian still.

Further trouble meanwhile developed. The three children were crying, and although the two older ones presented no problem, only a mother could care for the youngest, a nursing infant. However, the wife of one of the interpreters, who herself was nursing a child, cared for the baby during the night. Sunday morning arrived, when a tall Sioux warrior appeared to report that Susan had spent the night in his lodge and was now gone to the American Fur Company post (Fort Berthold). Here she night's rest, but the hope was vain. The robes composing my bedding were old, having been well worn by their previous owners, the Indians,

sent for the baby and the immediate trouble was ended. Just before the fort gates were closed, Susan sneaked in and seated herself at McBride's door. The men inside, seated around the blazing fire, ignored her presence and she soon crept in with covered face and went to bed. "She was one of the prettiest squaws I have seen and McBride treated her too well. The devil has been getting into the women up here," wrote Boller.

But Susan's conduct was not wholly unreasonable. McBride explained that he had been watching the cook, who was passing biscuits through the pickets to a Crow woman outside, and was intending to reprimand him. Susan, whom he had supposed to be in bed with her children, had come upon this scene, and supposing he was courting the Crow damsel had retired to a dark corner of the yard, where she had brooded upon the wrong-doing until her Indian blood was up, and the attack followed.

Evidently all was forgiven on both sides, for McBride did take Susan and their children below, where in his letter of February 28, 1863 he expresses regret that Boller had not called upon Susan, "for nothing could have pleased her better," adding that she would have been glad to make the moccasins Boller had requested. Thirty years later, on August 10, 1894, the U.S. Indian Agent at Greenwood, South Dakota, wrote that Susan was living on the reservation with her family of three boys and four girls, all of them married save one boy. All the boys were farmers, and all were "pretty good boys" and doing well. The youngest, Benjamin, had graduated from the State University last year (1893) and was a very bright fellow. There were two other boys living at Crow Creek of whom the writer knew little. One of them had suicided a short time ago. Further information concerning Susan is lacking. Obviously she was a good woman, and a good mother and wife.

and as a matter of course were thickly populated by those minute specimens of animated nature with which savages are so bountifully provided. The active little creatures kept up their attacks most vigorously, and in such numbers that after vainly battling with them for several hours I was fain to give up the unequal contest and retreat to the floor, where I spread my blankets and hoped to snatch a little sleep.

But very soon my tormentors discovered my new location and renewed their assaults until, completely worn out and irritated, I began to think that the romance of Indian life was one thing but its reality another. However, after a few weeks I became in a measure invulnerable to these pests and paid but little attention to them, regarding them in the light of an unavoidable nuisance. Finding sleep impossible under these circumstances, I went out into the area of the fort and climbing to the roof of one of the houses contemplated the unaccustomed scene. The surrounding prairies were wrapped in uncertain darkness, and not a sound escaped from the Indian village close by.

The morning-star shone brightly, high in the heavens, and I felt the freshness of approaching dawn. Soon a faint reddish streak became visible in the east, brightening even as the eye gazed upon it, and long rays of light shot upwards.

Hazy and indistinct the outlines of the village appeared, and gleams of rosy light illumined the prairies, bringing into strong relief the scaffolds supporting the bodies of those now sleeping their everlasting sleep. The mournful howl of a dog, mounted on the top of one of the lodges, breaks the almost death-like stillness. The notes are instantly caught up by others and directly every cur in the village is taking his part with commendable energy. Commencing soft and low, the noise grows louder and deeper until it finally dies away in a prolonged wail. Modulated by distance, the sound is not unmusical.

This canine matinée rouses up the sleepers, a stir is evident in the village, and soon the curling smoke from the lodges floats in the morning air. The squaws, old and young, followed by the usual retinue of dogs, hasten down to the river to fill their kettles, while the warriors from the tops of the lodges anxiously scan the prairies to discover signs of enemies. Everything appearing quiet, the horses are driven forth, each band guarded by a young brave, who takes them where the best pasture is to be found and brings them back at sundown. As the horses in the course of the day often stray to a distance of five or six miles from the village, the guards act also as scouts, and ranging over the surrounding hills, serve not only to discover game (*i. e.* buffaloes) but also the approach of a war party. Timely alarm can thus be given and the horses hurried in while the warriors prepare for battle. As horses constitute the principal wealth of an Indian and are the chief incentives to depredations by one tribe upon another, the untiring vigilance used in guarding them is an imperative necessity. An Indian without horses is reduced to a pitiful strait indeed, crippled in hunting and unable often to carry home the meat he may kill, or to move his family when the camp travels.

When thus situated he will usually act as hunter for some relative rich in horses, who by giving him a few robes now and then, in payment as it were for his services, affords him an opportunity of regaining his former position. Horse-flesh is uncertain property in any part of the world, and nowhere more so than in the Indian country. A fine horse is an overpowering temptation to a redskin, and if the possessor of one to-day, to-morrow may find him many miles away, having changed owners quite unceremoniously.

The idlers, the *gentlemen* of the village, having taken their morning bath in the river and made their toilets, which at this season seemed to consist simply in readjusting the breechcloth, wend their way to the fort, loitering around and peering into the different houses in hopes of being

asked to eat, an invitation which they never consider amiss, and always cheerfully accept.

Conspicuous in the van is old Mi-ran-tah-nour-
eesh, or Raising Heart, a tall war-worn veteran,
bearing in the scars with which he is covered the
traces of many a hard-fought battle, besides being
lamed and badly crippled in his hands. He is our
soldier, chosen on account of his friendly feelings
towards the traders and his influence and ability
to protect them from the many annoyances to
which they are often subjected. He is, of course,
a regular *habitué*, and is dressed and fed at the
expense of the post. But although of a pleasant
and smiling disposition, any injury done to the
property or persons of the whites under his care
is instantly resented. More than once have I seen
him punish a young buck by striking him with
the flat side of his tomahawk, as a gentle reminder
that he cannot play the same pranks in the white
men's lodge that he can in his own village, while
the Raising Heart is their soldier.

The old man was not a chief, although his
many dashing exploits when he trod the war-
path richly entitled him to that distinction. He
preferred to keep a large band of fine horses,
make plenty of robes, and provide well for his
family, instead of giving away nearly everything
he possessed, although he would thereby gain
the much-coveted distinction of being a big man,

which distinction is too often acquired at the sacrifice of wealth and comfort, compelling the family to live in a straitened way and in a great measure shift for themselves. But the Raising Heart, though not a chief, was very rich, and had an extensive circle of influential relatives, who, according to Indian custom, were obliged to make common cause in protecting one another and in taking up any quarrel which concerned one of their number. Without a soldier it would be almost impossible to conduct trade or to transact business in this country.[35]

All the wild Indian tribes look upon the whites as an inferior race, pretty much in the same light that we formerly regarded plantation Negroes. They have the idea that the earth is one vast plain resting upon four huge turtles, and that the whites occupy a very small corner of it, while the rest is the exclusive and illimitable

[35] On the subject of the functions of the soldier among the Indians see Charles Larpenteur, *Forty Years a Fur Trader*, 333–35 and *Uncle Dick Wootton*, 29–30, the Lakeside Classics volumes respectively for 1933 and 1957. See also Boller, index entries. Among the Sioux the soldiers were chosen by the chiefs from among the most reputable warriors, and they exercised an authority somewhat comparable to that wielded by civilized police officers. Larpenteur, who certainly was intimately acquainted with them, affirms that their authority exceeded that of the chief. The details he recites are more than ample to support this generalization.

domain of the Indians. One might talk to them for hours on this subject without being able to convince them one iota to the contrary, but would infallibly gain for himself the reputation of being an unmitigated liar if he persisted in asserting that the whites were as numerous as the leaves in the forest, and cunning and skilful beyond all expression. The poorest vagabond of a redskin that roams over the prairies, with little else than a breechcloth to hide his nakedness, thinks himself infinitely richer and better in every respect than his Great Father, the President of the United States, supposing him to have some definite idea of such a personage. The Indians look upon all Americans, or "Long Knives," as a nation of traders, who get their goods from a cunning people beyond the big water; and entertaining such a contemptuous opinion of them, it follows naturally that they will take every opportunity of showing by petty annoyances their much-vaunted superiority.

The knowledge that an influential man with a host of relatives is soldier for the whites renders the young bucks disposed to conduct themselves usually in an orderly and quiet manner, being well aware that any imbroglio that might arise from misconduct on their part would end in Indian being arrayed against Indian, and not the whole tribe against a handful of whites. Thus it will be seen how the prosperity and success of a trading-post is dependent upon the efficient and conciliatory measures of the bourgeois, or commander, and the friendship and support of a powerful interest in the tribe.

Another of our regular visitors was Noc-pitt-see-top-pish, or Four Bears, one of the shrewdest men, all things considered, that I have ever encountered.[36] Had he been a white man, he would have made a consummate politician, for while keeping in good favor with both the rival companies he never failed to enrich himself greatly by so doing. Four Bears was a tall, noble-looking man, with long black hair trailing nearly to the ground, an ornamental appendage valued almost beyond price. He was usually accompanied in his

[36] The Hidatsa (Gros Ventre) Chief, Four Bears, should not be confused with the earlier Mandan chief of the same name, to whom George Catlin devotes much attention, who died at Fort Clark during the smallpox epidemic of 1837. His eloquent and pathetic dying address to his people is printed in *Miss. Valley Hist. Review*, XVII, 299 (Sept. 1930). Four Bears, our present subject, was a native Assiniboine who was taken prisoner in childhood and reared among the Gros Ventres, where by reason of his warlike exploits in combats with the Sioux (his relatives by blood) he rose to the chieftainship of the tribe. His name is still venerated by his people of the Fort Berthold Reservation. When the highway bridge across the Missouri near Elbo Woods was under construction they urged that it be given his name. The Mandans were no less urgent that the bridge be named for their Four Bears. Where-

visits by his favorite son, a hopeful boy of seven summers, who had, when only four years old, shot his mother with a gun, killing her instantly. This exploit was regarded as an evidence of indomitable spirit in the youth, who, it was expected, when old enough would greatly distinguish himself on the war-path.

The Chief invariably entered the Bourgeois' house with a bland smile upon his countenance, and seating himself upon a chair proceeded to retail the news of the day: how badly his people talked against their traders, and how disinterestedly he took the part of the latter and pointed out to his young men that the traders were not only a convenience to them, but in reality a necessity. They were dependent upon them for guns and ammunition to hunt with and to defend themselves against their many enemies, for blankets and scarlet cloth to dress their

upon the Solomonic decision was reached to name the southern end of the bridge for the Gros Ventre chief and the northern end for the Mandan. A plaque was placed at each end bearing their respective names, to which for good measure several more Mandan and Gros Ventre dignitaries were added. The Arikaras (third member of the allied tribes), not to be outdone, now added the names of several worthies of that tribe, bringing the total number in whose honor the bridge is named to nineteen. De Trobriand, *Army Life in Dakota*, 270–71; *North Dakota State Guide*, index entries. For the death of Four Bears, our present subject, see Boller, *post*, (p. 422).

women and children, and reminded them of the
trouble the women had in the olden time to boil
a piece of meat. Unsupplied then with camp kettles, they were obliged to dig a hole in the ground
and after lining it with a raw skin throw in heated
stones to make the water boil.

Having thus succeeded, as he says, in con-
vincing his young men, he expatiates at length
upon the great advantages derived by the tribe
from having two trading-houses and the necessity
of dividing their patronage between them for the
support of both. He takes occasion carelessly to
remark that from his position as head chief any
acknowledged leaning to one side or the other
would exert an undue influence over his people,
yet in his heart he favored the Opposition Company, because they had not been so long established and their presence prevented the American
Fur Company from charging the exorbitant prices
that prevailed before there was competition.

After talking in this strain a cup of coffee is
given him, to get which has been the principal
object of his visit. Then wrapping himself in his
handsome buffalo robe, on which were painted
the head dresses of war-eagle feathers he had given
away in the course of his life, the chief stalks over
to Fort Berthold, there to repeat his remarks, with
modifications to suit the change of locality. He
expresses his great attachment to the American

Fur Company because of its long establishment in the country and its ability to reciprocate substantially any influence which he, the Four Bears, might exert in its behalf.

Thus both whites are assured to his own satisfaction of his disinterested friendship, and the Chief returns to his lodge to gather a circle of his political cronies around him. Here the social pipe passes from hand to hand, and the conversation turning on public affairs, they discuss the expediency of inducing the traders, if possible, without pushing them too hard, to pay higher prices for their robes and peltries. After his horses were brought up for the night he would pay us another visit, incidentally remarking that the cup of coffee given him at Fort Berthold in the morning was sweeter and stronger and the biscuit larger than those he received from us, expecting us, of course, to improve upon the hint. If not too late, he usually wended his way to Fort Berthold to try his diplomacy there again.

The heat gradually grows more intense and the bright July sun beats down from a cloudless sky with an almost tropical fervor. The Indian idlers have all disappeared, and stillness reigns supreme where a short time since resounded the stir and hum of busy life. The very dogs are quietly sleeping in the shade of the lodges. On the prairie not one of the many hundreds of horses that were driven forth at the break of day can now be seen. They have wandered off to shady dells where the grass is always fresh, watered by never-failing springs. The parched and smoking prairie fairly radiates under the intense heat of the noonday sun, and the deathlike silence that reigns is broken only by the sound of the rushing waters of the Missouri.

CHAPTER V

Nightfall and Repose

WHEN the noontide heat is over, the village rouses into full activity and the idlers resume their seats and pass their accustomed criticisms. Nothing escapes their notice, and many and hearty are the laughs they enjoy at the expense of some *wah-see-chu* or little Frenchman.

Sundown approaches and the day's work is over. In the eddy at the base of the bluff quite a number of Indians of both sexes and all ages are indulging in an evening swim and a variety of aquatic sports extremely amusing to the lookers-on, if their hilarious mirth be any evidence. Crowds gather on the bank to watch the gambols of these water-sprites, and a line of squaws is constantly passing and repassing to and from the river with their kettles for water to cook the evening meal.

Droves of horses cover the prairie, slowly driven towards the river. When they approach, the bathers leave the water and their places are quickly filled by the restless, half-wild horses, who, urged by the yells and cries of their drivers, rush pell-mell in. After drinking and swimming about they scramble out, and forcing their way through the incoming droves, quickly rejoin their companions. When each band is collected again, they are driven up to their owner's lodge and secured for the night.

Farther down the bank several men are fishing. The one that appears to have the best luck among them is a blind Mandan who goes regularly twice a day, following the path along the edge of the bank and avoiding with wonderful skill all unsafe places. I have never known him to miss his favorite spot, and he always found with unerring accuracy the rod which he had hid in the bushes after using it. The Indians claimed that he was gifted with supernatural powers—that he was Medicine.

Warriors who have completed their evening toilet now make their appearance on the roofs of the lodges. With paint and feathers, bright blankets, and tinkling hawk-bells, they stand, their gaze apparently fixed on some far-distant object, but in reality fully alive to the interest they excite among the young squaws, who eye them with ill-concealed admiration.

Tall forms stalk through the area of the fort with proud and measured tread, or leaning carelessly against an open door observe all that passes, with seeming indifference. But let them catch sight of any preparations for cooking and they will quickly enter and seat themselves upon the floor. A pipe is sure to be forthcoming and passed around, while they converse with one another with great animation upon the ever-fresh topics of war and hunting. Thus they sit and talk and smoke, and are sure to remain until the cooking is done, when, after eating the portion given to them, they rise, uttering a satisfied "how!" and take their departure, usually turning their steps toward the village to tell their comrades, without loss of time, of the feast they have just eaten in the white man's lodge.

On one occasion, during the long and seemingly interminable days that always preceded the arrival of the annual steamboat, my house was filled with Indians as usual, being, in fact, the headquarters of the élite of the Gros Ventre village. Meat was plenty in camp, so there was no immediate necessity to hunt. No enemies had been seen around for several weeks, and besides, the *mah-ti-she-sheesh* (steamboat) was daily looked for. It was a season of absolute repose, of masterly inactivity for both traders and Indians, and lounging from the trading-post to the village and the village to the trading-post was the only business to be thought of.

I had become completely tired of the incessant loafing that never gave me a quiet hour during the day and for a little diversion to kill time filled a large coffee-boiler with water and set it on the hearth close to the embers of the fire. My friends soon began to drop in and before long the house was uncomfortably crowded. In the anticipation, however, of a cup of coffee they did not mind it in the least, but cheerfully, and with well-timed remarks, made room for every one that entered. Pipe after pipe was smoked, and an animated conversation kept up all the while.

An hour passed, but no one left the room, being afraid to lose the expected treat, and I was ostensibly too busy with some writing to pay any attention to the thirsty souls. They waited with unfailing good-humor, attributing the delay to my being occupied, and indulged in a brisk conversation about engaging in a general war with the Sioux after the departure of the steamboat.

Time wore on, my circle of guests was still there and had not manifested any inclination to diminish. I now purposely left the room for a few moments and on returning found them drawn as close around the fireplace as they could possibly crowd. One gentleman, known among us by the sobriquet of the Gambler, was just setting the boiler down, having evidently been testing by its weight, for his own satisfaction and that of his comrades, whether it was full or empty. That it was full of coffee was the only inference they could draw. One, unable to remain any longer and not wishing to forego the pleasure of tasting it, drew my attention to the boiler and plainly hinted at what was expected.

I cheerfully assented. Tin cups were quickly produced, and the Gambler was deputed to do the honors, which he undertook with great alacrity. The peculiar clearness of the liquid drew forth a remark from some one of the party and the cup already drawn was poured back, while the supposed grounds were vigorously stirred with a stick, but with no improvement in the result. A brief consultation ensued, and they were unwillingly forced to conclude that they had been "sold," but without manifesting the slightest displeasure they quietly left the room. It was soon noised through the village, and ever afterwards the Gros Ventres were satisfied to see a coffee-pot standing near my fire without waiting half a day to investigate its contents. The joke had a lasting effect.

Young bucks parade about on their fancy horses, some of which are spotted in a remarkable manner. War-eagle feathers float from the forelock or tail of many of the steeds, denoting speed and the high estimation of the owner. Those who are so fortunate as to possess one, use the heavy Spanish bit with its long iron fringes, jingling with the slightest movement of the horse. Shrinking and fretting under its cruel pressure, he arches his neck, curvets and prances to the great delight of his savage rider. Preëminently conspicuous among the chivalry of the Minnetarees was the second chief, Chaeshah-hor-a-hish, the Poor (or lean) Wolf, mounted on his magnificent charger, black as a raven and adorned with gay barbaric trappings, the Chief himself clothed with the insignia of his rank and exploits as a warrior. Horse and rider would stand motionless as a statue before the gates of the fort, and it was next to impossible not to admire this perfect living picture.

The Poor Wolf was an Indian to the backbone. He scorned the dress, food, and merchandise of the traders as much as he felt himself their superior. At all the public dances and ceremonies of his tribe he was invariably present, and entered into them with his whole heart. Like the Four Bears, he ranked high in the estimation of his people, but unlike him, though poor, he neither courted the traders nor feared their power.[37]

[37] Poor Wolf was born in 1820 in one of the Gros Ventre villages at the mouth of Knife River. He lived to an advanced age, and when eighty-six years old (in August, 1906) dictated his autobiography to a spokesman of the North Dakota Historical Society. According to his story

The crowd gathering on the prairie close to the pickets of the village shows that something unusual is going on. A horse-race must be the cause of the excitement, since five or six young men are galloping away in the direction of the creek, fully half a mile distant. They are naked, with the scanty exception of a breechcloth, and control their spirited ponies with a lariat tied around the lower jaw. From the tops of the lodges eager eyes are directed towards the starting-point and a few brief sentences announce to the expectant throng that the riders are coming this way. In one moment the competitors are spread out in line. The next they are hid from view by an intervening roll of the prairie, but the quick strokes of their horses' hoofs grow rapidly more distinct. Now they are close at hand. The excitement is at its height, for the horses are neck and neck. So closely is the race contested that it is impossible to tell who will be the victor.

The friends of the competitors yield to the impulse of the moment and make bets, throwing down robes, blankets, and guns in the most reckless manner. The riders lean forward until they

he removed to the Gros Ventre village at the site of Fort Berthold in 1844, when the trading post was established there. Old-age memories of dates, however, are often inaccurate. In May, 1893 Poor Wolf was baptized and joined the Christian Church at Fort Berthold. *North Dak. Hist. Colls.*, I, 437–43.

lie almost flat upon their horses, yelling, thumping their heels into their sides, and using the heavy Indian whip with a will. Fifty yards more will decide the race, and a breathless suspense prevails. Gathering all his energies for the decisive moment, the Crow-that-Flies shoots far ahead of the rest, amid the wildest exultations of his friends, and careers on at full speed until within a few feet of the edge of the precipitous bank of the river. Then, checking his horse so suddenly as to throw him back upon his haunches, he wheels sharply around and canters back to receive the congratulations of his friends, who are loud in their praises of his black and white spotted steed.

The young squaws are playing a game of ball resembling shinny or football, inasmuch as curved sticks and feet are called into service. The girls are generally dressed in a *metukee* (petticoat) of blue or scarlet cloth, some being trimmed with rows of elk's teeth, a scarce and highly prized ornament since it is only the two tushes of an elk that are used. On account of the difficulty of obtaining them the value of a dress ornamented with several hundred of these teeth is at once apparent. The crease of the hair is painted with vermilion, as is also a round spot on each cheek. The little boys amuse themselves in shooting at different objects with blunt arrows.

In another direction we see three young Indian dandies dressed and painted in the height of fashion, with bunches of shells surmounted with small scarlet feathers fastened to a lock of hair on each side of their foreheads. They wear false hair ornamented with spots of red and white clay and ingeniously glued to their own, and sport bright scarlet blankets lavishly garnished with white and black or white and blue beads. The long fringes of their deerskin leggings trail their whole length, and a foxtail dragging from the heel of each moccasin completes the costume.

This trio of worthies is mounted upon a stout pony, whose plaited tail is adorned with eagle feathers and the impress of a hand stamped with white clay upon his flanks. In this style they wend their way slowly through the village, the first one guiding and urging on the steed, who by his sluggish gait plainly shows his disapproval of this style of equitation. The middle one is singing at the top of his lungs, assisted by the third whenever he is not obliged to give his whole attention to avoid sliding over the horse's tail.

Those invaluable but greatly abused members of the community, the dogs, take advantage of the temporary inattention of the women to prowl among the lodges in hopes of being able to steal something edible. One has found a slice of meat and is bearing it off, foolishly thinking to enjoy it by himself. In an instant a hundred hungry, wolfish curs seize upon it and there is a prodigious uproar, a grand flourish of tails, and much snapping though but little biting. In the confusion, some cunning old dog, watching his chance, picks up the coveted morsel and bolts it down while the rest are blindly fighting for it.

The disturbance, however slight, is sufficient to draw the attention of one of the squaws, who picks up whatever comes first to hand, be it a billet of wood, a kettle, or an axe, and hurls it at the assembly with the complimentary remark "Nar-har-ah-suk-kuk," (Go away, you fools) which advice is promptly heeded. When meat is plenty in camp the dogs get fat and look well, but in times of scarcity they have to pick up whatever they can find and are often driven to the most revolting means of satisfying their hunger.

The sun has long since gone down, but the rays of his departing splendor illumine everything with a soft golden light. The tall cottonwoods across the river look fresh and green as in early spring-time. The prairie is deserted, the last band of horses has disappeared within the picketed enclosure of the village, the gates of the fort are closed and locked, and the sounds of life in the Indian camp grow fainter and fewer. Will night and darkness ever come? It is late, quite late, yet so pure is the atmosphere that one is still able to read by the light of the stars glittering in the calm, clear sky.

A woman is wailing by the dead body of her husband on one of the scaffolds. The sound is mournful in the extreme, as if her heart was broken with a grief that could not be comforted. Her husband had fallen in a battle with the Sioux. More than twelve moons have waxed and waned since he started with his warriors on that fatal warpath. Her eyes are tearless and there is little real sorrow in her lamentation. When she has cried long enough she will return to her lodge and enter into any domestic occupation or amusement that may be going on. Should there be a dance in the village she will quickly rub a little vermilion on her cheeks and join in the revelry, to all appearances as gay as the gayest. As the sounds of grief die away, the voice of a young buck is heard singing a love-ditty, which an inexperienced ear might find difficult to distinguish from a lament for the dead.

The night advances, and even these sounds are at length hushed. The perfect stillness that reigns over everything is broken only by the sullen, ceaseless roar of the Missouri, or the occasional whistle of an elk, borne faintly on the evening breeze. Now and then a crash tells of some portion of the river's bank, undermined by the rushing of the current, crumbling in, often bringing with it some noble forest-tree, which is swept into the whirl of angry waters to be carried along until, stripped of its fair proportions, it is cast a shapeless log upon some distant sand-bar.

The scene varies. Bright and dazzling the Northern Lights flash up high into the starlit sky, dimming the evening's early glories by their greater splendor. Gradually they too fade away, but the stars still glitter in the heavens and the full beams of the rising harvest moon shed their soft, silvery light over forest and prairie. Insensibly

"Sleep and oblivion reign over all."

Such were the scenes and such often the routine of a midsummer's day and night in the far-off wilderness of the Northwest.

CHAPTER VI

The Trading Post and a Buffalo Hunt

FORT Atkinson was, at the time I speak of, a new erection and but partially finished. The buildings formerly occupied by the Company had been put up some years previously and had become so dilapidated with age and neglect as to be almost unfit for use, making their renewal an imperative necessity. The new fort was one hundred and twenty feet square, which was sufficiently spacious for all the requirements of the trade. It was built on the lower end of the high bluff bank, about two hundred feet from the river and nearly the same distance from the Indian village.

A row of four houses of hewn timber, one story high, was already completely finished. The first house was used as an Indian room. Here the pipe was kept, and here the two interpreters, Paquenaude and Malnouri, dwelt, with their Indian wives and half-breed progeny.[38] Rude

[38]Charles Malnouri was a native of Illinois who evidently came to the Upper Missouri some years before the arrival of Boller in 1858. He was one of the seventeen white defenders of Fort Berthold against the determined assault of the Sioux on Christmas Day, 1863. In his later years he lived at Elbowoods on the Fort Berthold Reservation where he died on June 7, 1904. In 1898 when Boller

benches were placed around the sides to accommodate the Indian visitors, who constantly dropped in at all times to smoke and gossip. It was, in short, a kind of Exchange, where the news of the day was retailed from one to another.

The building adjoining was intended for the men's quarters, but at present was used as a storehouse. The one next above was the Bourgeois' house or headquarters. Here McBride and I dwelt in glorious independence. The interior arrangements of this abode were in a style suited to the place, and very cosy and comfortable. Two rough bedsteads of cottonwood slabs stood in opposite corners. The bedding consisted of buffalo robes, and the rough frames of the bedsteads were partially concealed by curtains of gaudy calico, which gave a certain finish to the interior.

The wide-spreading horns of an elk occupied a conspicuous position on the wall, from the

was engaged in revising his book he learned of Malnouri's address and sent him a friendly letter. Evidently it was in response to this that Malnouri sent his old-age picture to Boller. Although he had lost a leg at the hands of the Sioux many years before this, he was prosperous in his later years, owning large numbers of horses and cattle.

Charles Paquenaude (variously spelled) was a native of Canada who came to the Upper Missouri in the early forties. Like Malnouri, he served as an interpreter at Fort Berthold and participated in its defense on Christmas Day, 1863. He died about the year 1872, *North Dak. Hist. Colls.*, I, 373–76.

antlers of which hung powder-horns and bullet-pouches, with shoulder-straps of scarlet cloth elaborately worked with beads. Bridles, mountain saddles, apishamores, lariats, and other equipment decorated the walls, from which were also suspended rifles and shot-guns, always loaded and ready for use, protected by fringed deerskin covers. There were also a few rough chairs, the seats being formed of raw-hide cords. These, with a clumsy table, completed the furniture.

A barrel of water stood by the door and a tin pan, hanging from a nail close by, afforded a convenient substitute for a wash-bowl and appurtenances. The appearance of all the houses was greatly improved by being washed, both inside and out, with the white clay that abounds in this region, which is generally used by the Indians to clean their robes and dresses from grease and dirt, also rendering them soft and pliable.

Adjoining the Bourgeois' house was the kitchen and mess-room, the presiding genius of which seemed to take greater delight in declaiming against the Indians and waging war upon the innumerable flies than in the discharge of his duties, about which, if the truth must be told, his knowledge was not over-extensive. On the opposite side of the area a row of similar length was begun, intended as a storehouse for goods and furs. Sufficient material was on the ground to finish all these improvements before cold weather set in. Three sides of the fort were enclosed with a substantial stockade of hewn timbers, sixteen feet in height. Each picket had a face of about twelve inches by six in thickness, and was strongly set three feet in the ground, secured at the top by a heavy wooden plate or sill. The unenclosed side was occupied by the remaining buildings of the old fort, which eventually would all be removed and rebuilt to correspond with the new part. The work was pushed on vigorously, exciting great interest among the crowd of idlers, who watched the proceedings with the untiring patience of the Indian.[39]

[39] At this point in his projected revision Boller inserted the following description of the carousal which followed the departure of the steamboat.

"The steamboat had hardly disappeared from view around the bend of the river when the yearly Saturnalia began. No whiskey was brought up by either company but individuals managed to smuggle it ashore in quantities sufficient to start everybody, both white and red, on a good old-fashioned 4th-of-July drunk. At our post all hands were kept too busy to allow of much indulgence, so there was comparatively little drinking, but at Berthold and through the village it was a lively week. Naked Indians, brandishing weapons and uttering terrific yells staggered around, making it difficult for their families to restrain them from committing deeds of violence.

"It was the custom for enough of the principal men to remain sober in order to keep a close watch on the revellers, and they had their hands full. One day a number of Indians, fairly crazed by fire-water, met in the Fort,

An Indian riding in hot haste towards the village one morning created a great excitement, while the guards at the same time could be seen hurrying in the horses from every direction. "The enemy! the enemy!" was the cry, and a general rush to arms followed. Whoops and yells resounded on all sides and the alarm was fast spreading, when the scout, dashing up on his foaming steed, announced that a large band of buffaloes had been discovered at some distance across the river. Preparations for the chase were at once actively begun, and in high glee at the anticipated feast of fresh meat the squaws carried down to the water's edge the bull-boats in which to ferry the hunters over. These boats, which are necessary adjuncts to every Gros Ventre lodge, are made of the fresh hide of a buffalo bull stretched over a framework of willow. As the hide

and for awhile it looked as if a general free-for-all fight was imminent. At such a time the whites kept out of the way as much as possible, leaving to the sober Indians the difficult and dangerous task of controlling the madmen. . . .

"A week wound up the carouse, and there were many 'sick' Indians anxious to sober down. All were thoroughly ashamed of the uproar they had been making. No one was better pleased at the return of affairs to their normal condition than the old Raising Heart. The angry gleam faded from his eye and the friendly smile, so habitual to his countenance, returned. It was a pleasant change to an excitement of a far different and legitimate kind [the reported approach of a Sioux war-party]."

dries it shrinks, binding the whole together with great strength. In shape they resemble large wash-tubs, and will bear astonishing loads, considering the frail manner of their construction.

With proper care in keeping the hide dry and free from holes a well-made bull-boat will last a couple of years. They are ticklish craft to navigate, however, and unless the voyager is extremely careful to preserve an equilibrium he will suddenly and most unexpectedly find himself treated to a cold plunge. These bull-boats are always paddled by the squaws, and very laborious work it is, since the paddle is thrust into the water only about two feet in advance and drawn towards the boat, thus impelling it slowly forwards.[40]

In embarking in one of these frail canoes the saddles, guns, and other equipment are carefully placed in the bottom. The hunter next steps in, holding the ends of his horses' lariats, which are

[40] Viewed as a vehicle for navigation the defects of the bull-boat were many. However it possessed two offsetting advantages. It could be easily and quickly constructed from materials commonly everywhere available, and it could navigate, even when burdened with considerable cargo, in water too shallow to admit the passage of any other type of vessel. Boller's description applies, of course, to the native or "Squaw" bull-boat. At the hands of the white man it underwent a marked development. Constructed chiefly for use on such shallow rivers as the Platte and the Niobrara, it might be as much as 30 feet long and 12 wide, with a carrying capacity up to 3 tons.

fastened with a double running noose around their lower jaws. The squaw then pushes the boat off and wades out with it until the water becomes sufficiently deep, when, steadying herself with her paddle she carefully takes her place and the horses, two or three of which are usually crossed at once, being urged into the river by the shouts and cries of the bystanders, slowly and reluctantly yield themselves to the guidance of their master.

For a while, although the squaw paddles with all her might, the boat makes no headway, but whirls around like a top. The struggles and plunges of the unwilling and refractory horses retard its progress and momentarily threaten to upset the frail vessel, until the very violence of their exertions carries them out into deep water. The strong current bears them swiftly along and the horses, guided and supported by their master, swim after, only their heads and elevated tails being visible.

Yet its draft in the morning (when the hides were dry and newly patched) would be but 4 inches, and at the end of the day, when water-soaked and perhaps suffering from leakage, but 8 or 9 inches. But the Platte and the Niobrara were whimsical rivers, with ever-shifting currents. The bull-boat crew which camped for the night beside the river might awaken in the morning to find their craft stranded high and dry far remote from the current. See Chittenden, *Hist. of Early Steamboat Navigation on the Missouri River*, I, 96–102.

The boats always start from the upper end of the village and strike directly across, but as soon as they get into the current they are drifted down some distance before they can make the opposite shore. After effecting a landing the squaw drags her boat out of the water and helps her hunter to saddle. He canters off on one of the pack-horses, leading his runner to keep him fresh for the chase, and striking through the timber halts at a convenient rendezvous previously agreed upon. When all are assembled the leader of the hunt takes command and arranges the details. The squaws, inverting the bull-boats over their heads, carry them to a point above the village and then set out on their return, reaching the shore considerably below the starting-place. The women with their boats over their heads resemble huge black beetles crawling along the sand-bar.—

An animated sight it was as the hunters cantered on their dripping steeds through the forest glades, their bright-colored blankets and glittering equipment forming a strong contrast to the dark green foliage of the cottonwoods and the brighter hues of the red willows. The buffaloes were in plain sight, feeding quietly, unconscious of the impending danger. They had divided into two bands, the smaller of which was much nearer than the other. Some were lying down, others were rolling and pawing the ground with their hoofs, causing a thin cloud of dust to float over the herds, while their deep bellowing sounded like distant thunder. Many of the bulls were butting and fighting each other.

The band of hunters emerged from the timber and after riding a few hundred yards out on the prairie came to a halt. A party was now detached and sent against the wind, keeping parallel with the forest. These were mounted on the fastest horses, those able to catch buffaloes under any circumstances. The main body continued cautiously on, having two scouts in advance so as to be instantly notified of any change in the position of the buffaloes. A second party now made a flank movement on the small band and halted. The rest of the hunters rode on and soon disappeared behind a heavy roll of the prairie. They then made a semicircular movement, which brought them close to the rear of the large herd.

The pack-horses were now hobbled and left, blankets and every superfluous article laid aside, and all being ready, at a given signal the three parties dashed forward at the top of their horses' speed.

In an instant the buffaloes appeared strung out in a long line, while the hunters, in an irregular body, dealt destruction everywhere. The fast horses soon distanced the others and brought their riders alongside of the "fattest meat." The dust raised by hundreds of hoofs hung in a thick, suffocating cloud, while the booming of guns, whizzing of arrows, and rush of the maddened herd, with the reckless riding of the excited Indians, formed a thrilling spectacle.

The cloud rolled away, but many of that band of buffaloes were lying dead upon the prairie and the hunters were busily engaged in butchering, their horses quietly feeding near with trailing lariats. A few survivors were fleeing rapidly over the hills and here and there a wounded cow stood at bay, savagely charging at her pursuer, while the well-trained horse skilfully avoided the shock.

In a little while the pack-horses were loaded and the hunters set out on their return. The close of the day saw them gathered on the sand bar, preparing to cross back to the village. Masses of reeking flesh were flung into the boats. The saddles, apishamores (old buffalo rugs used under the saddles, soiled with blood and sweat) were thrown on top with the rest of the equipment, and the hunters taking their places, re-crossed, the exhausted horses swimming passively behind. At the landing the squaws again saddle the horses and pack the meat, leaving the hunters to pick up their weapons, without giving themselves further concern. The shrill cries of the women scolding at one another and driving away the dogs that are hovering around to snap at the meat hanging from the pack-saddles add to the general confusion and excitement.

When the returning hunters were first seen on the hills fires were kindled in the lodges, over which the squaws hung kettles of water. No unnecessary time was therefore lost before a general feasting was in progress throughout the entire camp. The very opportune supply of meat which this hunt afforded would, however, last but a few days, and another was therefore proposed as soon as a war-party should return which had been out for a long time and for whose safety great apprehensions were felt.

The next morning two white medicine flags were flying on the prairie, each bearing a rude painting in vermilion of the sun and moon, to which they were offerings. An Indian walked in a circle around them all day long, crying and praying to the Great Spirit to grant him success in war and the chase. Near him was a small pile of human skulls, around each of which was bound a strip of scarlet cloth. His lance, thrust into the ground beside them, supported his shield and medicine bag. During the time that he was making this Medicine he dared not eat nor speak to any one for fear of breaking the spell and thereby displeasing the Great Spirit.

Chapter VII

A Raid and a Medicine Man

WE were enjoying the usual noontide siesta. The day was warm, and the village had quieted down to a state of general repose. A sudden discharge of firearms across the river changed the scene. In an instant all is excitement. Warriors seize their weapons and rush to the edge of the bluff, eagerly seeking the cause of the alarm. Thirteen Indians have just made their appearance on the sand-bar opposite. It is the long looked-for war-party. They are returning in triumph!

Their faces are painted black and one carries a scalp on the end of his lance, while another leads a fine horse. They form a single rank and march up and down the bar, singing and firing off their fusees. Bull-boats are quickly sent across, in one of which is the Long Hair, who, as soon as he hears the news, announces it across the river and is heard without difficulty. Soon the whole party are brought over and receive the warm congratulations of the old men, as well as the smiles of the squaws, and are objects of envy to the *bannerêts* and boys who have not yet had or sought an opportunity of distinguishing themselves on the war-path. For the rest of the day and all night nothing else was thought of but singing and dancing the scalp. Towards sundown the Long Hair (so called from the length of his natural hair which trailed on the ground as he walked), celebrated as a haranguer, came into the fort at the head of a party of young squaws to entertain us with the scalp-song and dance. All had painted their cheeks with vermilion and yellow clay and wore their finest dresses. As they had been singing and dancing before every lodge in the village, the girls appeared rather tired and the Long Hair decidedly out of breath with his exertions. They danced around in a circle, with a jerking, shuffling step, the Long Hair beating a drum which resembled a very large tambourine and singing "hi, hi, hi-yah, hi-yah," to which the squaws echoed shrilly, "he, he, he-ee, he-ee."[41]

This war-party had started out several weeks before in connection with a small band of Rees, making altogether about thirty young and daring braves. Their destination was Fort Pierre,

[41] An abundant growth of hair was highly prized by certain of the Upper Missouri tribes. Another well-known Long Hair was the Crow chieftain of this name in the thirties. Reliable contemporary testimony affirms that his hair was over ten feet long, unmatched by that of any other member of the tribe. R. G. Thwaites (Ed.), *Early Western Travels*, XXII, 353; *Montana Hist. Soc. Contributions*. VIII, 224–28.

in the neighborhood of which a few lodges
of Sioux were usually encamped, and they designed lurking around until an opportunity
offered to "count a coup," *i. e.*, steal a horse
or take a scalp, in both of which they had been
successful.

Carefully and stealthily they made their way,
subsisting upon dry pounded meat or toro
which had been prepared for them before leaving
home. Lighting no fires when they camped, lest
they should attract the notice of their enemies,
they kept on, day by day, until after a toilsome
march they beheld, from a distant bluff, the
long-sought Fort Pierre, and near it eight or
ten lodges of Sioux.

Here they remained concealed until nightfall,
quietly awaiting the decisive moment when success or defeat would attend them. It came at last
and with cautious tread they crept within an
arrow's flight of the lodges.

The gray dawn is breaking, and before the
inmates of the trading-post are astir the Sioux
have loosened their horses and are driving them
off to pasture. The women take their kettles to
the river's brink for water and one old squaw
comes unconsciously towards the lurking-place
of her deadly foes to pick service-berries, which
grew there in abundance. A start, and the hand
extended to pluck the berries is motionless for

an instant. Instinctively she turns to flee, but the winged arrow is swifter and she falls headlong, pierced through the heart. The scalp is torn off with a quick jerk of the knife and each warrior strikes the body, thereby counting a coup, to be emblazoned on his battle-robe and placed on the Indian roll of fame. Flushed with success and heedless of the weary distance to be traversed before they see their own village again, the victors rapidly and warily begin their return.

Dire will be the consternation that seizes on that little encampment when the mangled corpse shall be discovered. Who can tell but that her increasing age and feebleness would ere long have rendered her unfit to keep up with her people when they travelled, when she would have been abandoned to a fate more horrible. Better for her was instant death than to be deserted by her kin and left to perish miserably, or be torn piecemeal by wolves.

Continuing their retreat, they found a very fine horse which had probably been lost from some Indian camp and was in good order, or as they expressed it, rolling fat. Highly elated with their success they returned in safety to their respective villages, where they met with a warm welcome, the more cordial since they had been given up for lost. After leaving the

Ree village every step of their route lay through
an enemy's country, whose numerous scouts
and hunting-parties could hardly fail to discover them.

A season of comparative quiet now set in. The
horses were luxuriating upon the rich grass and
rapidly recovering from the fatigues of the last
hunt. The squaws were hard at work hoeing their
cornfields, and exulting in the prospect of an
abundant crop. Our storehouse was by this time
completely finished. It was divided into three
compartments, one for storing away the robes and
peltries, and which was, of course, at this season
nearly empty. The middle part was fitted up as a
trade-store, with a high counter set back a few
feet from the door, just giving space enough to
admit two or three Indians at a time. Rude
shelves of rough plank at the rear contained a
small assortment of the various goods needed,
blankets, knives, gayly-ornamented bridles, fusees
with their stocks profusely studded with brass
tacks, blue and scarlet cloth, beads, calicoes,
and all the glittering trifles that please the savage taste. In the remaining apartment were kept
the provisions and goods in bulk, from which
the trade-store was supplied as its necessities
required.

After storing and arranging the goods there was but little to do until the winter trade began. The work of enclosing the fort with pickets had also been completed, new and substantial gates hung, and after the haying season was over it was designed to put up an ice-house and plunder-rooms. These improvements had done away with almost every vestige of the old fort. One magnificent structure alone remained. It was about eight feet by ten, with not space enough between the floor and roof to admit of a middle-sized man standing upright.

This building was at present occupied by an old Santee (Sioux) named E-ten-ah-pen-ah, (the-Face-that-don't-run) a highly accomplished sinner, and a worthy inhabitant of the old cabin. He was a boundless liar, but always told his stories with such a serio-comic air, that it was impossible to listen to him without being greatly amused. For many years he had dwelt among the Rees and Gros Ventres, and was regarded by them with great awe as a medicine man, or doctor, of extraordinary skill.

Besides his squaw, a rather fine-looking young Yankton woman, and his boy, there were four or five old hags, habitual attachées of his establishment, who made it their regular headquarters and lived there with bag and baggage. So it is obvious, from the very limited size of this dwelling, that there could be but little room to spare. All day the old Doctor, as we styled him, would sit, surrounded by a coterie of his friends, regaling them with numberless lies, but all so plausibly told that his delighted auditors listened with gaping attention. The kettle was constantly on the fire, for the Doctor's hospitality as a host was proverbial, and as long as there was anything in the cabin to eat he entertained plenty of company.

His son and heir, a hopeful urchin of three summers, who rejoiced in the title of the Muskrat, was usually called in to finish the remains of the feasts, which, with the willing assistance of two or three puppies, his constant companions, he quickly and thoroughly accomplished. The Muskrat ran about with nothing but his own skin for a covering, which was generally spotted in a tasteful manner with white clay, and after a meal his rotundity would assume such bursting proportions as to most justly entitle him to the enviable distinction of being a "Gros Ventre," regardless of his Dacota parentage.

Doctor E-ten-ah-pen-ah came into my room one morning and found me poring over a book. Here was a new idea! If he could only get one! Much amused, I presented him with it, and then, at his urgent solicitation, wrote some sentences in Sioux, which he dictated, on one of the pages, and chuckling to himself over his prize the old rascal hurried back to his abode.

In the course of the morning, while strolling around I noticed an unusual crowd in front of his residence, and curious to know what ceremony was in progress, looked in. There was the Doctor with the book open before him, his eyes intently fixed upon the page, moving his lips as if reading, and occasionally turning over a leaf. He had on a pair of heavy silver-rimmed spectacles, and, as might be expected, looked profoundly wise. With difficulty suppressing my mirth I was turning to go away, when one of his guests, who was evidently skeptical as to the Doctor's literary attainments, called me back and asked me if he could read. Prompted by a glance from the Doctor I nodded affirmatively, whereupon with consummate adroitness the old fellow repeated the lines I had written at his dictation, and then pushing his glasses up over his forehead, handed the book to me. I at once read off the same sentences and his triumph was complete. After casting a quizzical glance at me, as if to say that we understood each other thoroughly, he closed the book, and looking around with an air of intense self-satisfaction complacently received the undisguised plaudits of his friends. So the Doctor continued to flourish until it was necessary to pull down the architectural pile in which he dwelt, when he removed to the village and purchased a lodge, giving one of his two remaining horses for it. He was, however, constantly in the fort, and frequently got medicines from me, with which he performed some wonderful cures.

About this time five or six "big men" came into the Bourgeois' house and said that it had been determined in council not to let the whites make hay this year. An interval of profound silence ensued, which was broken by one of the party asking that a kettle of tea be made for their refreshment. The interpreter was forthwith ordered to tell them that as we were not to be allowed to cut hay this season it would be necessary to save our tea to feed our horses on during the winter. This unexpected reply entirely upset their remaining ideas upon the subject, and after a short and awkward pause they gathered their blankets around them and made a rather undignified exit. A day or so after, the Fat Fox, who was the principal spokesman on that memorable occasion, stopped in to see us in a most friendly way and casually remarked that what had been said about not allowing us to cut hay was merely a little fun—only squaw's talk, and consequently nothing more must be thought of it. So this attempt to levy blackmail from the luckless whites resulted in a complete failure.

A drowned buffalo floated past, when some young Indians swam after, and succeeded in landing it about a mile down the river, where it was butchered. When carried by, the meat was rank and almost putrid, but not too offensive for the delicate palates of the savages.

Chapter VIII

A Buffalo Hunt that Failed

GOING to Nickaway[42] in two nights, near the Square Hills in the big bend."[43] So the Hawk told us when he came to beg some powder and balls, making the usual promises to pay liberally in meat when he returned. It was to be a general turn-out, he said, of all the able-bodied men, each accompanied by one or two squaws to cut up and jerk the meat. The old people, who would be compelled to remain behind, were already in great trepidation lest the Sioux, after reconnoitering and finding nearly all the men away, would devastate the corn-fields, and perhaps the village itself. Even the General, as we called the valiant Paquenaude, asked permission to accompany the hunting-party, for the sole pur-

[42]When the Indians go on a single hunt, they call it a "surround." When they go with their squaws, intending to make a number of surrounds until they have secured as much dry meat as they want, they call it "going to Nickaway." Boller.

[43]Lieutenant G. K. Warren's map accompanying his *Report of Explorations . . . . in 1855–57* shows the Square Hills on the western side of the Missouri some ten miles by land below the site of Fort Clark, in present-day Oliver County. But the "Nickaway" of Boller's narrative, to which the hunters were going, was near the head of the Grand Detour, in present-day Mountrail County. See *post,* 225–26.

pose, as he said, of securing a supply of superior meat for the use of the fort, but others, less charitable, said it was simply a strategic move on his part.

The whole morning resounded with the busy note of preparation. Towards afternoon the horses were driven up and the work of crossing them commenced. The confusion and bustle were at their height when Paquenaude began saddling up. He intended taking his squaw and child along, and as many of his effects as could be conveniently packed on his horses, three of which were loaned him from our stud with the understanding that one-half the meat they brought back was to be turned over to the Company.

The General put on his helmet, in the shape of a black handkerchief tied around his head, and shouldering his gun when everything was ready, bade us farewell with a lengthened countenance which was irresistibly ludicrous. No inducement could have been held out sufficient to keep him with us in the fort while so many of the Indians were away. He took his departure with the settled conviction that we were doomed men, and would undoubtedly fall victims to the immense war-party of Yanc-toh-wahs, which *he knew* was lurking near by, only waiting until the hunters got off to make an onslaught upon the village, and expecting when he returned to find nothing but charred timbers and mangled corpses.

By evening all the hunters were across the river and everything had settled down into more than its wonted quiet. Our store was filled with Indian valuables temporarily deposited for safe-keeping, while many women and children, as well as old men, asked and obtained permission to share the security of the fort until their friends returned.

The Nickaway people camped on the edge of the open prairie, where their cheerful fires at nightfall lit up the surrounding gloom. But few closed their eyes in the village that night. The slightest sound was anxiously listened for, and when morning broke and revealed no trace of the dreaded foe the alarmed Indians breathed more freely and felt as if a respite had been granted them.

Relieved of the presence of so many idlers, our building was pushed on rapidly, and we congratulated ourselves on the prospect of having everything nearly finished before their return. They expected to be gone on this hunt about one moon. The long line of the hunting-party had scarcely disappeared behind the swells of the distant prairie before a small war-party was discovered on the heights beyond the southern bend of the river. Their boldness in showing themselves in broad daylight led all to suppose that they were merely the scouts of a larger party, so numerous that they did not feel concealment necessary. The alarm was therefore great. The horses were hurried up to a safe distance and every one prepared for the expected conflict.

Another night of anxious suspense to the watchers in the village followed and the morning light discovered three arrows shot into the body of a squaw on one of the scaffolds. She had been the wife of old Ara-poo-she, the Rotten Bear, an elderly Indian of immense corporation and of the mildest and most inoffensive disposition possible. To the astonishment of every one the Rotten Bear appeared in a new character. Naked to the clout, with war-paint and weapons, he waddled around and harangued for all whose hearts were strong to follow him to glory or the grave, and avenge the wrong he had sustained in the insult offered to the body of his old woman.

His futile rage and impassioned appeal to arms excited only laughter and ridicule, for the Rotten Bear was as harmless and far less offensive than his namesake could have been. Two or three turns around the village in the hot July sun took all the martial spirit out of him, and when rallied about it he seemed to consider it as rather a good joke than otherwise.

An interval of perfect quiet succeeded, but it was the calm which precedes the storm. In the dead of night, (it was the tenth, I think, since the Nickaway people had left) we were all startled by a most unearthly noise and yelling in the village. It seemed as if every old hag and every dog had had their vocal powers strengthened a hundred-fold for the occasion, to say nothing of the yells of the men and reports of fire-arms. We concluded, as a matter of course, that our friends had one of their regular paroxysms of fear, when a number of guns were discharged in rapid succession and amid the most tremendous uproar that I ever heard we made out to learn that the hunters had been completely routed by an immense war-party of Sioux, and a remnant only had succeeded in effecting their escape.

Bull-boats were at once put into service and the exhausted and panic-stricken fugitives were safely brought over. The General's eagerness to bring us the news was such that very few crossed before him. The poor fellow looked jaded and haggard, and the black handkerchief was disordered, as if by the sudden uprising of his hair. He was, in fact, completely demoralized.

McBride, with the slightest possible approach to a smile, asked, "Are all the horses back safe?"

"Yes."

"Did you bring a pretty good load of meat with you?"

"None! I had to throw it all away when the Sioux *faunced* on us."

"The Sioux *faunced* on you, did they—how many did you kill of them?" (Great interest manifested by all of us to hear.)

"Yesterday afternoon near sundown we were camped near the Square Hills when Red Tail discovered the enemy rushing on us. Every Injin yelled and shouted and went on like mad, and some began to throw away their meat and got on their horses and *mooshed* for the village."

"Did you yell any?"

"Me! Of course I did. Every one around was yellin' and screechin', and there was no use tryin' to keep quiet."

"I want to hear if any were killed."

"Don't know. I let go my horses as fast as they could run. It was so dark you couldn't see ahead, and me and my woman fell into a deep hole. It is terrible how my chest is bruised."

"Who was at the head of the party?"

"The Injins told a squaw to go ahead, as they could better spare a woman than a man if they fell into a trap."

"You've played——on this hunt, sure," McBride remarked, a conclusion to which we all assented, and left the General to take care of his inner man.

At early dawn the air resounded with the voice of the old Dry Pumpkin, haranguing, and calling upon every one to prepare to revenge the terrible defeat they had just sustained.

"Men of the Hee-rae-an-seh, a black cloud covers our village with darkness. The Great Spirit is angry with us. Our hearts are buried deep in the ground. Where are our brave warriors? Our women and children are crying. Rouse yourselves, sharpen your arrows and seek the enemy! Strike them so hard with your tomahawks that both hands will hardly pull them out! Make strong Medicine, and the Great Spirit will grant you a successful return with plenty of scalps and horses. Then will the women dance and not feel ashamed. Men of the Hee-rae-an-seh, if your hearts are strong, hear me! It is I, the Dry Pumpkin, that speaks. He is not a child any more. His head is whitened with many snows. Rouse up, rouse up, young men! If you are wise, listen to my words. Go and wipe out this disgrace, or the Sioux will laugh at us and call us dogs and old women!"

In this strain the Dry Pumpkin continued, walking around the village, and occasionally mounting upon the tops of the lodges to make himself better heard. But unfortunately, his warlike antecedents were by no means calculated to stir up a feeling of fiery revenge among his people. In truth he might just as well have talked to the winds, for none listened to him.

Years before, when a young man, as he was returning with his squaw and several Gros Ventres from a visit to the Crows on the Yellowstone they were attacked by a war-party of Assiniboines. At the first sound of the conflict the Dry Pumpkin made off and his hurry was such that he stopped not until he arrived at his village, where he told how his friends had been attacked by an overwhelming force of the enemy and after a desperate struggle he alone had effected his escape. It seems that the Dry Pumpkin ran away with such celerity that no arrow could possibly have flown fast enough to hit him, and his squaw, in attempting to keep him in sight, was overtaken and ruthlessly butchered and scalped.

As he had never ventured upon the war-path after this heroic achievement his opinions and advice had very little weight. After haranguing until he was wellnigh exhausted he came into my room complaining of feeling unwell and asked for some medicine. I administered, accordingly, an enormous dose of Epsom salt and saw nothing of him for several days, when he came crawling into my quarters again, leaning on a stick and looking considerably reduced. He remarked simply that the medicine I had given him was very strong.

By-and-by the Gros Ventres showed signs of returning reason, and upon mustering their forces none were found missing! All were safe, minus their stock of dry meat, which was lost owing to a senseless panic. They were in a splendid hunting-ground with every prospect of success, when one evening a smoke was discovered and also the form of a man, supposed to be a spy.

The alarm was given, and the wildest confusion prevailed. One frightened another, and amid the most heathenish yells and screams it was determined to move camp at once and the pell-mell retreat commenced. It was now ascertained that the fire had been kindled by one of their own hunters who had been looking for a stray horse, and stopped to cook some deer meat that he had killed. The Nickaway was a complete failure. Their horses were run down and would require rest. They had lost all their meat and were in a starving condition again.

CHAPTER IX

The Mandans Make Medicine

TO atone for the past, and in the hope of pleasing the Great Spirit so that He would send the buffaloes close to their village again, the Indians determined to make their great Bull Medicine.

The necessary preparations for this important ceremony now engrossed the attention of the entire community. The squaws were busy in arranging a large and spacious lodge and cleaning off the area in the center of the village where the principal ceremonies and dances would take place. The making of this medicine occupies four days, during which time all who take part observe a strict fast.

The first day, the old Mandan medicine man, A-mah-she-kee-ri-pe, the Buck Eagle, came into the fort and seated himself upon a pile of lumber in the middle, followed by a crowd who arranged themselves around at a respectful distance, while in a subdued and plaintive tone of voice he commenced an invocation to the Great Spirit. With the exception of a white wolf-skin over one shoulder he was entirely naked. A fillet of the same was bound around each ankle and two wolf's tails dragged from the heels of his moccasins. A cap made of a piece of white buffalo robe, trimmed with the claws and tail-feather of an eagle, covered his head and his withered limbs were painted with red clay. Some trifling presents were placed before him, and after his adjuration was concluded he gathered them carefully up and took his departure.

In the afternoon of the second day I went to the lodge where the ceremonies were going on. It was filled with young men, some of whom had passed through the ordeal before and were now merely fasting. The others were those who were to undergo the terrible torture, and around the interior were arranged their shields, lances, and medicine bags. The men mostly reclined on their backs and a few were even asleep.

The Buck Eagle sat in the center, near the embers of the fire, smoking a handsome pipe and occasionally calling upon the Great Spirit. The warriors who were to take part in the dance were painting their bodies with alternate bars of red and white and dressing themselves in a piece of shaggy buffalo robe, with a large bunch of green willows bound on their backs and smaller bunches in each hand. They represented the bulls, and were six in number. At regular intervals during the day they came forth and danced around the open area, or public square, in the middle of the village. In the center of this area was a circular structure, resembling a very large hogshead. Suddenly the Buck Eagle appeared from the lodge with his pipe in his hand, and leaning against the tub commenced crying in a loud voice to the Great Spirit. Rattles sounded from within the lodge and three men ran out in a crouching position, carrying drums garnished with feathers, and seated themselves on the ground close by him. Two others bearing rattles followed, and the signal was given for the dancers to appear by a prolonged drumming and rattling.

All the people of the village now congregated to witness this ceremony, which they considered their most important one after the dance of the Calumet, and covered the tops of the surrounding lodges, from one of which I had an excellent view of the proceedings. The assemblage behaved with the utmost decorum. There was no jostling or pushing, setting in this respect an example which could be followed with infinite advantage elsewhere. Then, from the Medicine Lodge, in pairs, with a jarring, shuffling step in regular cadence, with their fantastic dresses of buffalo robes and willow boughs, came the bull-dancers, and commenced to circle slowly around the tub.

On the afternoon of the third day the most thrilling part of the ceremonies occurred. The rattles sounded, the drums beat, and the bulls executed their stamping, jarring dance with un-

wonted energy. The Raising Heart conducted
me to a seat on a log among the dignitaries of
the tribe and seated himself close by among some
of his old cronies, with whom he kept up an
animated conversation. All eyes were turned towards the Medicine Lodge, whence came pouring
forth, and dispersing in all directions, a band of
antelopes, fifty or sixty in number. They were
men and boys of all sizes, entirely naked and
painted all over with white clay. Willow twigs
were bound on their heads in the shape of and to
represent horns. There were also frogs and several nondescript animals.

After dancing for about twenty minutes the
bulls suddenly broke away in different directions,
mostly taking their course through the groups of
women and young girls, who scattered upon
their approach, with screams of laughter, to
lodges where refreshments, consisting chiefly of
boiled mush, were prepared for them. Buck Eagle
and his musicians returned at once to their
lodge, and after eating, the bulls followed their
example, to repeat the dance within an interval
of half an hour.

The band of antelopes rushed hither and
thither, anywhere and everywhere, one moment
on the tops of the lodges, the next dashing
through the groups of squaws, and then clustered together plotting fresh mischief. The frogs

kept near the big tub, around which they danced and hopped in a most grotesque manner. An old woman now came forward with a large wooden bowl of mush, which she handed to one of the frogs, but scarcely has he lifted it to his mouth ere it is snatched from him by an antelope, when the rest of the band dash forward and in the scuffle that follows the earth receives most of it, while the old woman retreats with feigned indignation to her lodge.

In retaliation for this insult, and with more agility than one would suppose them to possess, the frogs pursue the antelopes, but seldom succeed in overtaking them. Another old woman now comes forward with another bowl of mush, but before she has advanced many steps an antelope trots up quickly behind her and suddenly snatching it out of her hands attempts to swallow it, but is thwarted in this by his companions and the mush is again spilled. Sometimes, however, the old woman will turn suddenly around and throw the mush over such antelopes as happen to be near, which exploit is hailed with intense satisfaction by the squaws.

So the sports go bravely on while the bulls keep up their dance with unabated vigor. But there is a pause as one by one in Indian file, with slow and measured tread, forth from the Medicine Lodge come the young men who have been fasting. All are naked, with the exception of a scarlet breechcloth, and their bodies and limbs are painted with yellow clay. Each one carries a lance decorated with fluttering pennons and war-eagle feathers, and a fancifully-painted and garnished shield is slung over the shoulder.

They looked emaciated, but showed no signs of weariness, walking with a slow but firm step to the middle of the area, where they prostrated themselves in a regular line with their faces flat to the ground and continued thus in silent prayer to the Great Spirit for about a quarter of an hour. The bulls still kept up their dance, but the sports of the antelopes had for the time ceased, and they clustered in groups on the tops of the lodges, silent and attentive spectators. Slowly rising from the ground, the young men retraced their steps to the lodge.

The bulls now exerted themselves vigorously, the antelopes resumed their pranks, and two old warriors, Chae-shah-ou-ketty (the Bobtail Wolf) and Mush-shuka-hoy-tucky (the White Dog) emerged from the Medicine Lodge, closely followed by a couple of the young men. Going up to two stout poles about twelve feet high and firmly planted in the ground, they disengaged cords of raw hide hanging from them. One of the young men knelt at the foot of the pole resting his thighs on his heels, and throwing his head back and his breast forward, supported himself in this position by his hands. The old men now, one on either side, with a common butcher-knife cut through the skin and flesh on each breast, and thrusting splints under the sinews attached the thongs to them. The other young man was quickly served in the same way.

Not a muscle of their countenances changed expression and not a sound escaped their lips while this painful operation was in progress. Each rose to his feet and throwing the whole weight of his body upon the cords, with the blood streaming from the wounds, tried to tear himself loose. One, as soon as he was left alone, sprang wildly to the full length of the cords and then, hanging with his full weight upon the sinews of his breast, swung back, striking the post violently.

Again and again he swung himself off and around the pole, calling in the most agonizing tones to the Great Spirit and praying that he might hereafter be a successful warrior and hunter, and that his heart might be made strong to enable him to bear his present sufferings. After being self-tortured in this way for some time he fainted, and hung, to all appearances, entirely dead. The strain on the splints finally tore them out and he fell to the ground, when his relations came forward and took him in charge, carrying him off to a lodge where, after he revived, food would be ready for him and he might then receive the congratulations of his friends.

The other youth uttered not a word. He was quite young, not more than seventeen or eighteen, and for some time walked around the pole, shrinking from the fearful test. At last, having nerved himself up to it, he suddenly swung off with all his strength, and returning, struck the post with such violence that he, too, fainted, and hung, a sickening sight, with the blood streaming from his self-inflicted wounds.

In no instance can the splints be pulled out. To do so would be fatal to the Medicine. In some cases, where the sinew is very strong, it is necessary to suspend them entirely off their feet and even increase the weight by hanging buffalo skulls to their limbs. One Indian was compelled to walk around for nearly an entire day, dragging after him six or eight buffalo skulls. All who can pass through this ordeal without flinching are looked upon as brave men and strong-hearted warriors and hunters. The Four Bears himself had gone through it four or five times, as the scars on his breast and limbs testified.

The fourth and closing day was mostly a repetition of the third. Those of the young men who had not succeeded in tearing themselves loose from the poles were dragged in a circle by the hands until the buffalo skulls fastened to their legs were torn out by the violence of the race, and it has happened more than once that the tough sinew, defying every effort to break it, rendered it necessary for the unfortunate sufferer to crawl off on the prairie and there remain until it had rotted completely out.

It is not my purpose, beyond a few general remarks, to enter into any speculations or theories as to the origin of this or other rites and ceremonies. I shall confine myself to narrating simply and accurately such scenes and incidents in Indian life as came under my notice, for the reason that all such speculations and theories would be for the most part vague and unsatisfactory.

There are of course exceptions, but the majority of the interpreters, through whom such information can only be obtained, are usually ignorant, unlettered men, who have originally been brought into the country as common voyageurs, and after a time, preferring the lazy life of the Indians, they fall into their ways and thus by degrees pick up enough of the language for ordinary intercourse. It cannot be expected, therefore, that interpreters of such limited intelligence would be able to enter into lengthened and profound explanations of these and kindred observances, however well fitted they may be to act the part of translators. When not in the employ of either company they live with the Indians, whose estimation of them is measured only by their ability to make presents and keep their squaw-wives and their interminable set of "cousins" well dressed and provided for.

The Bull Medicine is intended to ask the blessing of the Great Spirit upon the tribe, but more especially upon the participants, that they may have plenty of buffaloes close to the village so that they need not go far away and be in danger from their enemies. Also, that success in war and horse-stealing may be granted them, and they may thus become distinguished among their people. Their fasts and self-imposed tortures are public evidences of the sincerity of their belief, and faith in the power of the Great Spirit to support them in these terrible trials and hear their supplications.

I have always considered the North American Indians a highly religious people, according to the light they have. They practise as well as preach. They all believe in an overruling Power, which they call the Great Spirit, and that He dwells in a beautiful country beyond the skies. To go to this beautiful country, or Happy Hunting Ground, is the crowning point of an Indian's hope. It is his expected reward for the faithful fulfillment of his obligations to the Great Spirit during life, by stealing horses, taking scalps, and general success as a warrior and hunter. There he will be rewarded for all his trials and privations on earth. There it will be always early summer-time. The grass will ever be green and fresh, watered by cool mountain springs. Game will abound in the greatest profusion, and the hunter need never fear the whizzing arrow or whistling bullet of his foe. His lodge will always be amply stored, his wives will raise abundant crops of corn and pumpkins, and his children will never cry for hunger. All will be contentment and happiness.

But, on the other hand, if he has excited the displeasure of the Great Spirit by refusing to undergo the Medicine ordeal, by laziness in war and the chase, and by his general worthlessness and neglect of all his duties, he will go to a land abounding with enemies, where he will suffer hunger and cold. There it is always night, and snow thickly covers the ground and as if to add to the horrors of his condition he will be tantalized by the sight of the Happy Hunting Grounds, whose secure enjoyments might have been his.

Thus it will be seen that the Indians look to a future existence, either of weal or woe, as their conduct during life may determine. Their numerous dances and ceremonies are but feasts and fasts to please the Great Spirit and ask a continuance of blessings. Thus their religion is essentially the same as that of more enlightened nations, differing only in the mode of its observance.

Chapter X

Another False Alarm

THE great Bull Medicine having been made to the satisfaction of all, it now remained to be seen what effect it would have upon the Great Spirit. Day after day passed and still there was no sign of the near approach of buffaloes. The chiefs and old men were generally of the same opinion: that the Medicine was sufficiently strong, and the Great Spirit would soon send them an abundance.

Many, on the other hand, including most of the young and impetuous braves, took an entirely different view of it. It was, however, agreed that before any further steps were taken in the matter a proper amount of patience and self-denial should be exercised, in consequence of which decision there was a brief period of general repose and inactivity, but it did not last long.

One day, towards the middle of the afternoon, an alarm was raised that a large war-party of Sioux on horseback had been seen lurking among the distant bluffs that loomed up beyond the expanse of prairie in the rear of the village. An instant and terrible uproar was the natural consequence of this unexpected discovery. The Medicine was strong, of that there was no longer the slightest doubt. The buffaloes had been sent, but the approach of this war-party had run them off. Universal consternation arose. The men yelled, the women screamed, and the dogs howled lustily, while the scouts and horse-guards were riding to and fro over the prairie with the utmost activity, collecting the scattered bands of horses and rushing them at full speed towards the village.

The clouds of dust raised by the hoofs of the excited horses partially obscured objects on the prairie, and the commotion soon reached the highest pitch. Powder, balls, and flints were in the greatest demand, and as the shades of evening closed around, the frightened squaws came into both forts, bringing their dresses, medicine-bags, and valuables for safekeeping, looking upon the capture and plunder of their village as a settled thing. The Dry Pumpkin, the Snake-skin, and the Long Hair went about and ha-rangued for the fighting men to "strike for their altars and their fires," and teach the rascally Sioux a lesson that they would not forget for many a day. A dilapidated chimney, the last remains of the old fort, was torn down by the squaws by order of the Dry Pumpkin, so that no enemy could be concealed behind it.

Our corral was literally packed with as many horses as it could possibly hold. The gates of the fort were shut at the usual hour and strongly barricaded, and every one looked well to his weapons and prepared them for immediate service. It was not considered necessary for us to mount a regular guard, as all the Indians would be on the qui vive. Paquenaude got ready for action by tying his favorite black handkerchief around his head and giving his gun a fresh load, after which he took his station, fully prepared for the worst.

The evening was remarkably beautiful. The soft moonlight fell with striking effect upon the wild figures in the area of the fort, and grim warriors stalked silently about grasping their ready weapons. The half-alarmed horses in the corral crowded restlessly together. The squaws and children huddled here and there in groups, with their valuables close by and a retinue of their favorite dogs sleeping quietly beside them. The women talked in low tones about the expected attack and expressed great fears lest their corn-fields, upon which they had expended so much toil, would be destroyed by the ruthless invaders.

As the evening wore on they crowded into the houses until all vacant nooks and corners were filled with valuables and every available foot of space on the floors occupied by recumbent forms, too anxious to close their eyes in sleep.

The Bourgeois' house was manifestly the favorite. "Crowd in," was the order, and it was carried out to the strictest letter and with such a will that it was almost impossible to move without treading on the graceful proportions of some Indian maiden.

The night was warm and close, and the effluvia arising from the closely packed bodies of the highly-scented squaws was infinitely stronger than agreeable. It was late when I thought of retiring, and found that beyond making my bed a general repository for miscellaneous articles it was otherwise unencumbered. I laid down, after merely removing my pouch and powder-horn, and in trying to stretch out my feet struck something which I took to be a buffalo robe closely folded, and without more ceremony kicked it upon the floor. In falling it struck with some violence the rotund form of an ancient squaw, and commenced crying out with a vigor that fully proved the strength of its lungs and general soundness of constitution.

A commotion among the females was the natural consequence of my inadvertently kicking a baby out of bed, and all the other infants (of which I thought there was a goodly number) added their full quota of music to the concert. By degrees everything quieted down again, but I felt constrained to lie very quietly, not knowing but that the slightest movement on my part might result in a similar catastrophe, and the remaining bundles on my domain (whether living or otherwise) remained undisturbed.

At midnight Paquenaude came to the door and hurriedly whispered, "The Sioux are coming!" An Indian had crept over from the village and reported that the enemy were now cutting and destroying the corn-fields. All were immediately on the alert and a sleepless vigilance was maintained the rest of the night. The morning dawned bright and clear and revealed no traces of the ravages of the foe. Not till the sun was high, however, were the horses driven forth to feed, and even then they were not allowed to go more than a few hundred yards from the pickets of the village.

The corn-fields were not disturbed in the least, and when the mounted scouts returned, after an extended reconnoissance, without having discovered the slightest trace of an enemy it was generally admitted to have been another false alarm. A feeling of security being once more restored, the squaws removed their valuables to their lodges and matters went on as usual.

CHAPTER XI

A Trading Excursion

IT was now the latter end of summer [1858], and I passed a great deal of my time in hunting. It was, however, almost too early in the season, and from the number of Indian hunters on the range game was very scarce and wild. About three miles above the village, after passing through a heavy forest of cottonwood, my favorite hunting-trail led out upon a beautiful prairie bottom with a swift water-course flowing through it, which terminated in a lake. In the spring and fall wild fowl in great numbers and of every variety were here to be found, and Paquenaude and I enjoyed excellent sport. The ducks were now in their prime, as fat as butter, and made very acceptable additions to our larder.

The Indians went out to surround just often enough to keep from starving, but the green corn was fast ripening and with the quantities of small game daily brought in by the hunters we fared luxuriously.

The only wild prairie Indians that raise corn are the Riccarees, Mandans, and Minnetarees. It is a species of Canada corn, very hardy and of quick growth. It is of all colors, red, black, blue, yellow, purple, and white. Sometimes a single ear presents a combination of all these hues. When boiled green, with rich buffalo marrow spread on it (instead of butter) it is very sweet and truly delicious.

The squaws have a busy time harvesting. It is a season of joy and festivity with them, when their long and patient labor is finally rewarded by an abundant crop. In the spring, as soon as the frost is out of the ground the women break up their patches of land. Every foot must be turned up and loosened with the hoe, a slow and toilsome operation. After the corn is planted and begins to come up, slender fences of willow are necessary to prevent the horses from destroying the tender blades. These willows have to be carried on the backs of the women a long distance, a few at a time, until a sufficient quantity for the purpose is collected. While the operation of breaking ground, planting, and fencing is going on, wood has also to be carried for the lodges, for those great, round, earth-covered dwellings of the Minnetarees are very chilly during the early damp spring weather, requiring much fuel for warming, as well as cooking.

Day after day, until it is gathered in, the corn must be regularly hoed, more to counteract the effect of drought than to keep down weeds, for on these dry and elevated plains rain seldom falls after the spring has passed. All these duties devolve upon the women. Hence it will be seen that when an Indian has a plurality of wives he is enabled to live by the distribution of their labor in comparative ease and comfort. From early morn until sunset the squaws, old and young, may be seen passing to and from their corn-fields with rudely woven willow baskets slung on their backs, in which they carry the corn to their lodges.

Fires are blazing in all directions, around which gather merry groups to feast on boiled and roasted ears. When the harvest is gathered in, the ears of corn are plaited into a trace (like a rope of onions) and hung upon scaffolds to dry. The variegated hues of the often tastefully arranged traces hanging from the scaffolds give the village a gay and holiday appearance.

Each family reserves a number of the choicest ears to make sweet corn for winter use. It is first parboiled. The grains are then carefully picked off the cob and dried in the sun upon a piece of lodge skin. Prepared thus, it retains all its juices and flavor and will keep unimpaired almost any length of time. It is then put away in skin bags and carefully hoarded for use on special occasions, or in times of scarcity.

The trace corn is câchéd. A hole is dug in the ground, usually near the lodge, some six or eight feet in depth and small at the top, but widening as it deepens, much resembling a jug in shape. Hay is next strewn over the bottom and sides, and when the corn is thoroughly dried it is taken down from the scaffolds and packed away. The câche is filled up with hay, dirt is then thrown on and firmly trodden down, and every sign carefully obliterated.

Each family has one or more of these câches, and as they leave their summer village early in the fall for winter quarters the corn remains undiscovered and undisturbed until their return in the spring. They also raise black beans, pumpkins, and squashes, but in spite of these vegetable resources, hemmed in as they often are by enemies and consequently unable to obtain by hunting a full supply of buffalo meat, they sometimes suffer greatly for food. Well may the season of green corn be one of festivity and gladness, for it is then only that the women enjoy a brief respite from their severe toil.

About the middle of September a party of thirty Assiniboines arrived to visit the Gros Ventres. The new-comers had been sent from a camp known as the band of Canoes by the chief, Broken Arm, to beg a little tobacco (*i. e.* a handsome present) from the traders, and induce them, if possible, to send to their camp on the River of Lakes, about three days travel, to traffic for such robes and skins as they had on hand at present, of which they declared, of course, that they had a great plenty. Quite a number of Gros Ventres decided to embrace this opportunity of visiting the Assiniboine camp to smoke the pipe of peace and friendship and exchange horses. Our Bourgeois, thinking it would be profitable, determined also to send an expedition.[44]

That night after closing the gates we began preparing a small but well-assorted outfit and drew rations for a ten days' journey, the length of time we expected to be gone. Roasting coffee comprised most of this preparation, and we soon had everything in readiness to leave at daybreak. Bright and early we were up, the wagon loaded, and our horses harnessed and saddled, so that before the sun had fairly risen we were several miles on our journey, taking a northerly direc-

[44] In the winter of 1844–45 Broken Arm had sent a similar request to Fort Union and Charles Larpenteur was dispatched with a small stock of trade liquor to visit his camp, which was somewhere on Woody Mountain in present-day southern Saskatchewan. *Forty Years a Fur Trader*, 155–80. The River of the Lakes, shown on Lt. Warren's map of 1856 was the Mouse or Souris, which rises in Canada and after making a long southward detour into western North Dakota (the city of Minot is near its southerly extreme) returns to Canada through central Bottineau County. Since the Assiniboines had almost no fixed villages, it is impossible to identify the routes taken either by Larpenteur in 1845 or Boller in 1858. It seems apparent, however, that Larpenteur's journey to Broken Arm's camp in 1845 was considerably longer than Boller's journey in 1858.

tion. I had charge of the party, which consisted of Paquenaude for interpreter and a long-haired mountaineer named Bostwick.[45] We soon overtook some of the Assiniboines, who were all on foot, and travelled along together in the best possible humor.

One old fellow took the lead, dragging a broken-down bay horse heavily packed with corn, the gift of his Gros Ventres friends. He kept up a measured jog the livelong day, with his eyes steadily fixed on a distant butte or pile of stones, landmarks by which he shaped his course, seemingly oblivious of the existence of any beings beside himself and his forlorn steed. At noon we halted by a little spring of clear water and turned the horses loose to graze at will while we regaled ourselves with some cold meat, and after a short rest proceeded on our way.

Our route led us through a rather uninteresting

[45] H. S. Bostwick, "the long-haired mountaineer," had guided the hunting party of Sir George Gore in 1854 and 1855. Although Sir George was quick to resent attempted impositions upon him, he was no less quick to deal generously with those who treated him fairly. Upon parting with Bostwick at Fort Union, Gore pressed upon him several hundred dollars' worth of goods for which he asked the very nominal price of $12. See Lt. J. H. Bradley's account in *Montana Hist. Soc. Contributions*, IX, 246–51. Bostwick was killed Aug. 9, 1877 in the Battle of the Big Hole, in which Chief Joseph's Nez Percés administered a severe defeat to General John Gibbon's command.

country, chiefly high rolling prairie, totally destitute of timber. Early in the afternoon we crossed a fork of a creek called Rising Water and encamped to await the arrival of the rest of our fellow-travellers, who had been detained by some dancing and other ceremonies at the village. Our horses were hobbled and turned loose with trailing lariats so that they could be caught up at a moment's warning, and resting our guns against the wagons, with powder-horns and bullet-pouches hanging from the muzzles, we began our preparations for supper.

The Assiniboines who were in company had but the one forlorn steed to look after, and all of us were soon busied in collecting dry buffalo chips for our camp-fire, there being no wood within miles. Before long it was blazing cheerily and Paquenaude, leaving Bostwick to pile on the chips, took the coffee pot and filled it with brackish water from the creek. Our coffee having been roasted before leaving the fort, I put a little into a leathern bag and pounded it with an axe on the tire of a wheel until it was crushed sufficiently fine for our purpose. By our united exertions our supper, consisting of coffee and dry buffalo meat slightly warmed through, was soon ready and as quickly dispatched. The Assiniboines built a separate fire, and as they had no coffee to make finished their meal before we did.

At dusk the rest of our party joined us, consisting of sixty Gros Ventres and the remaining Assiniboines, all well mounted and leading extra pack-horses. The Four Bears with his favorite squaw, the Hawk, and several other principal men rode up. The first eager inquiry of the Four Bears before unsaddling was, "Have you made coffee yet?"

The horses were driven up and secured for the night by being either hobbled or picketed, our arms examined, and enough buffalo chips collected to keep a little fire throughout the night. The Assiniboines gathered around and commenced playing a game of hand, while the Gros Ventres boiled a kettle of sweet corn, of which, after it was cooked, the whole party were invited to partake. Two of the Assiniboines were so absorbed in their game that they kept on playing in preference to indulging in the (to them) unwonted luxury of green corn. After the feast was over we wrapped ourselves in our blankets and the last sounds I heard before losing consciousness were those made by the horses cropping the short rich grass and the monotonous chant "heh-ah-heh" of the gamblers.

Toward morning we were roused up by a cold driving rain, and throwing fresh chips on the fire we prepared our breakfast of coffee and meat, so that by daylight we were en route again. The morning was bitterly cold and raw and we rode with our robes and blankets wrapped closely around us. We travelled at a rapid pace, and an old lame Assiniboine, who had been residing with his family among the Gros Ventres during the winter and had embraced this opportunity of returning to his people, found it exceedingly difficult to hobble along fast enough.

He had one horse and a travée, upon which his three children and all his worldly goods were transported. His squaw led the wretched animal and old Lousey, as the matter-of-fact Bostwick styled the unfortunate Assiniboine, toiled painfully along in the rear, using such exertions to keep up that the perspiration rolled in streams down his rueful countenance, notwithstanding the chilliness of the morning. All his efforts, however, were in vain and he was finally left behind, loudly protesting against being abandoned in such a dangerous country and so far from his people's camp.

A squaw with three small children was also left. She carried one on her back and another in her arms, while the eldest trotted along by her side. Some time after, a young Indian who had loitered behind came up and reported that the squaw had just killed the youngest because it was too small to travel.

A grizzly bear was discovered a short distance

from the line of march, but the whole party were in too much of a hurry to run the risk of delay by attacking him, so he was not disturbed. Our course took us through a most barren and uninteresting country, abounding in rugged hills and dales, making it very laborious for the wagon-team. Our advance roused two lean old buffalo bulls, and the partisan or leader of the Assiniboines, the Red Snow, gave chase and killed one after a short and spirited dash. When we reached the place where the animal had fallen, only a few hundred yards off, he was already butchered and half a dozen hungry savages stood over the carcass greedily devouring the warm and quivering flesh. A halt was made, the horses turned loose, a fire of dried buffalo dung kindled, and in almost the twinkling of an eye the kettle was boiling. The meat was so warm and fresh as to require very little cooking. It was too fresh, in fact, to be good.

As a titbit, the Four Bears' squaw made a boudin, *i. e.* an intestine filled with chopped meat like a sausage, but without seasoning of any kind. In the preparation of this dainty morceau, economy both of time and labor was well studied, for as the intestine was gradually filled up at one end the original contents were forced out at the other. A few moments' immersion in the kettle sufficed to cook it, and a much shorter time was required for the surrounding epicures to discuss it, which they did with indescribable gusto.

This delectable meal over, we were off again, leaving a fine feast for the wolves, whose forms could everywhere be seen sneaking over the adjacent hills. The whole affair—the run, the butchering, cooking, and eating—did not occupy an hour. We toiled on until afternoon, when a cold, driving storm of sleet and rain set in. At one time it was so severe that the horses turned their tails to it and refused to proceed, whereupon, wrapping our robes and blankets around us for protection, we patiently waited until it should abate a little. The Indians lit their pipes and enjoyed a social smoke, and as soon as the storm moderated we hastened on as quickly as possible to make up for lost time.

When evening came, cold, tired, and hungry, we made our camp at the head of Shell Creek, the scanty fire of buffalo chips not warming us, but merely serving to boil some of the bull-meat and coffee. Quickly dispatching our supper we turned in and slept soundly, with the exception of several of the Indians, whose fears led them to expect being rushed upon during the night by a war-party. My slumbers were not the less sound for having such vigilant sentinels.

We started early the next morning, as usual, but in crossing Shell Creek one of the wagon-horses mired and fell and was only extricated after much trouble and delay. The country still continued bad for wagons. It abounded in innumerable lakes or ponds of stagnant water, and all more or less highly flavored with buffalo urine. Wild fowl were present in countless numbers and as they were very fat at this season we enjoyed rare sport, and feasted in true hunter style. So plenty were they and so tame that it was like shooting into a flock of barnyard fowls, but no more were killed than we actually wanted. Buffaloes were plenty about the head of Knife River, but no stop was made for hunting as they were yet poor and thin and plenty of ducks could be obtained with but little trouble.

The sun, which had been hidden behind dark and threatening clouds all the morning, adding to the indescribable dreariness and desolation of the wild and barren landscape, suddenly shone out in all his splendor just as we were about to leave the ridge and descend the sloping prairie to the crossing of the river, at this place not more than fifty feet wide. The grass looked greener and fresher than on the sterile plains we had quitted, and a few stunted trees growing on the margin of the little stream, the first which had been seen since leaving the Missouri, and the towering bluffs by which the valley was surrounded on all sides added greatly to the extreme beauty of this fairy dell.

I reined in my horse to admire its quiet and seclusion. Bands of buffaloes were scattered here and there, some grazing, others rolling, and evidently enjoying themselves, while many were indolently lying down ruminating. A large band of antelopes started up and fled swiftly away. The wind was blowing from us and the buffaloes, sniffing the tainted air, sprang to their feet and rapidly disappeared over the distant bluffs.

As we climbed the steep heights after crossing the river I looked back. The scene was changed. The fairy dell was deserted and had relapsed into its former stillness without sight or sound of animal life. Continuing on, this enchanting scene was shut out from my sight, but not from my memory, by the rugged defiles through which our course lay. After winding around lakes and passing through gloomy ravines we made our noon halt beside a pond of water so brackish and stinking that our thirsty horses refused to drink.

From here the Red Snow said we ought soon to see the Assiniboine camp, and the Indians busied themselves in making their toilets. Four Bears painted the face of his favorite squaw (the only one that had accompanied him on this trip) with vermilion, and then his own in true warrior style. His long hair, which had been clubbed up behind for convenience, was loosened and carefully combed out. He then dressed himself in his splendid shirt ornamented with long scalp-locks and dyed horse-hair. When all these preparations were completed we resumed our journey, and after some hard scrambling got clear of the *mauvaises terres* and stood upon the *coteau de prairie*, the great dividing ridge that separates the tributaries of the Missouri from those of the Red River of the North.

Here the Red Snow called a halt and consulted with his comrades as to where the camp was likely to be. A butte was pointed out a few hundred yards off, near to which the chief expected to find it, but not a sign was visible. In vain our eyes swept the prairie until, dimmed with the intensity of our gaze, we could no longer distinguish in the distance the faint line that marked the meeting of earth and sky. A pipe was lit and smoked, after which we climbed to the top of the highest butte, whence by the aid of my spy-glass we had the satisfaction of discovering a number of barely distinguishable points against the sky, which the Indians unhesitatingly pronounced to be the lodges of the Assiniboines.

Whether we could reach them by nightfall was the question. They were a long distance off and our horses were jaded, but it was determined to make the attempt. The whole party pushed forward vigorously, some of the Indians singing, and all rejoiced at the approaching termination of our trip. I was riding alongside of the Red Snow when he called up one of his young men and ordered him to precede us and announce our coming at the camp. The fellow was on foot (like most of his party) and had been trotting along for the last hour at a brisk gait, but he immediately quickened his step and went on ahead.

A dark line of trees marked our approach to a running stream, the River of Lakes. It was a fork of Mouse River, and for a wonder in this part of the country had a hard rocky bottom, making a very good crossing. Toiling up the steep and stony bluffs on the opposite shore, we reached the broad plateau that stretches away to Mouse River, about half a day's farther travel. Our party, instead of keeping in a compact body, was strung out over the prairie, the footmen well in advance and the special messenger far ahead of all.

The conical skin lodges were now plainly in sight, not more than five miles off, and Indians galloped out from the camp to meet us and escort us in. Buffaloes, they said, were plenty. Nearly all the hunters were away surrounding, and had not yet returned. Crowds of women and children rushed out, attracted by the novelty and rattling of the wagon as we drove up to the chief's lodge. The old man was out with the hunters, but his squaw stirred around and soon carried everything inside, so that when we returned from watering and picketing our horses near by, the kettle was already on the fire and a delicious *bos* (or hump ribs) cooking.

By the time supper was eaten the hunters returned, and the squaws were busy unloading the meat and taking care of the horses. The dogs, which were very numerous, as is particularly the case in an Assiniboine camp, hailed the arrival of so much meat with a series of prolonged howls. After smoking a pipe with our host and briefly detailing to him the principal news we rolled ourselves in our blankets and slept soundly, without being troubled by the abundant insect life with which an Assiniboine lodge is especially favored, or by the proximity of several squaws, members of the chief's family.

CHAPTER XII
Return to Fort Atkinson

THE sun was high when we rose next morning, and after inspecting our horses (which were under the chief's care) we returned to the lodge for breakfast. Large bands of buffaloes were in plain sight from the encampment and the hunters went out to surround again. The squaws were cutting up the meat which had been brought in the day before in thin sheets and drying it on poles resting on crotches. Two or three of them would sit down with a piece of skin between them, upon which the meat was placed. They wore the usual elegant style of dress which appeared to be the mode with the ladies of the Canoe band of Assiniboines; viz., a garment of skin originally ample, but from being frequently taxed to furnish material for patching moccasins it had become very low in the neck, very short in the sleeves, and of so scant a pattern that it was in many instances a mere apology for a covering.

Chatting and laughing all the time, they cut the masses of meat with wonderful quickness and skill into large and thin sheets, with the fat judiciously mixed, and then hung it over the poles to dry. After exposure for a couple of days to the sun and pure air of the prairies the meat turns black and hard, and in this condition will keep for a long time perfectly good. The best meat is made in the winter. It is then fatter, and is partially dried in the smoke of the lodges, which greatly improves its flavor.

The encampment was in the middle of an open plain without a stick of timber in sight, and the superannuated squaws sat in the shade of the lodges nursing the children and scolding at the dogs, who kept prowling around watching their chances to steal. Other squaws were scraping the hair from the buffalo skins and dressing them to make new lodges, of which by the way very many families were sadly in need. Some had cut down their lodges little by little to supply pressing demands until there was barely enough left for a shelter. Sixteen skins sewed together with sinews, somewhat in the form of a cloak, and stretched over a framework of poles, form a very fair-sized lodge, sufficiently large to accommodate eight or ten persons with their effects. But owing to the scarcity of horses among this band of Assiniboines and the necessity of using dogs as their beasts of burden, most of the lodges consisted of from six to ten skins only.

At this time they were comparatively rich, having recently concluded a treaty of peace with their old enemies the Gros Ventres of the

Prairie (a band of Blackfeet), and obtained a number of horses from them in exchange for the annuities which they had received from the Government.

While strolling around, I caught a glimpse of Bostwick eating in one of the lodges and trying to make himself agreeable to a rather fine-looking squaw. In the Broken Arm's lodge Paquenaude was preparing a feast, to be given at the council which we intended to hold with the principal men in the evening, after their return from the surround.

When the feast was ready the camp was harangued to call the soldiers to it. In a little while they came, each one bringing his bowl and cup, and the lodge was soon crowded to its utmost capacity. All sat with their knees huddled up to their chins and deep in communion with their own thoughts. The feast, consisting of Indian sweet corn and tea, was set before them and Paquenaude addressed them, urging them to winter with the Gros Ventres, which they had some idea of doing, telling them to give us all the trade they could, and concluded by laying before them half a dozen large plugs of tobacco.

They all responded with hearty emphasis, "How," and then lifting their pans of tea to their lips commenced sucking it in with a loud noise, more like a herd of swine feeding than anything else. After the tea had been drunk the Broken Arm brought out his pipe, made of a soft black clay, and after carefully cleaning and charging it with a mixture of tobacco and a weed which grows plentifully on the northern prairies, and is used by the Assiniboines and Blackfeet instead of the red willow, drew a few whiffs through it and then handed it around.

When it had circulated a few times the chief gave the signal that the feast was ended by smoking with the bowl of his pipe to the ground and each one, taking his pan of corn, quickly and quietly left the lodge. There were over thirty men crowded in that lodge during the feast, where there seemed barely room for four or five to move about comfortably.

Large bands of buffaloes were in sight next morning and the hunters went out again. The whole country seemed fairly alive with the moving herds. The squaws were kept very busy in consequence, and the dogs, gorged to repletion, lay sleepily basking in the sun, and, contrary to their usual custom, took not the slightest notice of me as I sauntered about.

The old lame Assiniboine and his family, whom we had left on the way hither, reached camp during the forenoon, all looking as if they had found it a very hard road to travel. Old Lousey's temper was not improved by the danger to which he had been subjected by being abandoned on the prairie to shift for himself, and as soon as he gained the middle of the encampment he commenced loudly exclaiming against those who had left him, and for whom, when they were young and before he was an almost helpless cripple, he had hunted and assisted in defending against the enemy. Very little attention was paid to this harangue and he was suffered to vent his indignation upon the four winds.

A buffalo bull, furious with his wounds, was driven close to the camp and his dying struggles attracted all the idlers to witness them. Weakened by the loss of blood streaming from several arrow wounds in his side and from his mouth (a sure sign that he had received a vital shot) he tottered feebly and as his pursuer rode up to within a few paces made a desperate lunge upon him, which was easily avoided by the activity of the well-trained buffalo horse. Recovering himself with difficulty the bull stood at bay, trembling with rage and maddened with pain. In a moment he fell gasping and struggling, but before the breath had fairly left his body the hide was torn off and the quivering flesh cut away with astonishing rapidity. The choice bits only were taken, the proximity of the herds and the abundance of meat in camp making the savages dainty in their selections. A splendid feast was left for the dogs, numbers of which were skulking around eagerly waiting their turn.

It came. There was for an instant a prodigious uproar, a snapping of jaws and flourishing of tails, and the pack dispersed, leaving only the skull and some of the larger bones and a patch of prairie clotted with gore to mark the place where the noble animal met his fate.

The next morning the squaws picked out the dryest pieces of meat and the trading began. The lodge was entirely cleared of Indians, except the chiefs and a couple of soldiers who sat at the entrance, as much to preserve order by preventing the squaws from rushing in en masse as for anything else. For the next three hours we had a lively time. Powder, balls, knives, looking-glasses, hawk-bells, brass tacks, vermilion, awls, and other trifles were in demand, and when we stopped trading, having obtained as much meat as the wagon could transport, the pressure became very great, the squaws fearing that our stock of goods would become exhausted before all were supplied. Many of the women were exceedingly angry when they found we would trade no more, and one old virago even went so far as to talk of cutting our goods to shreds in revenge. A few trifles judiciously given, aided by the determined effort of the soldiers, finally quieted her down. The customary present to the chief for the use of his lodge was made, to which were added a few trifles for his squaw, which pleased her immensely.

The Gros Ventres were getting ready to return, and we set about loading up the wagon and saddling our horses. When everything was ready the Four Bears and several others were called in to the Broken Arm's lodge to eat and smoke before leaving. The Four Bears and Broken Arm exchanged horses, the latter giving a fine one and receiving an indifferent animal in return.

Making our way through the dense crowd, comprising both sexes and all ages, we left the Assiniboine camp and struck out over the broad and sloping plain between the camp and the Rivière au Lacs, when the conical lodges with their wild population were lost in the distance. Descending the rugged and stony bluffs, we recrossed the river and travelled on until sundown, when we encamped by a pool of brackish water so strongly flavored and discolored by buffalo urine that it exceeded anything we had hitherto met with and our coffee was, in consequence, scarcely drinkable.

A beautiful starlit night succeeded and I was glad to sleep in the fresh free air of the prairie in exchange for the smoky and crowded lodge of the Assiniboine chief. The following day we plodded steadily on through an uninteresting country.

Not a tree was visible. No limpid, cooling streams, with their verdure-clad banks, gladdened the eye. We saw only innumerable sedgy lakes of stagnant rainwater, the edges muddy and trampled into a quagmire by the buffaloes.

Near sundown we struck the pebbly shore of a very large lake of clear water (the only one I had seen on this expedition) and after proceeding some miles farther halted on Shell Creek, not very far from our old camping-place. After passing a quiet night, free from any alarm, we started again at early dawn, and soon leaving the rugged and desolate country of lakes and hills were once more on the broad rolling prairie. Buffaloes had recently roamed here in great numbers, for the grass was eaten quite short and other traces were everywhere visible.

Large flocks of swans and pelicans were continually passing over our heads in graceful, undulating flight, together with immense numbers of ducks and geese, all taking their departure for more southern climes. A few bulls lazily walked along the base of the distant bluffs, and sneaking wolves, roused from their lairs by our approach, trotted sulkily off after stopping an instant to look at us. Animal life abounded. It would have been delightful to have stopped and hunted for a few days but the country was extremely dangerous, being constantly overrun by war-parties of

Sioux, Assiniboines, and Chippewas, one of which might cross our path at any moment.

Our Indians hurried on and the Four Bears would not allow a gun to be fired, since the sound could be heard a long distance in these still regions and might be the means of discovering us to the enemy. The recent hoof-prints of a band of buffaloes in full run were plainly distinguishable, which the Indians closely examined in great concern, and called a council of war. Buffaloes never "raise" without cause. Therefore they must undoubtedly have been disturbed by a roving band of Indians, but whether friends or foes we could not tell, most probably the latter.

A young Gros Ventre crawled to the top of the next roll of the prairie and took a long and careful survey. Nothing was discovered, so we kept on, well together and ready for any emergency.

At sundown we recrossed Rising Water and bivouacked. No fire was kindled, and each man looked well to his weapons. Not a sound, except the gentle ripple of the stream, broke the silence of the night. Bostwick and I made our beds together and laid down with our guns in our arms. Paquenaude spread his blankets close by and we found much amusement in watching his preparations for the terrible conflict which he was sure was impending. His famous black handkerchief was tied tightly around his head and his naturally sallow countenance looked ghastly enough by the light of the stars. He carefully reloaded his gun, putting a half-ounce bullet in one barrel and nine buckshot in the other. The latter he dropped in one at a time, and as each rolled slowly down it sounded ominous of danger. Woe to the "Injin" that should chance (by accident only) to get that charge into his lights. The General's martial spirit was now aroused and he was fully determined on counting such a coup as would make him glorious for the rest of his existence. Four Bears crawled off quietly and was quickly lost to view in the surrounding gloom. The Hawk, by command of his chief, sat a little apart, gun in hand, on the alert to detect any signs of enemies. The rest of the party lay scattered around in seemingly careless groups of twos and threes.

The Northern Lights flashed up and glowed until the prairies were almost as bright as day, and revealed the figure of a man seated upon the edge of the bank, guarding against surprise in that quarter. It was not the Hawk, for he was close by us. Could it be the Four Bears? It must be, for he had gone off in that direction early in the evening.

But why is there such uneasiness among the Indians? Wherefore are they gazing so earnestly

at the skies, and talking to one another in subdued whispers? In the northeast a comet, with
its tail spreading over a vast arc of the heavens,
was distinctly visible, and with all the surround-
ings, the bivouac on the lonely prairie, the
startled groups of Indians, and the consciousness
of impending danger, caused all that I had read
of comets being the heralds of wars and tumults
to flash through my mind, until I could not help
sharing in the superstitious fears of the Indians
and wondering what it boded.[46]

Morning came at last and roused us all into activity. A fire of buffalo chips was soon kindled
and we commenced preparing our breakfast,

[46] This was Donati's comet, one of the brightest which
has appeared in the last 150 years. It was named for
Giovanni Donati, an Italian astronomer, who discovered
it on June 2, 1858, and was visible to the naked eye in
the United States in early September. It increased in
brilliance until October 10, and disappeared from view
ten days later. Professor James C. Watson, University
of Michigan astronomer, estimated its distance from the
earth (on Oct. 11) as 50,000,000 miles and the period of
its revolution as 2400 years. Thus it had last been seen
over 500 years before the beginning of the Christian era,
and its next visitation may be anticipated about the middle
of the forty-third century A.D. Data adapted from information supplied by Prof. F. Clever Bald and Prof.
Freeman D. Miller of the University of Michigan. The
frontispiece of Prof. Watson's book, *A Popular Treatise
on Comets*, published at Philadelphia in 1861, presents a
telescopic view of Donati's comet as seen on October 15,
1858.

which, as it consisted of a piece of jerked meat, simply warmed, was not a tedious operation.

I went down to the creek for a cup of water and saw, as I thought, the Four Bears still keeping guard on the bank. On my return I passed close by and was amused to find the supposed sentinel nothing more nor less than the robe and head-dress of the chief, cunningly placed upon a stick and so arranged that in an uncertain light it presented an admirable counterfeit of a human figure, well calculated to deceive and hold in check the advance of any foe from that direction.

The comet was the universal theme of con-versation and the Indians expressed the liveliest apprehensions as to what might happen. Some even predicted an attack upon the village, and all showed anxiety to get back as soon as possible, which we hoped to do by afternoon. We travelled all the morning, and when within six or seven miles of the village were discovered by some of the advance horse-guards, who, after signalling our approach to the rear, came riding toward us at their highest speed, dashing recklessly up and down hill. We drew up in a body to meet them as they charged headlong towards us, without attempting to slacken their speed until within a few paces, when they checked their horses so sud-denly as to throw them back on their haunches.

A few hurried words to the Four Bears, and an

intense excitement was immediately visible throughout our party. All dismounted. The pipe was lit and passed around, and the following news elicited. The hunters had crossed the river the day before to surround, and after a very successful run were returning in scattered parties heavily laden with meat. While passing through the belt of timber before coming out on the sandbar they were fired upon by a war-party of Sioux in ambush and several slightly wounded. The reports of the guns roused those who had remained in the village, and seizing their weapons they hurried across the river. Here they were strongly reinforced by the rest of the hunters, who had hastened up at the first sounds of the fray, when the Gros Ventres became in their turn the assailants and tracked the enemy through the woods to where they had entrenched themselves behind a rude breastwork of logs.

Contrary to their usual custom of advancing warily, the Minnetarees, maddened by the presence of their hated foes and conscious that they had them in their power, rushed forward to the attack. After a short but desperate struggle during which the forest rang with the rattling of arms and the whoops of the combatants the assailants charged up to the breastwork and carried it, killing almost instantly its brave defenders, only nine in number.

Several Gros Ventres lost their lives and a number were wounded, some mortally. While this information was being received mounted Indians continued to arrive every moment, all riding as if their lives depended upon it. We kept on after a brief delay, leaving the Indians smoking and relating the particulars of the fight. Upon reaching the fort the reports we had heard were confirmed.

The whole party of Yanktons, nine in all, were killed, and their bodies hacked to pieces. Each of the victors brought as trophies fragments of the bodies, fingers, ears, and scalps. A hand mounted on a pole was set up on the prairie as a thank-offering to the Great Spirit. But the Gros Ventres paid dearly for their success. Four were killed on the field of battle and many wounded, some fatally. My esteemed friend Doctor E-ten-ah-pen-ah had suffered severely. Although a Sioux, he had lived among the Gros Ventres many years and was therefore anxious not only to prove the sincerity of his friendship for them, but also to display his prowess as a warrior. So he boldly sought the thickest of the fray. His left arm was badly shattered in two places and he was so weakened by the loss of blood that he had to be carried in a blanket from the landing to his lodge by four sympathizing squaws.

Chapter XIII

Goose Medicine and Visitors

AFTER the corn had all been gathered in, the Mandan and Minnetaree squaws made their Goose Medicine on the level prairie behind the village. This dance is to remind the wild geese, now beginning their southward flight, that they have had plenty of good food all summer, and to entreat their return in the spring, when the rains come and the green grass begins to grow.

The charms of most of the squaws in this Goose Band appeared to have faded long ago. They were evidently past the bloom of youth and their voices and tempers had not improved in consequence. However, on this occasion they endeavored to look their best with the aid of paint and finery, in which respect they are not far behind their white sisters of more civilized climes. A row of poles resting upon forked sticks is put up, over which are hung in profusion pieces of fine, fat, dry meat, which have been carefully saved for this occasion. A band of four or five drummers take their seats close to one end and a double row of squaws next to them, facing each other. Each woman carries a bunch of long seed-grass, the favorite food of the wild goose, and at intervals all get up and dance in a circle with a peculiar shuffling step, singing and keeping time to the taps of the drum.

The spectators keep at a respectful distance and enjoy the fun, which consists in the attempts of some of the young men to steal the meat from the poles, in which, however, they are often thwarted by the vigilance of a few wise old geese who are constantly on the alert to prevent theft. If successful, the meat is carried off in great glee to some lodge, where they cook and eat it at their leisure. These exquisites are elaborately gotten up with bunches of raven plumes fluttering from their scalp-locks, and stripes of white and yellow clay upon their bodies comprise their only covering.

Finally, one of the old men (who have been thumping assiduously on the drums all the while) takes his place a few hundred yards off on the prairie and a grand race by the whole goose band follows. All form in line together and run around the old gander before returning to the starting-point.

The race over, the scaffolds are taken down, a feast is prepared, and the meat remaining on hand cooked and eaten. For the rest of the day the band danced around among the different lodges and of course paid a visit to the fort before concluding. On these occasions a few yards of calico or some trifling gifts are always expected to be thrown to the Medicine by the traders.

Two more Indians died of their wounds, making the total loss by the fight six. The rest of the wounded were doing well, and in a fair way to recover. Doctor E-ten-ah-pen-ah made his appearance for the first time since the battle. His arm looked very bad, being broken in two places and poorly splintered. It was greatly discolored and smelt offensively, with every prospect of mortification speedily setting in. But this did not appear to trouble him in the least. His countenance wore an expression of the utmost self-satisfaction at the part he had taken in the fray, and he used his powers of romancing so judiciously that, coupled with the appearance of the comet, which he claimed to know all about, many of the Gros Ventres began to look upon him with awe as one who was really gifted with supernatural powers.

A large party of Gros Ventres had gone down to the Riccaree village and their return was anxiously anticipated, as they were expected to bring tidings of the whereabouts of the Blackfoot and Onc-pa-pa bands of Sioux, who, being just now on friendly terms, were likely, since the corn was gathered in, to visit the Rees and Gros Ventres to maintain the entente cordiale. These two bands are very powerful and warlike, rich in everything that constitutes Indian wealth, and conscious of their superior strength roam where they will, trespassing almost constantly on the hunting-grounds of the Riccarees, Minnetarees, and Mandans and sometimes even penetrating to the rich game country of their bitter enemies, the Crows, on the borders of the Yellowstone.

The Gros Ventres returned from their visit to the Rees and reported the Onc-pa-pas and Blackfeet camped on the head of Knife River, loaded down with meat and robes. It was expected, as they were distant only about two days' travel, that they would be in very shortly to trade. A begging party headed by the notorious partisan, the Black Moon, had already arrived at the Ree village and a similar party might be looked for at our post at any time.[47]

The next morning dawned bright and clear and the sun had nearly reached the zenith when the Indians discovered objects moving at a distance across the river, evidently rapidly coming towards it. There was some speculation at first whether it was a herd of buffaloes which had been raised by the hunters from the Sioux camp,

[47]Black Moon was the hereditary head chief of the Hunkpapa Sioux. He was one of the Indian leaders in the battle of the Little Big Horn in 1876 in which Custer met defeat and death. Although Boller characterizes him as "notorious," Linda W. Slaughter calls him "a man most respected and loved by all the tribes." *North Dak. Hist. Colls.*, I, 420; *South Dak. Hist. Colls.*, I, 152; Doane Robinson, *Encyclopedia of South Dakota*, 84: Lewis F. Crawford, *Hist. of North Dakota*, I, 308, 626.

or the expected visitors. As they approached, the gleaming of their polished lances and the glitter of the small mirrors, which in true Indian fashion they carried suspended from their necks, proclaimed them the party of Sioux.

While they boldly galloped down the bluffs that separated the high rolling prairie from the timbered bottom and were hidden from view by the intervening forest, there was great activity in the village. Bull-boats were carried down to the water's edge and the squaws prepared to cross over at a moment's notice. Soon the Sioux emerged at a gentle canter from the timber upon the broad and smooth sandbar, and leisurely dismounting, unsaddled their horses and shouted to their individual friends or comrades, declaring who they were and asking to be crossed over.

The Gros Ventres eagerly responded to the call, and in a few minutes the sinewy arms of the squaws were urging their unwieldy boats over the turbulent Missouri. The saddles and other equipment were loaded in and the guests, carefully taking their places in the frail vessels, were ferried over to the village. They were at once conducted to the lodges of their friends and something to eat set before them, generally corn, of which they partook eagerly, esteeming it a great luxury.

Their horses were carefully crossed over by the Gros Ventres and driven out to pasture, while all united in extending to their guests every hospitality which fear of a possible breach of friendship and the consequent evils of war could suggest. No sooner were the Sioux feasted in one lodge than they were called to another, and so it continued all day long.

There were about thirty in this party, all warriors, tall, noble-looking men of symmetrical form. Their long black hair was carefully combed and gathered into a plait on each side of the head, bound with scarlet cloth, while the neatly-braided scalp-lock was adorned with a strip of otterskin. They were clothed in finely-dressed deerskin shirts, beautifully worked with stained porcupine quills of various colors, and fringed with scalp-locks and dyed horsehair.

In form and feature these Indians seemed cast in one mould, and they had a wild and game appearance that told of a lordly spirit unsubdued and the consciousness of superiority to the smaller tribes, who might be said to exist only by their sufferance, and to the poor whites, to whom they traded those robes and peltries which they could neither eat nor wear, and would otherwise throw away. Each one wore a white blanket, and was completely armed with bow and arrows, fusee, tomahawk, and scalping-knife. Many also had lances in addition. The war-eagle feathers on their heads danced and fluttered in the wind and the hawk-bells and dried antelope-hoofs, with which their shirts and leggings were lavishly hung, tinkled and rattled with every motion as they stalked proudly about, literally monarchs of all they surveyed. Several wore the curiously striped and woven blankets of the Navahoes, obtained most probably in some freebooting excursion against the tribes south of the Platte.

Our usual Gros Ventre levee was but slimly attended, the elegant and dashing strangers being the centers of attraction. The cook was able to perform his regular duties without having the kitchen windows darkened by the women curiously peering in or the apartment invaded (if by chance the door was left open) by a crowd of impudent idlers who, in defiance of all the rules and regulations of the post, encamped around the fireplace until ordered out by the interpreter.

Late in the afternoon we called the Sioux to a feast, and as it was politic to keep them in good-humor in order to obtain as much of their trade as possible, McBride determined that the repast should be a substantial one. When they were all seated around the room the cook set before the chief a large kettle of coffee, hard bread, and pans of corn and meat. A present was also added, consisting of blue and scarlet cloth and a mirror and knife for each one. These liberal gifts caused the liveliest satisfaction, which they expressed by emphatically grunting "How!" The pipe was lit and passed around and a brisk conversation followed.

Running Antelope (the partisan) said the Sioux camp was on the forks of Knife River, about two days' travel from the post, and numbered over a thousand lodges. There were some Minne-con-jous and Yanc-toh-wahs with them. He also reported the buffaloes very plenty and added, "It is terrible how fat they are!"[48]

Our improvements in building excited their surprise and admiration, and the Crow's Feather thus figuratively expressed himself: "These whites used to dwell in a dirty brown lodge full of holes" (the old fort) "but now they have a fine, large white one."

They had noticed the comet and were greatly concerned thereat, believing it to be a forerunner

[48] Running Antelope, a chief of the Hunkpapas, was noted for his ability as an orator. He was commonly chosen by his people as a member of the committee to represent the tribe in treaty-councils. He commanded the Indians in the last great buffalo hunt in June, 1882, when 5000 animals are reputed to have been slaughtered. His face adorned the old five-dollar U.S. treasury note, and his portrait is reproduced in Lewis F. Crawford's *Hist. of North Dakota*. Crawford, I, 193, 229; Doane Robinson, *Encyclopedia of South Dakota*, 631; De Trobriand, *Army Life in Dakota*, index entries.

of wars and troubles. This party disclaimed all knowledge of the nine Sioux who had been recently killed by the Gros Ventres. The supposition was that they must have belonged either to the Two Bears' or Big Head's bands, now camped somewhere on the Moreau.

After the feast was ended the majority of our guests returned to the village, but several of the principal men remained with us all night. The third day after their arrival the Sioux left for their camp, making the most extravagant promises as to how they would act in the coming trade.

Two or three of our regular visitors commenced grumbling and finding fault, alleging that we "looked at the Sioux" (*i. e.* paid them unusual attention) more than at the Gros Ventres. A jealous feeling was evidently springing up, when the old Raising Heart struck a blow upon the floor with his tomahawk to arrest attention and declared that the whites acted perfectly right in treating the Sioux well; that they came only once, or at most twice a year to see them, whereas the Gros Ventres were with them all the time, and begged and received presents far greater in the aggregate than the Sioux ever had. This matter-of-fact statement, made the more impressive by the emphatic flourish of the tomahawk, speedily brought the grumblers to their senses and they tacitly admitted the force and justice of his reasoning.

The day following the departure of the Sioux was cold and stormy, with occasional spits of snow. The Indians assembled in council and determined to move into winter-quarters as soon as the Sioux should come in and make their trade. The squaws were making and repairing skin lodges which, when completed, they pitched on the prairie to see if everything was in order. The surplus corn had been câchéd and the scarcity of buffaloes around the summer village began to be severely felt. Had it not been for their crops the Indians would have been reduced to extreme hunger, and the supply of meat so opportunely brought from the Assiniboine camp was in great demand. All that could be spared was traded for robes to the starving Indians.

Summer was past. The autumn, with all its gorgeous splendor, had come. The grass on the prairie was bleached and withered and the leaves of the tall cottonwood trees and the red willows on the sand-bar were day by day more brilliant and beautiful in their dying glories. Travelling on the plains at this season is delightful. The creeks and streams are low, the air clear and balmy, and the wild animals in prime condition for hunting.

In a little while how changed will be the face of

nature! Snow will lie heavily on forest and prairie, on hill and valley. The once impetuous river will then slumber calmly in its icy bed and the fierce northern blasts, sweeping across the naked plain, will drive the bands of buffaloes to seek the shelter of the timbered bottoms.

Chapter XIV

A Friendly Visit

THE first snow of the season! October seventh dawned clear and cold, showing the ground covered with snow to the depth of three or four inches, but it soon disappeared under the influence of the noonday sun.

About eight Gros Ventres mustered up sufficient courage to go hunting. They returned well laden with meat and reported the buffaloes plenty and close, moving in toward the river. Encouraged by this news a large party went out the next day but came back during the evening in great trepidation, frightened by a herd. They had discovered plenty of buffaloes moving very rapidly towards them and without any further evidence concluded that there were enemies about and beat a hasty retreat. Buffaloes, as a general rule, never raise unless disturbed by man, but at this season they are usually very wild. The Indians say they smell the approaching storms of winter, and the slightest taint in the air alarms them. The hunters might, therefore, have invoked the aid of a little common sense before hurrying back in terror.

Mah-to-ta-ton-ka, the Bull Bear, came in reporting an abundance of antelopes close to the hills, about five miles off, and said he was going out to hunt them. This is considered an unfailing sign of the proximity of buffaloes. Just at dusk an Arikara Indian arrived from his village and said that he had seen five large bands of cows on the opposite side of the river, probably driven this way by the Sioux hunters.

October passed slowly. The Sioux were daily looked for and our Indians did little or nothing, being unwilling to hunt until settled in their winter quarters. The deer were now in fine condition and the fat haunches of venison that sometimes graced our board furnished a most acceptable change from the dried buffalo-meat, some of which, having been accidentally exposed to wet and not thoroughly dried afterwards, began to smell much stronger than was agreeable. Some pieces, indeed, became so full of animal life that it seemed almost impossible to keep them quiet on the mess-table.

The share which fell to the lot of our Canadian voyageurs excited their loudly expressed disgust. They were under the impression, when they engaged with the Fur Company, that they were going to a land flowing with milk and honey, where, among other luxuries, they hoped one day to possess "a lodge in some vast wilderness." But to be regaled on maggoty dried meat they considered beyond human endurance. Accordingly one of their number, who had been a tailor somewhere, was constituted a committee to remonstrate with the Bourgeois. The latter gave the committee such a stunning reply that on its report to the constituents they wisely concluded to endure what they could not help. At all events we heard no more complaints, and as we were subsisting on the same fare ourselves there was no reason for them.

An Indian arrived from the Sioux and said they would be here in "five camps—" seven or eight days. Pierre Garreau, the well-known interpreter, came up from Fort Clark to assist in the coming trade at Fort Berthold and to accompany the Gros Ventres to their winter quarters. Of this noted character I will speak at greater length hereafter.[49]

Horse-racing continued to be the principal amusement of the Indians in the afternoons, while the favorite game appeared to be one which we called billiards, and a space outside the

[49] Pierre Garreau was for many years a well-known character on the Upper Missouri. He was a man of great physical strength and of unsurpassed bravery. For accounts of his career, in addition to that of Boller, see De Trobriand, *Army Life in Dakota*, 69 and "Pierre Garreau at Fort Buford" in *North Dak. Hist. Colls.*, VII, 39–49. In 1881, old and infirm, he was living alone in his cabin, which caught fire and burned. His body was found inside the door, where, apparently, he had been smothered by the smoke.

pickets of the village was beaten as smooth and hard as a floor by those who engaged in it. This game is played by couples. The implements are a round stone and two sticks seven or eight feet long, with bunches of feathers tied on at regular intervals. The players start together, each carrying his pole in a horizontal position, and run along until the one who has the stone throws it, giving it a rolling motion, when each, watching his chance, throws his stick. The one who comes nearest (which is determined by the marks on the stick) has the stone for the next throw. Horses, blankets, robes, guns, &c., are staked at this game and I have frequently seen Indians play until they had lost everything.

The Pipe was a most inveterate player and usually an unlucky one. His oldest squaw, a sour-looking Mandan woman, entirely disapproved of this mode of spending time and would berate him so soundly that he was glad to go with her for the sake of peace, following meekly to the lodge where they stayed, for the poor wretch had none of his own. These exhibitions of conjugal discipline were always very amusing, and greatly enjoyed by his fellow-gamblers.

Four Bears came into my house one evening with his robe closely wrapped around him and contrary to his usual custom said not a word, but remained in an attitude of profound reflection.

After a time he spoke: "My heart is in the ground; my youngest wife is very sick; her life is very small; the breath has nearly left her nostrils." Upon being further questioned he said his squaw was far advanced in pregnancy and had complained of feeling unwell. Several old women undertook to treat her, which they did by kneading and punching her in the stomach (a favorite and universal remedy) until, as might have been expected, she was in a very critical condition.

Early the next morning the Raising Heart knocked at the gates before they were opened, to inform us that the squaw was dead, and that he wanted a scarlet blanket for her winding-sheet. There was the usual wailing and gashing of flesh around the grave by her relations, and the Four Bears did not come for his regular cup of coffee.

After the burial, old Doctor E-ten-ah-pen-ah dropped in and said he was called in too late to save her, although there were several other "physicians" in attendance. His course of treatment was certainly original. He wrapped her head in a blanket and burned a piece of dried buffalo dung in her face, uttering meanwhile an incantation. She died, however, in spite of all, but of course the Doctor was not to blame.

Several fresh arrivals came from the Sioux, bringing word that they had moved and would be in for trade in two more camps. As there was now a certainty of their coming the men were sent across the river to construct a temporary trading-house. An outfit of goods was prepared, that everything might be in readiness at a moment's notice.

The rival company also erected a post adjoining ours, and both parties were constantly on the alert that they might not lose, even for an instant, any supposed advantage. The excitement among the whites communicated itself to the Indians and countless rumors were in circulation respecting the treachery of the Sioux and apprehensions of a collision with them.

Riding out just before dark, I passed near the newly-made grave of the Four Bears' favorite squaw. Standing by it and crying in the most heart-rending tones was the oldest wife. She was almost nude, having cut her garments to pieces to testify to the intensity of her grief. Her hair was hacked off short all over her head and there was scarcely a spot on her arms and legs that was not gashed and bleeding from numerous self-inflicted wounds, made with a blunted butcher-knife which she held in her hand. Even her forehead was not spared, and altogether she presented a sickening appearance.

It is by no means uncommon in cases of violent grief to sacrifice one, or even more fingers. The

Four Bears made his appearance for the first time in the evening. He, too, had cut short his long and valued hair, and looked much altered in consequence. Just before she died he told his squaw that his heart would be buried in the ground with her and that when he was an old man and followed her to the Spirit-land he would have her again for his wife and their happiness would be eternal.

In the middle of the month a cold, driving snow-storm set in and lasted all day. The horses left the open prairie and huddled together in groups in sheltered places. At times the storm was so violent that we could not see the dead people on their scaffolds, only two hundred yards from the gates. Outdoor work was suspended and the men toasted themselves by huge fires and whiled away the time with song and story. In spite of the storm a Mandan came from the Sioux camp and confirmed the report of their being in shortly. He also said another party of visitors might be expected the next day.

There was nearly a foot of snow on the ground when the storm abated. The old mountaineers considered it one of the most severe within their recollection at this season of the year, and the Indians said that if the Sioux did not speedily come they would delay no longer going into winter-quarters.

Immense flocks of wild geese passed south all day, flying very low and offering excellent shots. By sundown a number of small moving objects were distinctly seen on the whitened plain, coming rapidly towards us. It was the expected party from the Sioux camp. They did not reach the sand-bar till after dark, and while waiting to be ferried over kindled blazing fires, which, with the groups of horses and riders, had a most picturesque effect, heightened by the surrounding snow-clad wilderness. Many Gros Ventres returned with this party and were loud in their praises of the hospitality of the Sioux. The weather moderated. The air became clear and balmy and the snow melted rapidly away.

The sun shone with dazzling brilliancy, and the reflection from the snow was extremely painful to the eyes. For several hours we were busy crossing over goods, and a party of men was detailed to remain with them as a guard. The Poor Wolf and Crow's Breast had a long talk with McBride, strongly urging him to extreme caution in his dealings with the Sioux, as they were apprehensive of treachery. They advised him to choose three or four of the most influential men for soldiers, adding that the whites and Gros Ventres would make common cause in the event of any difficulty arising, as their interests were identical—self-preservation.

A spell of pleasant weather succeeded and the camps had not appeared, although every day brought fresh arrivals and fresh reports. At last the Running Antelope returned, saying that the Sioux were all coming in. The purpose of his visit was to confer with the traders about prices, with the object of having them raised, and if their demands were not complied with, threats were freely hinted at, which the rascals were able and willing to execute.

One night after all of us were wrapped in slumber Four Bears came over from his lodge in hot haste and said he was afraid to sleep there any more, for he had heard the sound of footsteps softly treading outside and directly something was thrown at him, as he lay. Both of his women ran off immediately, but he declared he was so badly frightened that he could not stir for some time and he was sure that it must have been the ghost of his dead squaw come from her grave to trouble him because he had not buried her as deep as he had promised.

Day after day passed, and every one was cursing Indian dilatoriness and wishing the trade over. A few Sioux came from the camp and said that to-morrow, beyond doubt, they would be here. Several slept in our house and the mice (of which there were plenty) troubled them so much by running over them that they got up, lit their pipes, and declared they could not sleep because the mice were Great Spirits.

The next morning bright and early we were astir and making all necessary preparations to conduct the trade. The Indians were in a great state of excitement and very busy getting everything in readiness to receive their guests with all honor.

A large flotilla of bull-boats was soon in active service and traders and Indians entered heartily into the business of the day. The sun was high in the heavens when a long dark line came in sight on the southern prairies, at first faint, but gradually becoming more distinct until hidden from view by the forest, whence emerged a living stream upon the sand-bar. McBride had crossed over with his men early in the morning and as soon as the Sioux appeared I dispatched the interpreter, Malnouri, to join him, and remained in the fort with only two men. Not an Indian was to be seen hanging around the kitchen-door. All were engrossed with the preparations and attentions which they designed for their Sioux guests.

As evening approached, matters assumed a very lively aspect on the sand-bar. Numerous campfires had been kindled, which threw into strong relief the groups of gayly dressed and bedizened Indians gathered around them. Huge fires were also made on the bank below the pickets of the village, illuminating the dark river covered with bull-boats passing and repassing, as well as the crowds assembled at the landing-place. The gates of the fort were closed at the usual hour and for an interval there were no interruptions of any kind.

A heavy knock at the gate, and a voice calling out, "Coula! coula!" (my friend) attracted my attention. After a short parley to ascertain who it was I unbarred the gates to admit the Tobacco (Mandan) and two of his Sioux friends.

I received them in the usual manner, giving them the pipe to smoke and a bowl of black medicine (coffee) and hard bread. One of the strangers was called He-who-uses-his-heart-for-all, and had been appointed chief of the Onc-pa-pas, under the Bear's-Rib, by General Harney at a treaty held with the Sioux near Fort Pierre in 1856.[50] He showed me his certificate of the same,

[50] Hostilities with the Sioux were precipitated by the slaughter of Lt. Grattan's detachment near Fort Laramie, Aug. 19, 1854. Whether the primary responsibility for the tragedy rested upon the Indians or upon the white army seems still to be debated. In 1855 General Wm. S. Harney led a punitive expedition against the Sioux and at Ash Hollow, Nebraska, on Sept. 3, defeated them with terrific slaughter. Whether Ash Hollow was strictly a battle or more properly a white man's massacre remains likewise a debatable question. Some 86 Indians were

dated March 4th, which he carefully treasured in a leathern pouch wrapped in a piece of calico. He also had letters of recommendation from Mr. Charles Primeau and several other well-known Sioux traders, testifying that the bearer was a good young man and a devoted friend to the whites. The usual result of giving a well-disposed Indian letters of this kind is to make him an

---

killed and 70 wounded, with a white loss of 5 men. Mrs. Margaret I. Carrington, *Absaraka, Home of the Crows*, p. 38; Geo. W. Kingsbury, *Hist. of Dakota Territory* (Chicago, 1915), I, 60–62; Addison E. Sheldon, *Nebraska, The Land and the People* (Chicago, 1931), I, 133–35. Harney now marched his army of 1200 to Fort Laramie and thence to Fort Pierre, where it was placed in winter quarters while the Commander scouted the area in search of a more suitable location for a permanent military establishment. His decision fell upon the point lower down the Missouri where Fort Randall was established in 1856. Meanwhile at Fort Pierre in March, 1856 he negotiated a treaty with all the western Sioux which provided for a measure of self-government through an extensive system of Indian police. Regrettably, as the future was to disclose, Congress refused to ratify the treaty because of the expense the system would involve, and the promises General Harney had held out to the Sioux were nullified. Despite this some of the chiefs, notably Bear's Rib, remained staunchly friendly to the whites. Out of this discordant situation came the murder of Bear's Rib near Fort Pierre, May 27, 1862 by members of the hostile Sioux faction. *North Dak. Hist. Colls.*, I, 425–27. For an interesting characterization of Bear's Rib see De Trobriand, *Army Life in Dakota*, 118–23. The record of the council proceedings in negotiating the treaty is printed in House Exec. Doc. 130, July 25, 1856.

inveterate beggar, until his friendship is regulated by the amount of presents he receives.

His companion claimed to be a comrade and intimate friend of Paquenaude, seeming to expect great attention on that account. After sitting and talking a while they took their leave, saying that they would return early in the morning to trade some robes.

Paquenaude's friend, however, changed his mind as he was going out of the gate, and declared his intention of sleeping in the fort. He followed me closely when I made my tour of inspection to see that all was right, and finally wanted me to send him across the river again. I got rid of him at last by telling him to go to the bank and call for a bull-boat. Then closing the gates I went to sleep, leaving him to pound for admission, and yell "Coula" until he was tired.

By early dawn a number of Indians who had finished their trading came over to visit us, peering around and sharply scrutinizing everything. The Bourgeois, leaving Paquenaude in charge of the business on the other side, recrossed to finish the trade at the fort, chiefly for such articles as had not been taken over. McBride reported that the Sioux had conducted themselves very quietly despite their threatening talk, and that at least two-thirds went down to the Ree Village, where the bulk of their furs would be disposed of. The

Gros Ventres exchanged corn for dry meat and were now well supplied for some time to come.

I noticed a great many handsome women among the Sioux. As they have not such laborious work to perform as the Minnetaree squaws they retain what beauty they possess much longer, and are generally tall and straight, without the thick ankles, the ungainly walk, and the stooping shoulders of their less favored sisters. Taking them altogether, men and women, the wild prairie Sioux have no superiors among the Indians in appearance and domestic virtues.

In the afternoon they commenced moving camp, intending to join the rest of their band at the Ree Village. Soon the long, black line stretching away over the pairie grew more and more indistinct until it finally vanished in the distance. The robes and peltries were quickly ferried over and stored carefully away, and closing the gates, all gladly rested from the fatigue and excitement of the past two days and the perplexities and uncertainties of the preceding three weeks.

CHAPTER XV

Removal to Winter Quarters

IT was now the end of October and the glorious
balmy Indian summer had set in. The Gros
Ventres were preparing to start for winter-
quarters in a day or two and were consequently
in a world of bustle. The entire morning a
crowd of squaws surrounded the grindstone,
waiting their turns to sharpen their axes. The
store also was thronged by those who were supplying themselves with necessaries for the winter
hunt, and by as many more trying to beg or
obtain on credit such articles as they needed. A
few of known probity were trusted with goods to
the value of several robes, while others of doubtful standing were obliged to deposit dresses,
ornaments, and bonnets of eagle-feathers as
security. Thus, between the rival trading posts,
nearly every Indian was able to supply himself
with an outfit. The men were employed in
cleaning up the fort, while we prepared an outfit
for the trade at the winter camp.

The next day was a busy one indeed. The
Indians were preparing to move away and
abandon their village to its winter solitude. Many
deposited their valuables in our store for safe-
keeping and we soon had a motley array of

medicine-bags, drums, rattles, lances, saddles, and other articles, useful and ornamental. Dashing young bucks, decked out in all their finery and painted in the most fashionable style, pranced about on their gayly caparisoned steeds, whose tinkling equipment could be heard in every direction, while upon the squaws devolved the task of saddling and packing the horses with their household effects.

As each family was ready its head led the way, followed by a train of pack and riding horses, travées, dogs, women, and children. Thus, almost insensibly as it were, the village was deserted. As the last stragglers were departing the Long Hair ascended the roof of his lodge, dressed in his chief's coat of scarlet cloth trimmed with gold and silver lace, and harangued his indignation at their going so far to winter quarters and leaving such a dangerous strip of country to be traversed if any of them should have occasion to visit the village and the forts. The Poor Wolf, the leader of the soldier band, mounted upon his splendid black horse, remained behind to urge on the loiterers, so that before nightfall the village was entirely depopulated and a feeling of loneliness overshadowed us all. Several families of Sioux had remained behind when their camp moved, intending to winter with the Gros Ventres.

In the morning we started to overtake the

camp and accompany it to winter quarters. Our party consisted of myself, an interpreter and his family, four men, and two wagons loaded with goods. We intended remaining with the Gros Ventres to trade through the season.

The day was beautiful and the air soft as in spring. The prairie was dry, the creeks low, and travelling was in consequence delightful. After a short delay while passing through the timber, caused by the tongue of one of the wagons breaking, we overtook the teams of the American Fur Company in charge of Pierre Garreau, and travelled on together in the most friendly manner.

The Indians had made their first camp at the lake about five miles from the village. The ashes of their fires were still smouldering and many little temporary huts of willow-boughs standing. A short distance farther on an Indian pony with a broken leg was lying by the trail, having been abandoned with a strange kind of humanity— without being killed to put it out of its misery. The poor animal raised its head and whinnied as we passed, but we could afford it no relief, and to kill it would only be made a pretext for its owner to extort from us its full value. We were therefore compelled to leave it to its dreadful fate, which was easily foretold from the number of sneaking wolves that hovered around, just beyond gunshot.

Our course on the high prairie was parallel

with the river, though sometimes several miles from it, but always in full view of its wonderful scenery and tortuous windings. On one side the prairie stretched away until it seemed to join the blue sky in the distance. On the other were bold and precipitous bluffs of different-colored clay, interspersed with grass-covered hills sloping down to the edge of the forest, which, no longer clad in the gorgeous hues of autumn, looked dark and somber.

Beyond coursed the mighty Missouri, all the wild, rushing impetuosity of the early summer gone, and flowing slowly and silently, as if its bosom was already chilled by the cold embrace of winter. Farther on, across the river, was another dark line of forest from which lofty cliffs of fantastic shapes seemed to rise, and beyond these again others, loftier still, reared their sharply defined crests to the sky.

Before us extended a vast plain whose extreme boundary the eye could not reach. Behind us the black hills which encircled the bend of the river below the village, apparently almost within reach, though in reality miles away, from the tops of which the boundless prairie again unrolled itself. A thin smoke, barely visible to a practised eye, floated on the air. The Indians said it rose from the Sioux camp on Knife River.

The sun was already declining when we came

in sight of the Indian camp, picturesquely located in a wooded ravine of the Mauvaises Terres, about a mile from the Missouri. A small creek, which after many windings emptied into the lake we had crossed in the morning, afforded a supply of water for the encampment.

Our cattle were unyoked and our horses unsaddled and driven down to drink and then allowed to graze at will. A fire was kindled and our dinner (and supper) of dry meat, coffee, and hard bread was soon in course of preparation. Before it was ready I was called by the Bear-in-the-water (Mandan) to a feast in his lodge, which consisted solely of some very fine, fat dried meat. After doing justice to it I returned with my entertainer to our campfire and dispatched a second meal.

The young hunters were ranging over the hills and through the ravines in search of game or traces of enemies. A group of the principal men stood upon a high black hill which overshadowed the camp, forming a conspicuous landmark for miles around, and discussed their future movements. The red light of the declining sun shone upon the white conical lodges that dotted the prairie and with all the accessories to the scene made a wild and strikingly beautiful picture.

Darkness coming on, the horses were driven up and picketed in front of the lodges and our cattle securely tied to the wheels of the wagons. The noise of a drum in a distant lodge was soon the only sound that broke the stillness of the night. Having picketed my horse close by, I wrapped myself in my robe, with my saddle for a pillow, and fell asleep, to be repeatedly wakened by the starved Indian dogs tugging and gnawing at my covering.

The morning broke cold and raw. The sharp, biting wind drove the horses to the dells for shelter as soon as they were released from their pickets. The squaws bustled about, shouting at the dogs and scolding the children as they gathered fuel for cooking. For a long time everything was quiet, the smoke curled from the lodges, and no sign of preparation for departure was visible. When the hour for starting had come, the soldiers rode around the camp and harangued, "Pull down your lodges, and pack your horses!" In a moment the lodges, which had been tightly stretched over the poles, fluttered in the wind. A moment more, and they were flat on the prairie, and the squaws busy packing and loading their horses, which had been driven up in readiness by the boys. We also harnessed our teams, but dared not stir until the camp was ready and the word given. After saddling my horse I could not help admiring the celerity and skill with which the squaws packed their plunder, keeping up meanwhile a clattering accompaniment with their tongues.

Not twenty steps from where I stood was pitched the lodge of the old Mandan, Buck Eagle, before spoken of in connection with the Bull Medicine. He was very aged and feeble and could barely keep pace with the camp on the march, and had we been constantly travelling like the Sioux he must inevitably have been left behind and abandoned to his fate. The women of his lodge hustled the old fellow out of the way *sans cérémonie* and began packing their horses.

The Buck Eagle took himself off a few paces, just far enough to be out of danger of being struck by a lodge-pole, and sitting down on his robe, deliberately proceeded to divest himself of his shirt and leggings and appeared, without any unusual exertion, to make a very hearty (though not very substantial) meal upon the parasites that so thickly infested the seams of his garments. Leaving him to the enjoyment of his epicurean feast, I rode to the black hill, whence I had a splendid bird's-eye view of the whole camp.

When the head of the column moved I rejoined the wagons, and directly Red Tail, one of the soldiers, galloped up, shouting, "Nar-har-ah," (Go on). We quickly fell in with the grand cavalcade of warriors, mounted and on foot, and horses drawing loaded travées, upon which were sometimes tied two or three children and as many puppies, clinging together with the most ludicrous tenacity.

Dogs also dragged their full share upon miniature travées, occasionally joining in a grand skirmish with their unemployed companions, usually resulting in the complete rout of the latter. Indian dogs, like their wolfish progenitors, are exceedingly cowardly, all bark and none bite, but the moment one is harnessed to his *travée*, conscious of the protection it affords him he becomes very quarrelsome, and when a number get together they make the hair fly to some purpose.

The young colts and favorite buffalo horses ran at will, careering gayly over the plain and dashing through the crowds, frequently starting some well-behaved pack-horse to indulge in eccentricities until his load was disarranged and required readjustment, the enraged women on whom the task devolved bestowing left-handed blessings on everything within earshot. Some of the young men played their game of billiards as the camp moved, and every one seemed to enjoy immensely the change from the staid life at the summer village.

The soldiers rode about, hurrying up the stragglers and checking the head of the column when it moved on too fast. Thus we travelled, a compact body in three parallel lines. I pressed to the head and joined the old Raising Heart and his family and relatives, and as they were all supplied with fancy spotted horses the clan made a gallant appearance.

The old gentleman wore a felt hat, a gift from some of his white friends, and was urging on, by repeated applications of his whip, a very diminutive donkey, whose pack seemed nearly as large as itself. With every stroke of the whip the old man looked at me and smiled, flourishing meanwhile a fan of eagle-feathers. Attached to his party was Ara-poo-shee, the Rotten Bear, whose immense frame bestrode a little sorrel pony that fairly staggered under its unwieldy load. The Rotten Bear seldom ventured upon equestrian exercises, having a wholesome dread of a fall, and never travelled faster than a walk. He was obliged to give his undivided attention to preserving his equilibrium and heeded not the many sharp jokes that were flung at him without mercy as at every slight stumble made by his little horse his countenance involuntarily assumed an air of the greatest solicitude and apprehension, ludicrous in the extreme.

Our course lay along the edge of the prairie overlooking the Mauvaises Terres. We were elevated many hundred feet above the wooded bottom of the river. Huge bluffs of clay of every color (bright red predominating) and of every conceivable shape reared their lofty turreted summits, suggesting the resemblance to ruins of colossal proportions. On these bluffs and over acres of red clayey soil not a blade of grass met the eye, their barren and desolate character well deserving the distinctive title of Bad Lands.

The river made a sharp turn to the southwest and the vista of rugged bluffs appeared interminable, dome after dome and turret after turret rising up against the cold gray sky, presenting a scene of desolate grandeur beyond all powers of description. We had journeyed on in this manner for some time when, leaving the high prairie, the motley crowd under the guidance of the Poor Wolf passed quickly down into a well-wooded ravine and halting, prepared to encamp.

We did the same, being compelled, however, from the nature of the ground to make a detour in order to facilitate the descent of our teams. The high bluffs were a great protection against the cold winds and we made a very comfortable camp. The hunters were soon roaming over the hills, and several fat deer were not long in finding their way to the lodges. A large band of elk was raised, but they were off in a twinkling, their magnificent forms being in full view as they rapidly dashed over the brow of a hill and were lost to sight. We built a huge blazing fire and a number of our Indian friends helped to complete the jovial circle that gathered around it.

CHAPTER XVI

Building the Winter Quarters

NOVEMBER set in raw, cloudy, and cold, presenting a very great contrast to the delightful Indian summer we had just enjoyed. The soldiers having given us permission to travel on independently of the movements of the camp, we made an early start, intending to reach the proposed wintering-place near the mouth of Rising Water, by sundown.

Pierre Garreau and myself rode ahead some distance in hopes of seeing a stray bull and giving chase. While jogging along, Pierre entertained me with many anecdotes of his early life and the exciting scenes in which he had been a conspicuous actor. Pierre generally claims to be a half-breed, but such is not the case. He is a fullblood Arikara Indian, and has passed his entire life in the service of the American Fur Company as interpreter. His mother, being a very handsome squaw, was married shortly after her Indian husband died to a trader named Garreau, who adopted as his own the child to whom she soon gave birth, and afforded him every possible advantage. When a lad, he sent him to St. Louis and had him apprenticed to one Page, a baker and confectioner, with whom he lived, as he expresses it, "four years in the brick houses," and thoroughly learned his business.

But that fondness for wild life which can never be overcome by those who have once tasted of its pleasures impelled him to return to the Indian country, where he has since steadily resided. He was now over sixty years of age, and his great pride was in his horses, of which he had some very fine ones.

Pierre had three sons by different wives, all quiet, well-behaved young men, who, from having lived so much with the whites, were free from many objectionable Indian habits. He himself was very neat and particular in his person and his clothes, guns, and equipments were always in perfect order.

We reached the crossing of Rising Water at noon, when, leaving the wagons to follow, the Hawk and myself, with Pierre's three sons, rode rapidly over the hills and finally came to a heavily timbered point about four miles above the creek, sheltered by high bluffs and affording secure and excellent pasturage. The Hawk made a cautious survey before entering the timber and carefully examined the trail for any suspicious sign. After threading a bridle-path for some distance we came to a cleared space where the Indians had once wintered, and found several cabins still standing in a tolerable state of repair.

We took possession of one, and tying our horses to the trees kindled a fire and roasted a piece of venison that the Hawk had luckily brought with him, watching its progress with infinite satisfaction and keen appetites. When it was done we drew our butcher-knives and using a piece of bark for a platter attacked it, nor rested until it was completely demolished. It was one of the sweetest morsels I ever tasted, seasoned as it was with that best of all sauces, hunger.

The cries of the teamsters now heralded the approach of the wagons, which had been delayed by the heavy growth of underbrush through which it was necessary to clear a road before a passage could be made for them. After unloading and storing away the goods the oxen were turned loose and we betook ourselves to our robes and blankets and slept soundly.

Toward noon of the next day the Indians arrived, and all was then bustle and animation. As soon as the lodges were pitched the squaws began chopping down trees and the deep silence of the forest was rudely dissipated by the clattering of hundreds of axes.

A child of the Red Tail died, and the body was placed in a tree on the edge of the forest by the sorrowing parents. The squaws worked diligently, and lodge after lodge filled the gaps left by the destruction of trees. Some of the hunters went out to reconnoiter and reported buffaloes plenty, moving in towards camp, and a general surround was talked of in a day or so.

One bright morning I shouldered my rifle and set out for a stroll among the surrounding hills to enjoy, if possible, the view from the top of one of the highest. My course lay through a low prairie bottom that nestled between the timber and the bluffs. On the sides of the latter the Indian horses were grazing, well secured against danger by the vigilant scouts posted on all the prominent hills, completely commanding the possible approach of an enemy. I spent nearly half a day very pleasantly climbing among the rugged clay bluffs, and with the aid of my spyglass saw distinctly, at a great distance, bands of buffaloes quietly feeding.

One very steep bluff, towering high above all the rest, attracted my attention and after a tough scramble I gained the top. A glorious view rewarded me. At my feet lay the timbered point in which the Indians were building their winter encampment. The sharp strokes of the axe, softened by distance, saluted my ears, and occasionally a crashing and swaying among the trees told that one more had fallen.

Around me rose clay bluffs of every size and shape. Some were black and gloomy, as if a fire had swept over them, but the majority were tinted with a vermilion hue, vividly bright under the glancing rays of the sun. The Missouri swept the base of a range of cliffs even more picturesque, which towered on the opposite side. These receded gradually from the river in a graceful sweep and returned again a few miles higher up, holding as it were in their embrace a most beautiful little prairie upon which the Indians cast longing looks, wishing the river frozen over that they might cross their horses and pasture them on its rich grass.

A mile or so farther on a dark line of timber showed where Shell Creek emptied into the Missouri. Here was the beginning or foot of the Grand Detour, and as it wound its tortuous way through the Mauvaises Terres the Great Bend could be distinctly traced until it was lost in the faint blue line that marked the hills of Knife River. I could have enjoyed the view for hours, but the sun was getting low and a sharpened appetite admonished me that it was time to return. On my way I shot at a wolf that was loping along in an easy, impudent manner, and disturbed his peace of mind very materially.

Our houses or cabins, for they were nothing more, were well advanced, the rails laid, and rushes and dirt thrown on to finish the roofs. A chimney remained yet to be built of sticks and mud, and two days of hard work would complete everything.

But we had reckoned without our host. The sticks forming the framework of the chimney were tied across at regular intervals to the four upright poles with thongs or cords of raw hide, and the end of one happened to project from the mixture of mud and grass that composed the walls of the chimney. This attracted the notice of some starving dogs, who, while we were all asleep in the adjoining cabin, tore the whole structure to pieces and devoured the cords, leaving us to do our work over again. After this warning a door was made to prevent any similar catastrophe.

Our men, not daring to vent their anger on the dogs for fear of the squaws' interference, contented themselves with uttering unlimited "*sacr-r-r-és chiens!*" and as if on purpose to increase their already unbounded disgust at everything Indian, the old Buck Eagle came into the house just as they were ready to eat their suppers and without even saying "by your leave," picked up the coffee-pot and drank off its contents from the spout with the utmost *sang froid*. After draining it to the grounds he pronounced it "suck-itts" (good) and took his departure, leaving the "moshees" (whites) to reflect upon the uncertainty of all human expectations.

The Indians built their village in three camps

about a quarter of a mile apart. Most of them had small log cabins close together, opening into a large round dirt-covered lodge, which was used in common as a stable for their horses. The majority of the Indians had finished their houses at the same time as ourselves and the numerous well-beaten paths leading in all directions through the timber gave the place the appearance of having been long inhabited.

I had now seen all things completed, and on the ninth day after our arrival started with the men and teams on my return, to bring back from the fort the remainder of the goods for the winter trade.

At sundown we bivouacked on Rising Water. Our fire was kindled, and before long a side of fat, juicy ribs of buffalo meat was roasting before it. The coffee was speedily made, the ribs done to a turn, and we were soon in the full enjoyment of a prairie supper. The sky was overcast and the cold north winds swept fiercely over the open prairie. The oxen had been tied to the wheels of the wagons to prevent them from straying, and were thus partially sheltered. My horse came to the fire to share its warmth, and stood so near me as I lay closely wrapped in my buffalo robe that my head sometimes rested against his fore feet and the breath from his nostrils blew into my face as he slept and nodded over me.

The darkness grew more intense. Then the Aurora flashed and faded in the northern sky until the prairies glowed as if on fire. Wolves howled around us in numbers all night long, and the sparks from our campfire, scattered by the wind, fell among the grass (which at this season is as dry as tinder) causing it to blaze so furiously that it required our utmost exertions to prevent a conflagration.

Mounting guard by turns, we passed the night. At daybreak we laid our course for the fort, distant about thirty miles, which by hard pushing we accomplished before evening.

CHAPTER XVII

Winter Toil and Recreation

WE were soon ready to return again to the winter camp. The wagons had been loaded and all the necessary preparations made, when the weather became very cold and a severe snowstorm set in. Not caring to unload again, after consulting with the Bourgeois I determined upon starting and was fortunately able to secure the services of a Gros Ventre Indian, popularly known among the traders by the sobriquet of Bonaparte, as guide. He was a stanch friend of the white man and a warrior of tried prowess, and had also been a travelling companion on our expedition to the Assiniboine camp.

For several miles our route lay through the timber, which sheltered us in great measure from the weather, but after crossing the lake and ascending the hills to the high open prairie the storm struck us in all its fury. The snow fell thick and fast and already covered the ground to the depth of half a foot, while a driving north-east wind whirled it about and chilled us to the bone, in spite of our blanket capotes, leggings, capeshaws, and other wrappings. The snow deepened so rapidly that the cattle toiled heavily along and were badly stalled more than once in crossing a

hollow of the prairie, where the drift had accumulated.

The storm was what is called in the mountains
a *pouderie*, and so blinding that it was impossible
to see more than a few yards ahead at any time.
Night overtook us as we reached the ridge. The
wind had blown the snow away and travelling
was much easier in consequence. Our Indian
guide led us to a sheltered place in the bad lands,
where we encamped in a snug thicket of dry ash.
The moment we gained the friendly refuge of the
encircling hills and were protected from the
chilling blasts to which we had been exposed all
day a feeling of warmth and security took possession of us and all gayly set about making camp
without loss of time. Our oxen fared well on the
huge bundles of hay we had brought with us, and
after stripping my horse of his equipment I
led the noble animal to a cosy little dell, which
was completely covered from the wind by the
thickly interlaced and overhanging branches of
the trees.

Having supplied him with abundance of hay,
I turned to where Bonaparte was scraping away
the snow with his feet and collecting dry leaves
and twigs to kindle a fire. The pile was soon
kindled into a blaze, and crackling branches
piled on until we had a huge, roaring fire. Water
there was none, but melted snow supplied a

substitute and we were thus enabled to enjoy that great luxury on the prairies, a cup of coffee. Our moccasins were hung on little forked sticks to dry, after which we spread our robes and blankets and slept soundly, undisturbed by the howling of the storm or the serenade with which the wolves favored us. Bonaparte crept into a little hollow by the roots of a tree and made himself a very snug resting-place.

When we awoke the morning air was chill and raw, the fire had burned down, and everything was heavily covered with snow. As each man rolled out from his lair, shaking the white clouds from his robes, it seemed as though every snow-covered hillock around us would suddenly start up and reveal a wild, uncouth-looking human form hurrying to stir up the embers, and re-kindle the almost expiring flames. More fuel was piled on, the remainder of the hay fed to the animals, and our own breakfast soon prepared.

We regained the ridge with difficulty, and not until we had doubled the teams on each wagon were we able to proceed on our way. A very large band of antelopes was started by the creaking of the wheels and their light airy forms flitted by us like shadows. We crossed the fresh trails of buffaloes going in toward the river, probably driven by the storm, and discovered a small band at a short distance from our line of march. The close of the day brought us safely to the Indian camp.

The paths leading in all directions through the timber were beaten hard and smooth as a floor by the constant tread of moccasined feet and the passage of numerous dog-*travées* loaded with wood. The lodges were finished, and the new-fallen snow lay pure and white on the rude cabins, making them look fresh and clean and concealing from view aught that might offend the eye.

I found life in the winter camp very enjoyable, the constant stir and bustle and the pleasures and excitements of the chase causing time to pass by almost unheeded. Early on still, cold mornings, at the hour when the lodge-fires were being rekindled, the thick white smoke would rise up in a heavy column and float away lazily with scarcely any motion, resembling, except in color, the smoke from the busy foundries in the haunts of civilized man. The effect was striking, and visible for a great distance.

Before the sun was up bands of horses were driven out to the most sheltered places among the hills and the beautiful prairie across the river, which, admirably protected as it was from the winds and abounding with rich grass, afforded the best winter pasturage for miles around. The whole face of the country was now

well covered with snow, and when the sun's
morning beams tinged with crimson the whitened
hills and valleys the frozen crystals sparkled and
glistened with indescribable brilliancy.

While the hunters ranged over the hills in
quest of game, or watching their horses, the
squaws went off to cut fuel for the lodges and peel
cottonwood bark for the food of the horses at
night. They commenced their preparations by
belting their robes around them in such a manner that, while affording a complete protection
for their whole bodies, the free use of the arms
was not interfered with. Then harnessing up
some eight or ten dogs to as many *travées*, they
shouldered their axes and led the van, followed
by the dogs trotting demurely along in single file.

Before long the woods resounded with the dull
strokes of the axes, mingled constantly with the
shrill voices of the women scolding their dogs,
who very naturally liked to vary the dull routine
of every-day life by getting up a little rough-and-
tumble fight among themselves. When a dog had
his full load he was led to the main pathway, and
after receiving a couple of practical reminders on
his head from the axe-handle to attend to his own
business, started for his lodge, dragging his
travée with great steadiness. Unless caught on
some obstruction (in which case he patiently
awaits his release) he quickly arrives at his

destination and finds some member of the family
ready to relieve him of his load and turn him
loose to steal or fight among his brethren for his
dinner. Several hours later the squaws are seen
coming back in parties, with a retinue of dogs all
loaded as heavily as possible.

Each woman carries on her back, supported
by a band passed around the shoulders, a bundle
of wood of such size and weight that two would
make a fair load for an Indian pony. Yet the
women think nothing of it, and travel along,
talking and laughing, as if it was play. Every day,
year in and year out, this must be done and if
the lodge is large and the weather very cold it is
often necessary to make two, and sometimes
three trips a day. A large camp will very soon
consume all the small dry wood in the vicinity
and the women are then compelled to go a long
distance, often two miles, before they can obtain
the needed supply.

When they reach the lodges the wood is
thrown down and piled, the kettle put over the
fire, and cooking goes on again. Then the cottonwood bark is to be thawed and peeled in thin
strips to feed the horses, moccasins have to be
mended, and skins and robes dressed or handled.
After a hunt the labor is greatly increased, as the
meat must be cut up and dried and the fresh
skins prepared for future dressing.

An Indian who has three or four wives gets along very comfortably, for, provided the women do not quarrel too much, they divide the labor between them. The Bear Hunter, in whose lodge I lived the whole of one winter, had five squaws, but as they were all sisters there was very little discord among them. His family lived well. They had an abundance of horses, and could always command the services of a good hunter.

Each of these five women belonged to a different band or society, and as the lodge was one of the largest in the village it was in great demand as a rendezvous. The band of Bulls, the White Cows, the Wild Goose band, and other associations frequently assembled and made night hideous with their vocal and instrumental accompaniments while tripping the light fantastic toe, putting sleep entirely out of the question.

While the women patiently performed their daily drudgery the men who were not guarding the horses visited from lodge to lodge, feasting, smoking, and relating long anecdotes of war and hunting exploits. Sometimes they gambled, playing their favorite game of hand, in which they would get so excited that time passed unheeded until the sharp voice of an old squaw, vexed and angry at the losses her husband was sustaining, berated him so severely that they were often glad to bring their sports to a close.

In order to enjoy their amusement of billiards some of its devotees cleared off a level piece of ground between the two lower camps and planted a line of bushes and underbrush to form a partial barrier against the wind. Logs were placed on each side of the alley to keep the sticks (or cues) from glancing off. By constant use the table was soon beaten and polished as smooth as ice, and the game was played with greater satisfaction and spirit than ever.

At any hour of the day, no matter how cold it was or how keenly the wind blew, one might witness a couple of fellows, clothed only in their breechcloths, industriously following up the smooth rolling stone with their sticks and measuring and disputing the success of the throw with the most intense eagerness. On the curbing the spectators sat, muffled in their shaggy robes, passing the indispensable pipe from one to another and entering heartily into the spirit of the game, betting and losing with the same recklessness as the players.

The mania for gambling was by no means confined to the men. The women and young girls were equally imbued with it and, sitting down on a smooth place on the ice, they would roll a pebble from one to the other for hours together. Young infants were often kept on the ice all the while, their mothers, or those who had them in charge, being too much engrossed with their play to pay them any attention.

When the sun had set, and while its departing rays grew fainter and dimmer, the sound of the horses' feet could be heard crunching the frozen snow-covered roads as they were driven home from pasture. While crossing the ice they drank from large holes cut for that purpose and constantly kept open. Cheerful fires were kindled in the lodges used for stables, and by their light the horses were carefully secured, the restive ones and young colts being separated from the others to prevent injury.

The women passed to and from the river bringing water for domestic purposes, and the dogs invariably curled themselves up at the entrance to the lodge, where if one was not very careful he could not avoid trampling on one or more, apparently sleeping. For a while all is quiet. Cooking is going on in every lodge, and during that important operation no one likes to be absent. When the meal is finished the bustle and stir begin again. The trader's house, the Exchange where all the idlers congregate to hear the news, is then the great center of attraction. Visits are exchanged from lodge to lodge and the young bucks, dressed and painted, stroll about in parties, singing songs, or hover around the dwellings of their sweethearts, watching for them to answer the usual signal.

The sound of the drum and the yells and cries of the dancers proclaim what is going on in another part of the camp, and the dogs, as if by a preconcerted arrangement, join in a general wailing cry which lasts for several minutes, and gradually dies away. Just as one begins to hope for a brief interval of quiet some young puppy, anxious to try his voice, indulges in a whine. In an instant every dog is endeavoring to outdo his neighbor, who returns the compliment with untiring energy. It is late at night before all is quiet. The bright sparks no longer fly thickly from the chimneys of the cabins, and every dweller in the camp is buried in slumber.

When the snow lies deep on the ground and enemies are less numerous (from the fear of being easily tracked) most of the horses are left out at night, and only brought up when wanted for hunting. If the grass is plenty and they can get a fair allowance of cottonwood bark they may be kept in good order all winter, but if hard hunted and brought up every night, by the time spring comes they are so reduced that only the very best horses can then catch buffaloes.

Cottonwood bark is very nourishing, and if judiciously fed, a horse will fatten on it. A tree is cut down, the tender boughs lopped off, and after warming it to take out the frost the bark is peeled and torn into strips of various lengths resembling pine shavings, the knots and rough pieces are carefully thrown away, and it is then ready for use.

Chapter XVIII

Winter Activities at Fort Atkinson

AFTER remaining several weeks in the camp I went down to the fort for additional supplies. The men were in the height of the trapping season and had met with good success. I was fortunate enough to be in time for the trial of a new style of trap which one of them had contrived. It seems he thought that catching wolves in the old-fashioned steel trap was slow and uncertain. Besides, from its bulk a wolf of any sense would be sure to see it and defeat the hopes of the trapper by declining to be caught.

The simplicity of the new invention was one of its chief recommendations. It consisted merely of a stout iron hook fastened to a chain and well baited with cracklings (leavings, after frying out buffalo tallow). It was then to be secured to a post most cunningly set in the ground and covered with snow. Success seemed beyond doubt. Every one commended this ingenious arrangement and predicted great results. It was set for the first time on a raw and cloudy night, when the wind whistled and howled and beat against the pickets with great fury. The other traps were set as usual, but no one cared to go to bed until the new one was proved. At midnight the men sallied forth to make a tour of inspection, more particularly to see the practical working of Monsieur Gingras' patent wolf-hook.

It was near the witching hour of twelve when a feeble cry came from the direction in which this scientific master-piece was planted, and picking up their guns and hastily unbarring the gates the men rushed forth in breathless haste, Monsieur G. in advance, with a heavy club to dash out the brains of the luckless wolf. Sure enough, a small animal was impaled on the hook. "A coyote! a coyote!" was the cry, and rushing on it with uplifted club he dealt a blow that stretched it lifeless. It was triumphantly carried to the fort, where the light of the fire in the men's quarters showed it to be an unfortunate little dog which had been accidentally shut out in the evening.

But the trap was a success. No one could gainsay that. So without heeding any of the witticisms his comrades indulged in at his expense he persevered for nearly a week, catching nothing, while the old-fashioned trappers had their hands full, skinning wolves and foxes. McBride advised him to take his hook to the point above and suspend it from the limb of a tree over a well-beaten deer-path, where, by using hay for bait, he might very probably succeed in catching a deer.

This advice coincided exactly with his views and he fixed his trap in a splendid place about a mile from the fort, visiting it regularly morning and evening for several days, always carrying hay for new bait. The deer-tracks, he said, were very plenty and very fresh, and how he failed to hook one was beyond his comprehension. Finally he was induced to think that the first of April had been anticipated in his case and abandoned in disgust his attempt to catch wolves or deer with a cat-fish hook!

Around the fort it was dull and lonely, for while it was certainly a relief to be free from Indian society, yet, when the village was inhabited the constant stir going on served to break the monotony of the daily routine. It was a favorite amusement, on a bright moonlight night, to watch, gun in hand, upon the roof of one of the houses in hopes of getting a shot at the wolves and foxes which were always prowling around. While thus keeping watch one could not help contrasting the changed appearance of the village, since its desertion by the Indians.

The once cheerful fires have burned to ashes. The lodges are damp and chilly, and have an earthy, sepulchral smell. Tall medicine-poles bearing offerings to the Great Spirit rear their lofty tops like the spires and minarets of an Oriental city, while over all reigns a stillness, painful from its very intensity, broken perhaps by the melancholy wail of the wolves.

No one about the post took a keener delight in these nocturnal amusements than the cook. That worthy delighted to post himself, with his gun cocked and primed, to send a dose of lead into any wolf or fox that might be so foolhardy as to expose himself to the unerring aim of the accomplished *maitre de cuisine*. The frozen carcasses of the wolves the men had trapped, after being skinned were thrown into a pile outside the fort, where they often attracted the attention of their living brethren.

The cook met with such success that he was induced to continue operations for several consecutive nights. McBride and myself were sitting before a blazing fire, awaiting the cooking of a side of fat buffalo ribs by his squaw (as only an Indian woman knows how) when the conversation turned on trapping and finally led to speculations on our cook's performances and suggested a practical joke at his expense. While McBride went to the kitchen, ostensibly to give some directions and detain him, I slipped out of the gate and propped up a large white dog that had been crippled, and killed in consequence, a short time before. In the uncertain moonlight he looked for all the world like a wolf prowling among the carcasses. Before long the cook cautiously reconnoitered from his lookout and catching sight of the intruder thrust his gun through the pickets as far as possible, and after a most careful and deliberate aim, fired.

To his unutterable horror it moved not. He leaped back into the house, rolling his eyes wildly and spluttering out exclamations and inquiries in such haste as to be totally unintelligible. The men, attracted by the report of the well-charged gun, rushed forth to see what he had shot, none more excited than the man who had been fishing for wolves. "Look! look!" he exclaimed, "he is running off!" Bang! went the other barrel, and before the smoke cleared away, the gates were flung wide open and a rush was made to bring back in triumph this new trophy of a sportsman's skill.

As they stood over the inanimate form a few brief but powerful words were uttered. The cook, lifting up his fur cap, wiped away the sweat that was rolling down his face and meekly returned, followed by a quiet and subdued party of men, to continue those slumbers which had been so rudely disturbed.

A day or so after this exploit several bulls made their appearance on the bluffs, not more than four or five miles off, and as cords were needed to tie up the packs of robes and peltries which had accumulated, it seemed a favorable opportunity to get one or more skins and have them cut into cords by the squaws. A hunting-party was soon made up, headed by Jeff Smith, a veteran of over thirty years experience. He wore a close-fitting, white blanket skull-cap, coming low down over the forehead, beneath which peered the deep-set gray eyes and sharp countenance of the old Kee-re-pe-tee-ah, or Big Bull, as the Gros Ventres called him. A well-worn blanket capote, once white, but by exposure to the weather and the smoke of the lodges turned to a sickly yellow, with leggings and moccasins of elk-skin, completed his dress. An excellent rifle in a plain skin cover lay across the pommel of his saddle and the handle of a long butcher-knife projected beyond the parfleche scabbard in his belt.

Antoine, another member of the party, was buried in an enormous nondescript headgear made of a piece of buffalo robe and wore an elk-skin hunting-shirt, trimmed around the edge with otter. He carried one of Sharps' carbines slung on his back and rode a little mustang, which had a peculiar knowing twinkle in his eye and kept his ears pricked up like a rabbit.[51] We

[51] The Sharps rifle, a breech-loader, was invented by Christian Sharps about the year 1850. It acquired wide-

incontinently dubbed him Rabbit, which name he retained until his death by drowning the following spring, while trying to cross a creek swollen by the melting snows from the mountains.

In high good humor we kept on together, laughing at Antoine's wrath whenever his unfortunate Rosinante made a mis-step, sometimes almost jerking him over his head. Old Jeff volunteered the rather unnecessary information that he didn't intend to run, but "kalkilated on approachin'," in which, be it said, he was generally very successful.

When we were as close to the bulls as we dared go without alarming them we dismounted to tighten our girths and see that the weapons were in readiness. Smith crawled some distance up the ravine and endeavored to approach near enough for a shot, but finding it impracticable, came back. Remounting, we rode forward, to the great joy of our horses, who with uplifted heads and tails were impatiently pawing the snow. Crossing a ridge, we came in sight of our game, five immense old bulls, who were feeding, rolling, and otherwise enjoying themselves with the greatest gusto.

spread notoriety for its employment by Free State adherents in the Kansas Border War of the fifties. During the Civil War some 80,000 Sharps rifles were supplied to the Union armies. *Dict. Am. Hist.*

They sprang to their feet the moment we were discovered and stood eying us attentively for an instant, when they scampered off with that peculiar, rolling gallop which, awkward and clumsy as it appears, requires the best speed of an Indian horse to overtake. When they started we gave our horses the rein and dashed recklessly over the rough, uneven ground, as if the possibility of a fall was out of the question, each hunter pushing his horse to his utmost speed.

Malnouri and I, being both splendidly mounted, went ahead, and rapidly neared the bulls. Selecting one that appeared to have the best robe, we followed him up and soon separated him from the others, whereupon he plunged down a rugged defile through which we chased him at the top of our speed, clearing rocks and gullies as if they were trifles. As the bull sprang upon a high ledge I fired and leaped my horse after him, when the animal, closely pressed and enraged at the wound, turned savagely on me, his horn by a miracle just missing my leg and my horse's flank. The well-trained horse skilfully avoided the shock and led the chase for a short distance, when the bull, feeling the effects of the ball, turned off and lumbered down the valley in a contrary direction. Malnouri had whipped up to intercept him and was just raising his gun to fire when Antoine, followed at a little distance by Smith, came galloping over the hill at a speed that was certainly surprising.

Antoine was no rider, and less of a hunter. Moreover his horse was known to be afraid of buffaloes. To our united astonishment he rode straight for the bull, as if to bear him down by his impetus, and was within a few yards when the latter suddenly stopped and lowering his head charged. In an instant Rabbit wheeled on his hind legs, as if on a pivot, and hurried off in an opposite direction leaving Antoine to finish a somersault in the air and land almost at the feet of the maddened brute.

Seeing his imminent danger we all pressed on, shouting at the top of our lungs, old Jeff exclaiming through his clenched teeth, "Run like ——, Antoine!" a most timely piece of advice which was instantly followed, Antoine making the snow fly in clouds with hands and feet, and the bull continuing his flight, he was soon out of harm's reach. All this passed in a few seconds, and leaving him to regain his breath and hunt up his flying Rabbit, we soon caught up with our bull, who was now well-nigh exhausted. His uplifted tail flirted wickedly from side to side and his head was lowered, ready to charge. Malnouri incautiously attempting to cross his path, the bull made a lunge and took his horse under the flank. Horse and rider were both in imminent

peril, when Jeff wheeled short around and drew
the bull off by attacking him on the other side.
He ran a few yards farther into a hollow and the
blood poured from his mouth, dyeing the snow
crimson, his eyeballs turned a brilliant red, and
directly all was over.

The horse, a fine powerful animal, had sustained very little injury, to our great surprise and
Malnouri's unbounded joy, the bull's horns being
worn and blunt. We took only the skin and a few
pieces of meat and returned to the fort in good
spirits over the incidents of the hunt.

Parties of Riccarees frequently visited the post
from their winter camp near the Red Springs.
Buffaloes were very scarce throughout the entire
lower country, and there was a great deal of
suffering among the Sioux on Heart River and
Long Lake in consequence. Many were obliged
to kill their horses to avoid starvation and there
were rumors of the Medicine Bear's band desir-
ing to make peace with the Rees and Gros Ventres in order to procure corn, after which it
would not be long before the peace would be
broken. A couple of years previously the Yanc-
toh-wahs under Big Head, after a long period of
hostility, met the Gros Ventres at their village
and smoked the pipe of peace with them. While
the big men were sitting together in social fellow-
ship some of the young Sioux bucks stole a large

band of horses from the Gros Ventres and made off with their booty. Such proceedings made the peace a mere farce, for neither party had sufficient confidence in the other to wish to keep it.

The inextinguishable hatred between these two nations, Minnetarees and Yanc-toh-wahs, owed its immediate origin to an affair that happened some twenty years before, when the Gros Ventres, then quite a powerful tribe, lived on Knife River, just above the Mandan (now Riccaree) village. During a winter of unusual severity a small party of Yanc-toh-wahs numbering about sixteen lodges came to the Gros Ventres to make peace and relieve their pressing necessities by trading corn. Confiding in the friendship of the latter, the Sioux camped about a day's travel from the village, intending to remain until spring. A few of the ambitious spirits among the Gros Ventres thought it would be a glorious chance, by rubbing out these same lodges, to "count a big coup" upon their enemies, one that would "make them cry for many moons." It was done, and since that time all attempts to preserve a permanent peace between the Gros Ventres and the Yanc-toh-wahs have been unavailing. The old sore still rankles.

During one of the visits of the Rees a young Indian was seized with an epileptic fit in the night. He fainted, bloody foam oozed from his lips, and he whinnied like an elk. His comrades were afraid to remain with him and one of them told the interpreter that an elk had thrown his Medicine upon him, and at certain changes of the moon he had these attacks and imagined himself for the time being that animal. The next morning he was apparently as well as ever, but before taking his departure the rascal stole a scarlet blanket that was wrapped around one of the dead people, an act of vandalism which would have been severely punished had it been discovered by any of the deceased's relatives. The effects of the dead are usually held sacred, except by open foes.

Soon after these events I returned to camp, intending to remain there until spring.

Chapter XIX
Making Buffalo Medicine

WHILE at winter-quarters I made frequent hunting excursions through the neighboring points and often extended my tramps to a considerable distance. Deer were plenty, though very wild from being so much hunted by the Indians. A fat haunch of venison was always a most acceptable addition to our larder, and now that all kinds of game were in their prime we lived literally on the fat of the land. Prairie chickens were very abundant and enough for a savory stew could be shot at almost any time within a few hundred yards of the camp. In very cold weather they scarcely heeded the crack of a rifle and I have killed several off the same tree, commencing at the lowest that the falling body might not alarm the others.

Herds of deer were often chased from the timber onto the ice by the wolves. The buffaloes, although very plenty, were at too great a distance to hunt and return the same day, and how to bring them closer was a subject of much anxious consultation among the Indians.

Several young men, animated by the hope of success and the honors which it would confer upon them, made great exertions to achieve the desired result. Four Bears was at the head of the "bring buffalo" party. He was continually excusing his inefficiency by saying that he could not dream right, to which Iddy-weah-iddy-qush (He-who-strikes-the-women) dryly remarked that he would not dream right until the weather turned cold and stormy and drove the buffaloes close to the shelter of the timber, which was looking at the matter in a very practical light.

A young man, the Red Cherry, next offered to bring the buffaloes and, if successful, a horse was to be the reward, but he wisely deferred the time of action as long as possible, thereby hoping to increase his chances of success. Meanwhile, all prayed that the Four Bears might be able to dream to some purpose, which he said he could not do until a war-eagle of a certain size had been shot, and although every effort was made it seemed impossible to secure one.

Finally it was agreed to let the Red Cherry try *his* powers. The next morning before the sun rose Red Cherry went to the top of the highest butte that overlooked the camp and began to cry and pray to the Great Spirit. He was to make his Medicine for three days and nights, fasting all the while, at the expiration of which time, if it was good, the buffaloes could not fail to come.

That no counteracting influences might operate against him the soldiers forbade the chopping or cutting of firewood by the squaws and exercised the utmost vigilance to prevent all sounds. Any unlucky squaw who was so forgetful or reckless of consequences as to venture to chop firewood was sure to have her axe seized and her wood scattered, and if she escaped a sound beating might consider herself remarkably fortunate.

During this embargo the only fuel that could be obtained was dry brush or small twigs which could be easily broken by hand without making much noise. Singing and the everlasting sound of the drum for a time ceased. Even the dogs seemed to know what was going on and in a great measure suspended their vocal exercises. Travel and hunting were strictly prohibited and a young man who had gone after deer a few points below the camp, not far from the mouth of the Little Missouri, was met on his return by several of the soldiers who whipped him severely and destroyed his gun and bow and arrows, cutting his robe and meat to pieces. Scouts were kept stationed on the hills to discover the buffaloes, and two fine horses were ready to be given to the Red Cherry in the event of his medicine proving good and strong.

The evening of the third day came and brought no tidings of the approach of buffaloes. Opinions began to be freely expressed that the medicine was worthless and the Four Bears, who had not yet been able to dream, was gloomy and despondent. There was no meat in camp, some families began to experience the pangs of hunger, and the tide of popular feeling was setting in very strong against the would-be medicine man.

The unsuccessful aspirant for medical distinction said, in self-defense, that if a spotted running horse had been offered him instead of two common pack-horses his medicine would have worked to a charm and the hearts of all the people in the village would have been made glad by seeing the surrounding prairies black all over with a terrible plenty of buffaloes. His friends (for he had many) began to think he might be correct, and were disposed to grant him further opportunity.

I had been living for three days on parched corn, not even having coffee to help it down, and was extremely anxious that the buffaloes should come in, without caring whether it was by the dreaming of the Four Bears or the Medicine of the Red Cherry. The second attempt was prolonged over four days when Ou-keh-shay (The-First-Feather-on-the-Wing) announced that he had discovered something on the high hills in the direction of the lake. Every one's heart beat high with hope and joy and the Red Cherry's star was in the ascendant, when a more careful reconnoissance showed the objects to be a small band of horses that had been out in câche, and were now being driven up by their owner. So the Red Cherry was again unsuccessful, and the Last Stone intimated in unmistakable terms that he was a fool, a humbug, and even threatened to whip him.

Something must be done. Already a few of the malcontents talked of scattering the camp and moving about until they got into a better hunting-ground. In this emergency, when all was doubt and uncertainty, the White Cow band, the *corps du reserve*, took the matter in hand, and as their medicine was never known to fail a better and more cheerful feeling soon pervaded the entire camp. The restrictions on cutting and chopping were removed and everything soon fell into the old routine. The great secret of the success of the White Cow band lay in the fact that when they undertook to bring buffaloes the dancing was kept up vigorously night and day until buffaloes came.

The lodge of my host, the Bear Hunter, was its headquarters and his five squaws all belonged to the band. He had three log cabins opening into a spacious round earth lodge whose dirt floor was beaten hard and smooth. His horses and mine, twenty-five head in all, were kept in one part, which was fenced off for the purpose, leaving ample space for the Terpsichorean exercises

which were taking place almost every night, and
so used did I become to the constant singing,
drumming, and dancing that I scarcely noticed
it. On grand occasions the beauty and fashion of
the village assembled here, and it was consequently the most popular and frequented locality
in the camp.

The five tongues of the old Bear Hunter's
squaws were unsurpassed for the ease and
rapidity with which they reported all the news of
the hour. Two dogs could not get into a fight at
the farthest extremity of the village without these
women being almost instantly apprised of it. The
charms of the second one had long since faded.
She had lost an eye and was quite lame, but her
powers of speech remained unimpaired. In the
blissful moments, like angels' visits few and far
between, when a profound silence reigned in
Bedlam, this female Cyclops would be sure to
rise and kindle a blazing fire and let loose her
unruly member. It made not the slightest difference to her whether there were auditors or
not, the sound of her own charming voice was
company enough.

This lady was the presiding genius of the
White Cows, and she had now a world of
business to look after. Small boys, masked and
disguised so that it was impossible to recognize
them, and carefully muffled up in robes with the

hairy side out, were sent from lodge to lodge in the evening before the dance commenced. These were making Medicine to ascertain where the buffaloes might be found. On entering a lodge they would sit motionless and without uttering a word until some trifling present was given to the Medicine, when they jumped up and after going through a short shuffling dance took their departure.

The different members of the White Cow band began to assemble and soon the regular taps of the drum notified the camp that the great and important ceremony was in full progress. At one end of the lodge sat the musicians or drummers, three in number, who were untiring in their efforts, and aided their instrumentation by singing in a monotonous chanting strain. The women, comprising some forty or fifty matrons of the village, most of whose charms had unmistakably faded, were all attired in their quaintly garnished deer-skin dresses. Each had a spot of vermilion on either cheek and their long black hair, which was carefully combed out and dressed with marrow grease, fell full and flowing over their shoulders, confined around the forehead with a fillet of white buffalo cowskin. One of them had a white robe (which is very scarce, and held in the highest esteem) wrapped around her. This white robe was the common property of the band, and in its great power as a Medicine were centered their hopes of bringing in the buffaloes.

The dance was kept up at short intervals for over a week without any signs of success. Every night the lodge was densely crowded with eager and anxious spectators, and if good wishes exerted any influence the White Cow band had them in abundance. On the surrounding hills the scouts directed their eyes toward all the points from which it was likely the herds would come.

On the opposite side of the river was a lofty butte standing alone. It was several hundred feet high and almost perpendicular on the face, but was easily mounted from the rear by a long, gently sloping ascent. On the very summit were placed a couple of buffalo skulls, with pieces of scarlet cloth fastened around each horn. Two medicine poles were also set up with pieces of calico flying from them, gifts to propitiate the Great Spirit that he would send them plenty of buffaloes.

This butte was a famous lookout, commanding the prairies for many miles in every direction. The Black Hills near Knife River, marking the head of the Big Bend, were plainly visible, and appeared close at hand.

Among the rugged bluffs that rose one above another was a remarkable group known, and justly so, as the Square Hills, conspicuous and noted landmarks for miles around. The whole country on the opposite side from that on which the camp was located seemed spread out at one's feet, while on either hand the view extended for miles and any bands of buffaloes coming down from the upper country were certain to be discovered.

I was upon this butte one afternoon with several Indians, vainly hoping to discover something by the aid of my glass. The Indians were pointing out various places of interest, scenes of encounters with the foe, or exploits of the chase. We spent several hours very agreeably in this manner, and returning to the lodge I watched the dancers for a while, then, stretching myself on my robe, indulged in reverie, from which I was roused by an unearthly clamor among the dogs and a general rush outside by the Indians.

Hastily snatching up my gun, I ran out to learn the cause of the excitement. Strong Medicine! A huge buffalo bull was charging wildly about, not twenty yards from the lodge wherein the White Cow band were dancing! The old fellow was bayed by fully one-half the dogs in the village, and rushed hither and thither in his blind, impotent fury, tossing the dogs in front and kicking and plunging to avoid those in his rear. He dashed headlong among the lodges, seeing only his canine tormentors and of course paid no heed to the eager crowd of Indians.

All were astonished and delighted beyond expression at this remarkable answer of the Great Spirit to their prayers and offerings, and but one opinion prevailed, that the bull had been specially sent to show them that the efforts of the White Cow band were not in vain. Directly the report of a fusee was heard, and lumbering on a little farther the Medicine Bull fell on the sandbar and breathed his last, but while his limbs were yet quivering with recent life a multitude of knives were busily at work and in a few moments only a pool of blood, which the dogs were eagerly lapping up, remained.

The White Cows came forth from their lodge and danced around the village. While thus engaged, a young man rode up at full speed and reported that a fine band of cows had just been discovered close to Rising Water. The soldiers at once directed old Snake-skin to harangue, forbidding any chopping or noise, and for the hunters to bring up all their horses and be ready to surround in the morning.

Hearty congratulations on the wonderful strength and efficacy of the medicine of the White Cow band were exchanged on every side, and soon a tripod, over which was thrown the far-famed white robe, was set up on top of the lodge, and joy and gladness animated the entire camp.

The next day the hunters went out and surrounded with success, and it was well they did, for a terribly severe spell of weather succeeded, during which it stormed and snowed with such fury that none dared travel. When it cleared off the whole prairie from the dividing ridge near Knife River to the Rising Water, and beyond it as far as the eye could reach, was literally black with countless thousands of buffaloes.

The winter's hunt, thus auspiciously inaugurated, bade fair to be a complete success. Every few days the hunters went out, and returned late in the afternoon with their horses heavily packed with fat and delicious meat which was soon cut into thin sheets and hung on the scaffolds to dry, out of reach of the dogs, whose well-filled sides showed that they, too, were making up for their involuntary fast. I went out frequently with the hunters, and the novelty having long since worn off, looked upon it as a regular business and not merely an exciting pastime.

CHAPTER XX

A Mid-Winter Buffalo Hunt

THE spectacle of a buffalo hunt when the ground was covered with snow was even more thrilling than in the summer-time. The danger was also greatly lessened by the soft, white carpet spread thickly over the prairie, serving to break the fall of any unfortunate hunter whose horse by a mis-step might throw him. The night before a hunt takes place the band of soldiers meet in their lodge and appoint some one of experience to head the party. The leader thus chosen has full authority for the time being and every hunter must conform to his orders.

No sooner is this settled than some long-winded old fellow is directed to harangue through the camp, "Bring up the horses and prepare to go to the surround," naming the leader and the time of starting. The squaws bestir themselves to provide plenty of cottonwood bark that the horses may have something to eat during the long night, and see that the saddles and apishamores are in complete order, taking care to tie a bundle of raw-hide cords to the horn of each pack-saddle, by which to secure the meat. The hunters look carefully to their weapons and whet their butcher-knives to a keen edge.

Long before daylight all are aroused by the cry, "Get up, get up, and saddle your horses!" While the hunters eat their breakfast the women attend to this, and as soon as each one is ready he starts off, leading his horses, sometimes accompanied by a squaw to assist in butchering and packing the meat.

Every hunter takes from two to four horses, these being as many as he can properly manage. The favorite buffalo-horse trots along loose, carrying only a light skin pad stuffed with deer or antelope hair. The hunter rides one of his pack-horses, in order that his runner may be fresh for the severe labor of the chase.

Arrived at the rendezvous previously designated by the leader, who is there with his lance or insignia of rank, they halt until the whole party has assembled. All now ride in a compact body, taking care never to press too closely on the leader, who with several experienced friends keeps well in advance to discover the game before coming near enough to alarm it. The only sound that breaks the dead silence of these snow-clad plains is the crunching of the horses' feet as they break through the frozen crust or the occasional jingle of the equipment. We ride steadily on until our leader comes to a sudden halt, and the hunters eagerly gather around him. The band of buffaloes we intend to run is before us and more than a mile distant, and the wind is very favorable, blowing from them to us.

The customary deliberative pipe is lit and a plan of attack agreed upon and communicated to the hunters in a few words by the leader. We start again, trotting and cantering along by turns, more rapidly than we have yet done, each horse being fully alive to the exciting scenes that will soon be enacted. A wide detour is made and under cover of a deep roll of the prairie we approach as near as possible without alarming the herd. Not many words are uttered for each one understands his business. The pack-horses are quickly hobbled and left, together with everything superfluous. Mounting the runners, whose impatient restlessness can hardly be controlled, with bows and arrows grasped firmly in their hands the hunters are ready for the onset.

Many ride bareback with only a lariat around the lower jaw to manage the horse, who is so well trained and so perfectly understands his rider's wishes that it usually hangs loose upon his neck or trails behind. We ride abreast, gradually extending our front like the horns of a crescent to make the surround as perfect as possible. Insensibly we quicken our pace and are careering forward at full gallop. The horses snort impatiently, with heads and tails erect, and the quick glances of their eyes tell the excitement they fully share, evidently feeling, as the Indians say, as if their hearts were glad.

Faster and faster we go. We are close on the herd, which, now thoroughly alarmed, huddles together for a brief instant and then dashes madly off, directing its course against the wind, the fattest cows leading the van. Our leader's lance is lowered. Now is the time, and every horse is stretched out at his utmost speed. The buffaloes appear to rise out of the ground as we rush on, until what at first seemed but a small band has increased to an immense herd. In a few minutes the fastest horses have carried their riders among them in every direction and selecting their meat they pursue it until killed. An occasional shot is heard, but the work of destruction is chiefly accomplished by the bow and arrow.

In a few moments some of the cows fall behind, gradually slackening their speed until they come to a stand-still. The blood flows freely from their mouths and they soon lie down to rise no more. Perhaps here and there a severely though not fatally wounded buffalo has been brought to bay and shows fight, charging upon his pursuer whenever he rides too close and calling into play the agility of the horse, who, by skilfully wheeling, avoids the shock. A well-directed shot settles the question, and while bristling with impotent fury the crimson tide gushes from her mouth and she convulsively breathes her last.

The white prairie is soon dotted with the black carcasses of the victims. Wolves skulk at a little distance, impatiently awaiting their anticipated feast, and flocks of ravens, flying low and croaking hoarsely, make their appearance so suddenly that no one knows whence they come. Here a hunter has been thrown by his horse getting his foot into one of the many holes with which the prairie is filled, but the thick carpet of snow has saved him from receiving serious injury. The more expert hunters will kill from three to five cows in a chase, and claim their game by the marks on their arrows.

When the hunt is over they return and look up their meat, then driving up the pack-horses, begin the work of butchering. The buffalo generally falls in a natural position, as if lying down, and the hunter splits the skin down the back and twisting the fingers of his left hand in the long hair of the hump, pulls the robe toward him while he rapidly cuts the tissue with his knife. An Indian will skin a buffalo very rapidly, but always leaves more or less flesh adhering to it, which has to be removed by the women before dressing it. The meat is cut away from the bones in large pieces, some of them weighing over a hundred pounds. The two sides of ribs are taken off and tied together by a cord to balance each other on the saddle.

The tongue, heart, kidneys, liver, paunch, marrow-guts, boudin, and brains, being esteemed great delicacies, are carefully saved. When there is plenty of meat the large bones and coarse pieces are always thrown aside, but in times of scarcity there is absolutely nothing left but the head. Even the blood is regarded as a luxury and saved. The horses are next to be packed. Half of the green skin is thrown over the saddle, then the heavy boneless pieces of meat, after which come the ribs and miscellaneous portions, and over all the remaining half of the robe. The meat and robe of a cow is considered a fair load for a horse, but I have often seen a cow and a half packed on when the distance was short, or a cow and a heavy man riding on top. This kind of work is very severe on both horses and men, for, starting early, they are generally a whole day in the cold without eating anything.

From the hunting-ground to the camp the speed is a steady jog-trot, no matter what the distance may be, and party after party come together at the big trail made in the morning. As the sun gets low the horses are urged on, and when within two or three miles of camp the dogs, scenting the meat, rush out at full speed, noticing no one until they find their masters, when they trot along in company, occasionally tugging at the meat as it hangs temptingly low.

When the party descended the bluffs, following the trail that led to the well-sheltered bottom in which the camp was pitched, the tired and heavily-laden horses often slipped and fell in the steep and icy path. Sparks from the lodge-fires greeted the hungry hunters, and the dogs, smelling the fresh meat from afar, began their usual howling. As each one arrived at his lodge the squaws rushed out to take charge of the horses, unpacking the meat, removing the saddles, and placing a bountiful supply of cottonwood-bark before them.

While the tired hunter divests himself of his equipment a choice piece of meat is cooking for him. A comfortable pipe succeeds, and as friends drop in the feasting is renewed until all are fully satiated. The details of the morning hunt are given, how many men were out, where the buffaloes were first seen, whose horse was the fastest, and who had killed the fattest cow, all are discussed and commented upon with the greatest earnestness and gravity.

The women seize upon the titbits with avidity, and roasting marrow-guts and making boudin keeps them fully employed until a late hour. Indian squaws are the best cooks of meat in the world. They know exactly when it is done, that is, cooked thoroughly, yet retaining all the juicy richness and flavor. The hump-ribs or bos are delicious when boiled, and a side of fat ribs carefully roasted ought to satisfy anybody. But one of the very best pieces on a buffalo is a thin strip of flesh on the inner side of the ribs. It is simply thrown on a bed of coals. The thick skin prevents the flesh from burning and the juice from escaping.

The tongue, when roasted for several hours in a bed of ashes, is very fine, but a young calf before it is born is considered the greatest delicacy of all. When first eaten, early in the winter, it is never larger than a kitten and gradually increases in size until near spring, when it becomes too large and coarse. The idea of eating such a barbarous dish was at first revolting, but afterwards, when better able to appreciate these Indian luxuries, I found it very palatable, particularly the natural liquor or broth in which it was boiled, which with the addition of salt and pepper made an excellent soup.

After a hunt the horses are allowed a little much-needed rest. The women find active employment in cutting and jerking the meat for future use and stretching the skins to dry, after carefully removing the flesh which adheres.

The men strolled from lodge to lodge, marvelling greatly at the remarkable strength of the Medicine of the White Cow band, relating anecdotes of the chase, and commenting upon the skill of some of the most noted hunters in the tribe. The Last Stone, when younger, was one of the very best buffalo-hunters the Gros Ventres ever had. It was said of him that he could kill on any kind of a horse, or, in other words, he depended more upon his skill as a marksman to bring down his game at long distances than upon the speed of his horse to carry him to close quarters. Last Stone was a large, fleshy man and he told me that when in the full prime and vigor of life he could shoot an arrow on horseback entirely through the body of a buffalo, so that it would drop to the ground on the opposite side.

The Indians also talked about The Yellow, (now dead) who is said to have actually killed three cows with a single arrow. He was of course riding close up when he shot. The shaft passed entirely through the bodies of two cows, the point projecting several inches on the opposite side. The third cow jostled against it in the general scamper and the point penetrating her vitals caused her death.

It has often been a matter of surprise to me that more accidents do not happen in buffalo-hunting, when we take into consideration the reckless speed at which they ride over the roughest and most rugged ground, the danger of getting accidentally shot, or of being impaled on the horns of an infuriated cow. In the autumn when the ground is hard frozen and before it is covered with snow the hunter is constantly liable to severe falls from the horse stepping into holes. In the spring, also, when the snow has thawed away leaving the ground soft and very slippery, buffalo-hunting is attended with much greater risk than in midwinter.

The Indian horses are so well trained that they not only watch the buffaloes to escape a collision, but also keep a sharp lookout for holes and bad places on the prairie, avoiding them with surprising skill. When the rider has picked out his cow the horse follows it up with loosened rein or lariat trailing behind him on the ground. He runs boldly up on the right side within a few feet, and the instant the arrow is shot swerves off to avoid the charge which is almost sure to follow. As soon as the cow resumes her course he comes up again, after giving the rider time to fit another shaft, and no matter how fiercely the maddened animal turns upon him, skilfully wheels around as if on a pivot and allows the buffalo to pursue him, as it always does for a short distance.

I often rode an old, well-trained horse which we called Mac after Owen McKenzie, who was one of the very best buffalo-hunters, white or red, on the prairies. The old horse knew by long experience exactly how far to avoid a lunge, and was no more afraid of closing up with a wounded cow than of joining his comrades on the plain. Nevertheless, in spite of all the skill of both horse and rider the former is sometimes severely if not fatally injured.

The Poor Wolf lost his splendid black steed

in this way. He had wounded a cow and closing up had given her another arrow, when at the moment of the charge the horse plunged up to his shoulders in a snowdrift and was utterly powerless to escape. The Poor Wolf was thrown and the buffalo's horn made a terrible gash in the horse's flank. With a convulsive bound he sprang up and dashed wildly over the prairie, treading on and tearing out his entrails, and after running a short distance fell dead.

A similar accident happened at the very next hunt. A horse belonging to He-who-strikes-the-women was ridden by a young man who was considered an excellent hunter, but the buffalo crowded on him so closely that he had no room to maneuver and the sharp horn of a cow ripped the horse's belly, causing the entrails to protrude. The horse was instantly stopped, and assistance coming up he was thrown, the entrails replaced, and the rent sewed up with a sinew, after which he was able to be led back to the camp several miles distant, fed as usual, and eventually recovered. I saw him frequently afterwards. A scarcely perceptible scar was the only remaining trace of the accident, and this would not be noticed, even by a careful observer, unless especially pointed out. The horse ran as well and seemed to be in every respect as valuable as before.

After returning from a hunt the sweat-houses are freely used, the hunters seeking by this means to invigorate themselves after their exhausting efforts. Nearly every lodge is provided with one, being merely a low hut of willow-boughs just large enough to admit one or two in a stooping posture. When used, it is covered with skins and stones are heated in the fire and placed inside, the occupant divests himself of his clothing, and the opening being carefully closed, raises a vapor by pouring water from a kettle on the hot stones. After remaining inside until nearly suffocated and sweating profusely from every pore, he comes out and rubs himself over with snow, or, if the river is open, plunges in. He then retires to his lodge and wrapping himself in his robe enjoys a refreshing sleep.

Upon returning from a hunt of more than usual severity and complaining of fatigue to the Bear Hunter, he insisted upon my trying a sweat. I found the effect far beyond my utmost anticipations, and afterwards resorted to it whenever experiencing over-fatigue, always with the happiest results.

There was considerable rivalry at this time between the two companies on the subject of trading buffalo-tongues from the Indians, and the prices went up accordingly. The Indians were the gainers of course, and were shrewd enough to make good use of their advantage. For several days after a hunt the traders for both parties were constantly on the alert to get all the tongues they could and so recklessly was the competition carried on that profit was totally lost sight of. An Indian having two or three tongues would stop at one trading-house and mention the fact to ascertain what he could get for them, then going to the other he would tell the same story, of course magnifying the price offered. Having obtained another bid, he would return to the first parties and report. The original price would be increased, and perhaps after a good deal of talking the trade would be pretty equally divided, the Indians saying that it was to their interest to support two whites, which it certainly was.

The tongues are salted by the traders (not by the Indians, as is generally supposed) and after being dried are sometimes painted over with molasses and water to improve their appearance and give them a dark smoky color. They are shipped to St. Louis in the spring, together with the robes and peltries, and are eagerly sought after as great delicacies.

Chapter XXI

Smallpox Ravages and Indian History

THE buffaloes still continued very plenty around the winter-quarters and were often in plain sight. The clean, well-trodden paths, the curling smoke from the lodges, and the scaffolds heavily laden with the choicest pieces of meat drying for future use presented a very comfortable appearance. Every one appeared satisfied and a genial feeling pervaded the whole camp.

The lodge in which I dwelt was filled inside and out with meat, and when there was no more room on the scaffolds poles were stretched across the interior of the cabin, heavily loaded with additional supplies. As fast as that on the scaffolds was fit to pack away the meat inside would take its place, thus leaving room for fresh pieces.

I was constrained to crawl on my hands and knees sometimes to get to my corner, where I liked to recline upon my robe and listen to the gossip of the hour. The crowded condition of things had one advantage. It kept away all idlers, and those who had anything to trade never hung around, as was their custom, after transacting business.

Nearly every day I went to the lodge of my comrade and friend the Bobtail Wolf. The old chief was not such a politician as the Four Bears, but was still respected and listened to by all. He was very fond of teaching me the language, which I wrote down as he pronounced it, and by this means made rapid progress. He would unweariedly repeat a word over and over again until I had caught the correct pronunciation. Many of the principal men made his lodge their headquarters and the talk was always about Indian fashions or customs, very seldom degenerating into mere gossip. His squaw invariably provided something for us to eat, and many a piece of calf, or boudin, or bos did we enjoy at her hands. When at the summer village, the old man spent the best part of his time in my house and he was ever welcome for he had plenty to talk about and was an excellent hand to entertain the visitors that were constantly dropping in.

During the whole time that I lived among the Gros Ventres I never missed a single article, although I took no trouble to keep my things out of sight. My house would often be crowded with Indians. Sometimes only one or two would be present, yet if called away I felt satisfied that on my return I would find everything just as I left it. But when any Rees or Crows were about it was very different. They would steal anything they could lay hands on, and required constant watching. Even the Gros Ventres frequently complained of their thieving proclivities.

The old chief, Bobtail Wolf, was exceedingly solicitous for me to take unto myself a wife, and had settled upon several squaws whom he considered eligible. I put him off from day to day until he began to think it was high time for me to make a decided move in the matrimonial direction. "My son," said he one morning, after the customary pan of bouillon, "it is time for you to take a wife. There is the Long Hair's daughter, a good young woman who garnishes moccasins well, works hard for her father's lodge, dresses robes and carries wood. You told me that you had the heart of a Gros Ventre, that your blood was red like ours. Why don't you make your words good?"

This was certainly bringing matters to a point, and after due deliberation I replied that what he said was good and true. The Long Hair's daughter was all that he claimed for her, but I did not feel like taking such a responsibility at present. "But," said I, stripping up the sleeve of my shirt and showing him the difference between the white skin and the part tanned by exposure to wind and weather, "you see my arm is gradually turning darker and darker, becoming like an Indian's. When I am changed all over I will be ready to marry the Long Hair's daughter."

This ridiculous answer, strange as it may seem, pleased the old man amazingly, and from that moment he looked upon my marriage as a settled fact, the question being only one of time.

On one occasion some of the old men were talking about the changes that had taken place in their nation. Many snows ago they were a part of the Crows and left them because they were too numerous. Their language is essentially the same, with such modifications as a long residence with the Mandans and Riccarees would be likely to make. They once occupied five villages and the Bobtail Wolf was chief of one. Incursions of their enemies and the fearful ravages of smallpox and cholera so reduced their number that they formed at last but one village and dwelt upon the banks of Knife River, above the old Mandan (Riccaree) village. At last they determined to seek the Crows and unite with them again. They deserted their village, abandoned their corn-fields, left the bones of those once loved and lost, and severing all old ties crossed to the east shore of the Missouri and started on their pilgrimage.

It was in the fall when they arrived at the site of the present village. The Four Bears thought it would be a good place to winter in and they accordingly prepared to remain until spring. When spring came the Fur Company's steamboat arrived and at the urgent solicitation of the Indians a trader was left with a few goods. He took up his quarters in the Four Bears' lodge.

The squaws cut and dragged timber for a fort. The Gros Ventres gave up their idea of rejoining the Crows, and Fort Berthold was built. In time the Opposition Company took the field and established a post on the lower side of the village. With the whites on either side of them, and protected in their stockaded village, the Gros Ventres had little reason to fear the incursions of their enemies so long as they remained at home.

But the smallpox was an enemy that neither stockades nor bravery could keep away. That frightful disease is peculiarly fatal to the Indians, and was unknown to them previous to the advent of the white man. The Mandans, from a large nation, have become reduced to a mere handful. All the tribes have suffered, but the Sioux have escaped with the least loss as they, immediately upon the appearance of the disease, scattered in small camps throughout their country and thus confined it to a single locality.

The last time the smallpox made its appearance on the Upper Missouri was in 1856 and the accounts I received from eye-witnesses were truly heart-rending. The Gros Ventres and Mandans suffered, of course, although not so severely as in former times, as they scattered immediately upon its breaking out. Around Fort

William the Assiniboines lay encamped, threatening the whites with justly-merited vengeance. The houses in the fort were crowded with Indians in every stage of the disease. The moment they were attacked they sought the whites, feeling, doubtless, that as the latter had brought the pestilence it was but just they should suffer some of the inconvenience.[52]

Few, if any, of the employés of the Fur Company were attacked by the disease. The houses were kept as warm as possible and many of the Indians who avoided exposure to the cold and snow ultimately recovered. One case was peculiarly distressing. A whole family had been carried off. The mother had just died, leaving an infant a few months old. The well Indians had as much as they could attend to and there was no one able or willing to take charge of the little orphan. It was placed in the arms of its

[52]Boller's narrative sketches somewhat lightly the tragic story of the ravages of smallpox among the Indians of the Upper Missouri. Some definite figures of the shocking number of deaths in the several tribes resulting from the epidemic of 1837 are given in Burlingame and Toole, *Hist. of Montana*, II, 87–88. For a day by day contemporary record of the progress of the epidemic in the Mandan and Arikara villages adjoining Fort Clark see Francis Chardon's journal in *Mississippi Valley Hist. Review*, XVII, 278–99. For a vivid second-hand account see Maria R. Audubon, *Audubon and His Journals* (New York, 1897), II, 42–47. On the epidemic among the Blackfeet see Chittenden, *Hist. of Early Steamboat Navigation on the Missouri River*, I, 229–30.

dead mother, enveloped in blankets and a buffalo robe, and set up on a scaffold in the usual manner of burying the dead. Its cries were heard for some time. At last they grew fainter and finally were stilled altogether in the cold embrace of death, with the north wind sounding its requiem and the wolves howling in the surrounding gloom a fitting dirge for so sad a fate. Nevermore in the happy Spirit Land would that mother and her child be parted.[53]

[53] Some half-dozen years subsequent to the publication of *Among the Indians* a dispute developed between two feminine authors over the original author of the story here related by Boller. On Feb. 16, 1874 Sarah L. Larimer wrote to Boller, then living at Junction City, Kansas, appealing to him to make a deposition that he was the original author of the story. She had published two narratives dealing with her own life in the Far West, one of them a true recital of her experiences, the other a fictional account based upon an incident in her earlier book. In it she had included Boller's story of the dying baby, giving proper credit to him as her source. However, her manuscript had been stolen and utilized by Fanny Kelly, who purported to be its actual author, and a law-suit was being waged over this. Fanny Kelly had testified under oath that she had obtained the tale orally from Lieutenant Chatterton of Fort Sully, and the published version was her own composition which Chatterton had never seen in print or in writing prior to her own production of it; affirming further that Larimer had in fact stolen the tale from a manuscript Kelly had produced some years earlier. Quite possibly neither of the warring ladies was guilty of plagiarism, since Lieutenant Chatterton may have heard the story related by some Indian, in the same way that Boller heard it.

Chapter XXII

A Tragedy and a Feast

PIERRE GARREAU'S three sons who had gone out with the hunters full of life and spirits, splendidly equipped and mounted on their bounding steeds, were waylaid, killed, and scalped by a Sioux war-party. At one fell blow were swept away the young men and nine as fine horses as the Gros Ventre camp could boast of.

They were returning after a successful hunt, and when within only five or six miles of the camp one of their pack-horses threw his load of meat and ran away. The brothers stopped behind the main body of the hunters to recover the truant steed. Night came. The hunters were all in. Fat ribs were roasting before blazing fires in the different lodges and festivity and gladness prevailed, except in one. The next morning a numerous and well-armed party with Pierre Garreau at the head started out to learn, if possible, the fate of the missing hunters.

Near the place where the boys turned back a flock of ravens was seen circling in the air. The party proceeded cautiously, yet with anxious hearts, toward the spot. Their worst fears were realized—there lay John, the youngest boy, scalped and gory, stripped of his ornaments. He was completely riddled with arrows, but they were all front wounds, showing that he had made a gallant defense. A little farther on the remaining two were found, similarly butchered. Curses, not loud but deep, came from the hearts of that warrior band and they swore that when the early spring-time came they would strike such a blow as would cause a terrible wail in the camp of the foe, and would make them remember for many a day the revenge which they had brought upon themselves.

Without manifesting any emotion Pierre directed the bodies to be conveyed to camp, and they were temporarily buried on a mound at the entrance of the trail leading through the timber. The horses were gone of course, and from the marks on the arrows the enemy were known to be Sioux. Word was immediately sent to Pierre's relatives at the Ree village, and the moody silence throughout the camp expressed far more forcibly than words the vengeance that would be taken upon the perpetrators of the outrage as soon as the plains should be free from snow.

Pierre gave away most of his property, as is the usual custom among Indians, and his two wives, although not the mothers of the deceased, cut their hair in token of grief. Pierre was soon recalled to Fort Berthold, his great affliction rendering him totally unfit to remain in camp as a trader, and his place was supplied by Paquenaude, who was then living as a free trapper.

After Pierre's return to the fort he had the bodies of his three boys brought down from camp and reinterred in the presence of the whites from both posts. Not a sound broke the stillness as the bodies were carefully lowered to their last resting-place, but when the men commenced throwing on the earth the Indian women burst forth into their mournful cry. Pierre turned, and thanking those present for the kindness and sympathy which they had extended to him said that it was a common feeling among all mankind, whether white or red, to wish their bones laid among those of their kindred and not scattered to the four winds in some distant land. No news of the reinterment was sent to the Ree camp until it was over, as Pierre did not want a vast concourse of his relations crying and making a distressing affair of it.

Many moons had waxed and waned, the snows had long disappeared, and the air was soft and balmy before Pierre Garreau became as of old, and his conversation continually turned upon the vengeance that would be taken upon the Sioux.

It was on one of the coldest days I ever remember when I started to return to camp, after a brief sojourn at the post. Getting clear of the timber, a sharp, cutting head-wind whirled the frozen crystals of snow through the air and all the exposed parts of my face were cut as if by a knife. I was obliged to dismount, and leaving the trail turned into the bad lands, where I could make a snug camp and remain until the wind lulled and travelling became more comfortable. I had left the trail with this idea but a short distance when a faint column of smoke curling up from the middle of a point of timber on the opposite side of the river met my eye. I at once concluded that it was the lurking-place of a war-party, being midway between the forts and the winter-quarters and an excellent position from which to discover.

Without a second thought I remounted and travelled through the deep snow as fast as my horse could carry me and late in the evening arrived at the camp, but not until my nose and cheeks were slightly frozen, in spite of my fur wrappings. With one exception, I never felt the cold so severely as on this trip and the Indians expressed great surprise at my travelling in such a head-wind, for none of them had left the shelter of the valley during the day. I mentioned what I had seen and a party hurried off that same night to make further discoveries, but returned the following day without having seen anything. A couple of nights afterwards, however, a mule and three horses were missing and the moccasin tracks left no doubt as to their having been stolen.

Christmas, the Big Medicine day of the whites, was fast approaching and the Indians eagerly looked forward to it. For several years past it had been the custom of the traders to make a grand feast to the different bands, and the Indians usually acknowledged the compliment by throwing robes or other articles of value to the traders in return.

We made our feast a few days before Christmas and the rivalry between the whites as to who would give the grandest entertainment made it unusually interesting. Each band was called separately and it was a good day's work to go the rounds. Our guests, while loud in their praises of our liberality, usually pled poverty as an excuse for not throwing robes as freely as they would like, which same plea was as strongly urged by ourselves as an additional reason for their extending substantial patronage to us.

At the fort they celebrated the day with great spirit. The grand feature of the occasion was the dinner, at which ample justice was done to the prairie chicken and rabbit pot-pies, buffalo steaks, and puddings and dried-apple pie, the whole making a very fair spread-out for the mountains. The men of the rival posts joined forces in the evening and enjoyed a regular frolic, which they kept up until the small hours, one by one fairly dropping upon the floor from exhaustion and overloaded stomachs. Several dressed up as squaws and took the part of women in the dance. The day was remarkably fine and the celebration passed off with éclat. A young dog had been fattening for some time to supply the place of a turkey, but unfortunately, just a few days before, he was run over by the wood-wagon and crushed to death, which the squaws lamented bitterly. The Gros Ventres seldom or never eat dog but the Sioux consider it the very greatest delicacy and to be called or invited to a dog-feast is a high compliment to a stranger.

Buffaloes were as plenty and close to the camp as ever, but the Indians surrounded less frequently, as the severe work was beginning to tell on their horses. The weather, too, was extremely cold and at the last hunt, when the Wolf's Eye was partisan, many of the Indians had their fingers frozen and several were considerably hurt by their horses falling with violence. The Hawk had his ankle so much injured that it was several weeks before he was able to mount his horse again. Only about forty cows were killed, and even of these many were left untouched on the prairie, it being too cold to butcher them.

I was at the lake, about six miles distant from the camp, looking after some horses which we had in câche there, and finding them all right crossed over to Shell Creek to inspect some beaver lodges, with which the stream was filled. When about returning, a buffalo bull emerged from the willows not more than a quarter of a mile from me and leisurely started across the prairie, stopping occasionally to paw away the snow and feed. The wind was very favorable and I determined to approach him. Taking advantage of every inequality of the ground, I crawled on my hands and knees, dragging along my rifle (protected from the snow by a skin cover) and having a white blanket capote with capeshaw of the same drawn over my head, at a little distance I looked too much like a white wolf to excite the slightest apprehension in the bull, who continued cropping the grass in the most unconcerned manner.

I was gradually getting closer and closer to him, when a slight noise made in breaking through the crust of the snow alarmed him. He stopped and looked around, but seeing nothing to justify his fears went on feeding, gradually making his way toward some coolies or ravines not very far distant. I followed as fast as was prudent and soon had the satisfaction of seeing the bull climb a butte and disappear on the other side. Following after him as fast as possible I gained the butte and crawling cautiously up, looked over the brow and saw my bull eating away with the most perfect unconcern not twenty yards distant. I had by this time crawled nearly half a mile and was not at all grieved by the prospect of bringing my labors to a termination.

The first ball struck the bull fair in his lights. He gave a slight jump and then stood still. The blood poured from his mouth, and tottering forward a few paces he sank quietly down upon his knees. I watched him and seeing no further motion concluded that if not dead already he was very near it, and accordingly moved directly towards him, when to my horror and amazement he suddenly sprang to his feet, lowered his head, and made for me. I turned and fled with all possible haste as far as I could go, through snow up to my knees, and would have fared badly had not the friendly butte interposed and hid me from his sight just when I was expecting to feel his horn in my back. Stopping only from sheer exhaustion, I looked back and saw him stretched out in the last agonies. Making sure this time that he was actually dead, I returned and took his tongue as a trophy, leaving the rest of his carcass for the wolves, who were already in attendance in considerable numbers and only waiting for my departure to begin their feast.

Ravens, too, were circling in the air and when all had eaten their fill the remains of the bull would be scanty indeed.

Chapter XXIII

Indian Ideas and Winter Journeys

IT was time to return to the fort again with the robes, tongues, and peltries which had accumulated since my last trip. Early on the morning I expected to start we were roused by a great uproar in camp, men firing guns, women crying, and the dogs of course contributing their share to the general racket. I hurried out of the lodge to see what it was all about.

The night was clear and beautiful, but the silvery beams of the full moon did not fall as brightly as usual. Darkness was slowly drawing its veil over the scene. The old men harangued, and when the shadow passed away and the moon shone brilliantly out again a general yell of exultation arose at the strength of the medicine which had appeased the anger of the Great Spirit. The Indians have no idea of what causes an eclipse and believe that the shadow would always remain unless they drove it away by the power and strength of their Medicine.

We had a toilsome journey to the fort as the snow lay very deep in places, rendering it necessary sometimes to unload everything in order to extricate the animals. When the crust is frozen hard it is a pleasure to travel, but it is very wearisome when the sun's rays have sufficient power to soften this crust so that one step will be firm and the next break through, oftentimes up to the horse's belly. I was always glad when the promontory upon which the forts and village were built came in sight, although at a distance of five or six miles, and the tired horses moved more briskly, knowing well that their labors, for the present at least, would soon be over.

A party of Gros Ventres, chiefly squaws, came down from camp at the same time, bringing with them the body of the Black Parflesh, who had died a day or so since and must, according to custom, be buried on a scaffold in the rear of the village. The weather was intensely cold and the squaws experienced considerable difficulty in digging holes in the hard frozen earth to set up the scaffold. It was, in fact, necessary to build a fire and thaw the ground before this could be done.

Doctor E-ten-ah-pen-ah was of the party, and stated that the ghost of the Black Parflesh appeared as he passed by his lodge in the village and beckoned to him. The Doctor said that he felt his hair gradually rising up, and cocking both barrels of his gun he ran away as fast as he could.

Returning to camp, I found the buffaloes beginning to scatter, and the hunters had consequently much farther to go for meat. Scarcely had I unsaddled ere the Four Bears called me to a feast at his lodge and on obeying the summons I found some eight or ten Indians assembled, while a splendid side of fat roasted ribs was being skilfully cut up by the senior Mrs. Four Bears. After the well-picked bones had been carried away and the pipe lit and passed around, the Four Bears inquired what the Rees were doing and if any later intelligence had been received from the Sioux camp. I gave all the information I possessed, and the conversation then took an entirely different turn.

My comrade, the Bobtail Wolf, asked me if it was not almost time for the wild geese to return, for thunder and lightning, and the river to open. I replied that nearly three moons must wane before those events would happen and inquired if he could tell me what caused thunder and lightning.

He said that there was, high in air, far out of sight, flying continually and never resting, an eagle of terrible size. Upon his back he carries a lake full of water. When this aerial monster is out of humor he flaps his wings and loud peals of thunder roll over the prairie. When he winks his eyes it lightens and when he wags his tail the waters of the lake on his back overflow, producing rain.

I admiringly assented to this philosophical explanation and for several moments nothing was said, when the silence was broken by the Poor Elk declaring that the whites were bad. They brought sickness among the Indians. They were much better without the whites than with them. What need had they of traders? Did not the buffaloes supply them with all they required? When their ammunition was expended could they not fall back upon their bows and arrows? They were not raised like the whites to drink sugar and coffee and it was terrible to see how fond they had become of it. Now, their young men would sooner sit in the whites' lodges, hoping to get a cup of coffee, than follow on the war-path or hunt the buffalo. They would soon be no better than women. He was in favor of driving all the traders out of the country.

"My friend," I replied, "you have no sense. You speak with a woman's tongue. It is very true that you did without the whites once, but that was many snows ago when you were but a few summers old. Now, if you were to drive them away, when your powder and balls were expended you would fall back upon your bows and arrows. The arrows would not last forever and when you wanted new ones where would you get iron for the points? When your kettles wore out what would your women do? Many snows have whitened the prairie since your people last made pots of clay. You have almost forgotten about them. When your knives were gone the young men would find it very different from begging their whites for new ones to use sharp stones (flints) as they did in the long ago."

"What the Yellow Hair says is true," Four Bears remarked. "We would find it very hard to do as we once did before we had whites. We are now a small people. Our enemies are many and strong. We are almost afraid to go out on our own prairies to hunt the buffaloes for fear our village might be attacked and our women and children killed during our absence. We have got the whites (traders). We can't do without them, and we must take pity on them and give them life" (*i. e.* trade with them, and support them).

These remarks silenced the Poor Elk, who, in truth, did not mean what he said but was only a little out of humor at being refused something which he had asked and took this method of venting his displeasure.

Indians who have been long accustomed to enjoy the many little comforts supplied by the traders would, if wholly deprived of them, find it almost impossible to exist. Many years ago, it is true, when some of the patriarchs of the tribe were young men, and before the traders came among them, they lived in the most primitive style. Their knives and arrow-points were of flint and many tribes had no cooking-utensils. The Riccarees and Gros Ventres were, however, in more respects than one in advance of the other prairie Indians. Out of a peculiar kind of clay they fashioned large pots of various shapes. After a time, from the effects of heat and use, these became hard and black like iron and so strong that an ordinary blow with a stick or stone caused no injury. Some of the Rees still possess a few of these curious vessels and regard them as relics of great value.

The arrival of the winter Express bringing dispatches from Mr. Clark at the Blackfoot post, although expected for some time, was an interesting event. The Indians were anxious to learn the movements of the Blackfeet, Crows, and Assiniboines, and whether buffaloes were plenty between the camp and the Yellowstone. The Express was brought thus far by a half-breed named Dauphiny, with one other man. They were to proceed as far as our fort, whence they would return and the Express be forwarded by us to the Ree post on its way to St. Louis. From the Rees it would be dispatched to Fort Pierre, thence to Fort Randall (a U. S. post) thence to Sioux City, where it would be put into the mail. Its route for many hundred miles lay through a wilderness infested by hostile Indians, by whom, if discovered, the carriers' lives would be held of little account.

After resting over night the Express continued on to the forts and I went along, as it would devolve on me to carry it to the Rees. A day was spent in writing letters and preparing the requisition for goods for the coming year's outfit. The weather was cold and disagreeable, but having secured the services of a young Indian, the Pretty Wing, as guide, I felt no hesitation about starting.

We left early for we had a long and fatiguing ride before us, the snow being very deep in many places. For a few miles we travelled under the bluffs, which sheltered us from the wind, but when we crossed the river and gained the high prairie the chilling northern blasts had full sweep, blowing the light snow in clouds and making it utterly impossible to see more than a few yards in any direction. Fortunately it was a back wind, which greatly lessened its effects.

We plodded steadily on, making our way, sometimes with great difficulty, through the numerous ravines or coolies filled with snow, and more than once were compelled to take a detour to find a suitable crossing-place. Instead of following the summer trail across the open prairie, my guide kept the river in sight the whole time. This made the road a great deal longer, but to have attempted crossing the plain in that driving *poudérie* would have been madness. Had we been foolish enough to have tried it we might have lost our course in the blinding storm and perished on the open prairie.

We had progressed well on our dreary journey when we encountered a large party of Rees moving from their winter camp at the Red Springs, on account of the scarcity of buffaloes, in search of a better hunting-ground.[54] They were all completely enveloped in their robes and hurried on, anxious to gain the shelter of the timber, for they had the driving storm directly in their faces.

We kept on for some distance farther, when the high bluffs and sheltered dells told us that we could not be far from the Red Springs, where more than half the Rees were still encamped. Soon we saw horses feeding here and there on the hillsides, a cheerful contrast to the dreary waste through which we had passed, and descending a steep hill found ourselves in the timber with the lodges of the Riccarees close at hand. Very few Indians were stirring. Even the dogs took no notice of us as we rode through the village, stopping only long enough for our guide to ask some

[54] On Lt. G. K. Warren's map of 1855–57 the Red Springs are shown midway between the Big Bend of the Missouri and the mouth of Knife River in present-day Mercer County.

questions concerning the best route to the Ree post, where we arrived, hungry and tired, long after dark.

Major Hamilton[55] soon had a cup of hot coffee ready and after a substantial supper we sat until a late hour talking over the different items of news. Several Yanc-toh-wahs from their camp at the Painted Woods, twenty-five miles distant, were in the fort.[56] They had suffered severely for want of

[55] Identification of this official is uncertain. Charles E. De Land states that a Major Hamilton "seems" to have been in charge of the Indian Agency at Fort George, about twenty miles below the mouth of Teton (Bad) River in 1843, where John J. Audubon encountered him in this year. *South Dak. Hist. Colls.*, I, 328. Doane Robinson's *Encyclopedia of South Dak.* notes a Major Joseph V. Hamilton, a native of Iowa, who served as supervisor of Indian agencies on the Missouri in 1845. Presumably De Land and Robinson refer to the same man. Robinson further states that he settled in Charles Mix County, and died in 1867. The U.S. Army Registers consulted do not list a Joseph V. Hamilton. On June 7, 1894 D. P. Lamb, postmaster of Wheeler, South Dakota, reported to Boller that he was informed by Charles Marshall, one of the "old-timers," that Major Hamilton had died about twenty years earlier. "He lived about fifteen miles above this place on the river and the township, Hamilton, is named after him." For the strange story of another Hamilton who was stationed at Fort Union for several years from about 1853 on, see Larpenteur, *Forty Years a Fur Trader*, 359–71.

[56] In present-day Burleigh County, North Dakota, Painted Woods Creek flows westward across northern Burleigh and southeastern McLean counties and joins the Missouri a few miles south of the town of Washburn.

food and many were compelled to live on horse-flesh. The Onc-pa-pas and Blackfeet had not been heard of for some time, but were supposed to be in the vicinity of the Thin Hills with plenty of buffaloes, the great depth of snow in the intervening country preventing communication between the camps. The Sioux expressed themselves very anxious to make peace with the Rees and Gros Ventres, as they invariably do when starving, in order to trade corn, but the latter placed no confidence in their Punic faith.

The next day we laid over to rest our horses, and passed it in visiting. Mr. Hodgkiss of the American Fur Company entertained me with interesting reminiscences of his life, he being one of the veteran mountaineers, having come up in 1832 as clerk for Captain Bonneville, whose graphic narrative is before the world.

Long before daylight on the following morning we were in the saddle. I found to my inexpressible regret that my horse, from some cause or other, was so lame in one foot as to be scarcely able to put it to the ground, and the Major gave me the

Dr. B. F. Slaughter's diary kept at Fort Rice in 1871 relates that the place (Painted Woods) derived its name from a battle fought here between the Sioux and the Arikaras. Many of the trees in the vicinity were marked with Indian devices representing incidents which occurred during the battle. *North Dak. Hist. Quarterly*, Vol. I, No. 2, p. 40 (Jan., 1927).

comforting assurance that I would have to leave him on the road. As I was unable, from the scarcity of horses at the post, to obtain a substitute, I determined to push on as fast as possible, trusting to luck to get through.

There are few things so discouraging to a traveller as to find his horse unfit for duty at the very time his best powers are required. In this unpleasant state of affairs we commenced our homeward journey, and as if in sympathy with our rather forlorn condition the sky was overcast with dull, leaden clouds, while the wind whistled in a way that told of a rising storm. While recrossing the river at the little Mandan village my lame horse lost his footing on the smooth ice and after a struggle fell. The difficulty of getting him on his feet again delayed us a little, but when we reached the shelter of the bluffs and the hard frozen crust of the snow bore up our horses we pushed on at a good gait. By the time we got to the Red Springs we were in a regular storm and *poudérie*, the wind dead ahead of us and intensely cold. Not a human being was stirring in the Indian camp and we passed through without attracting the slightest attention, but when we emerged from the shelter of the high hills the fierce, wintry blast burst upon us with all its fury, fairly taking away our breath, and with great difficulty our horses were made to face it.

All signs of the trail were completely lost in the drifting snow, but nevertheless my Indian guide kept on his way without an instant's hesitation. Once only, for a short time did we lose our proper direction. So terrible was the storm that the figure of my companion, though only a length ahead, was at times invisible. I drew my fox-skin cap close over my eyes and with my capeshaw pulled over that was well protected.

As the shades of evening gathered the storm lulled for a while, and leaving the high prairie our route lay through a sheltered bottom which was thickly populated by a village of prairie dogs. About ten miles below our destination we again crossed the river and overtook half a dozen lodges of Rees travelling up to the Gros Ventres. We were almost within sight of the forts when the storm, as if it had gathered fresh strength by its temporary lull, commenced with renewed violence and although we had so nearly completed our journey it was next to impossible to proceed.

The next morning I examined my horse's foot and found he had snagged himself in the sole. All efforts to extract it being unavailing, a dressing was applied and he was turned out to rest and re-cruit. It was not until green grass came that sup-puration set in and the snag could be taken out, after which old Mac was as well as ever.

With but a single exception, that was the hardest day's travel I ever experienced, not from distance, though that was about fifty miles by the course we were compelled to take, but from the long exposure to such a terrible storm.

CHAPTER XXIV
A Sioux Raid

I FOUND on my return to the camp that the buffaloes had been driven in close by the severe weather and the Indians went out to surround almost every other day. On one of these hunts I wounded a fat young cow and although well-mounted she seemed for a short time to defy the speed of my horse. As we dashed on, the cow in advance, I saw her slip and fall as she climbed a butte, and not willing to run that risk myself I rode rapidly around it, expecting from the advantage her fall gave me to catch her on the opposite side. My horse was at his best speed to cut her off and my pistol drawn ready for use when we came suddenly upon a ravine right before us. It was wide, and its depth was hard to tell, since it was nearly filled by a snow-drift. To stop in time was impossible, from the speed I was going, so giving my horse every assistance with leg and rein he threw his energies into the leap and just cleared it. My pistol was still in my hand and having taken off a mitten to use it I found my forefinger (which had pressed against the cold iron) slightly frozen. To dismount and restore the circulation by rubbing it with snow was the work of a few moments, and then I galloped on after my cow, knowing she was pretty well run down by this time.

Following hard on her tracks, I at length came up with her and was surprised beyond all expression to find her at bay, surrounded by a gang of wolves. Some were tearing large pieces of flesh from her as the poor animal toiled slowly and painfully on, dragging her hind-quarters, for she had been hamstrung by these sneaking wretches. The blood streamed from the gaping wounds and many of the wolves were smeared with gore.

I had read of scenes like this, and given them partial credence only, but here was the reality being enacted before me. When I rode within a few paces the cow bristled up, flirting her tail, and essayed a charge, but fell upon her knees. A friendly bullet cut short her misery and taking her tongue I rode off a short distance to watch the actions of the wolves, who, unintimidated by my presence, could hardly be driven away. The instant my back was turned they rushed upon the body. In an incredibly short time there was but little left besides the head and the wolves sat around, complacently licking their chops.

As a parting benediction I favored one gentleman with a leaden pill to aid his digestion and then rejoined the hunters, who were busy butchering. My friend, the Bobtail Wolf, and his relations were loading their horses, and enjoying a great luxury in the way of a piece of fresh raw liver. The blood streaming over their faces made me think that the difference between two-legged and four-legged wolves was not so great after all.

Towards the end of February a spell of mild weather set in and the trails around the camp became wet and slushy, while the melting snow covered the ice with water. This created alarm in the minds of some of the Indians, lest by the speedy breaking up of the river the low point upon which the camp was located might be flooded and cause destruction of property. Some of the more timid ones worked themselves into a perfect fever and were almost afraid to sleep at night. The mild weather had the effect of making the buffaloes travel out into the "large," and moving camp was talked of in consequence. Meanwhile the thaw continued and there was so much water on the ice that the Indians were afraid to cross their horses. Some were in favor of going to the bluffs just back of the point, others of moving down to an eligible place midway between their present camp and the summer village.

For a time no determination was reached, until one morning the Last Stone's horses were brought up and his women began packing their effects. By noon he with his relations, numbering altogether some thirty or forty men, women, and children, started off, announcing their intention of going down to the bad lands and there remaining until the river should break up, when, the winter hunt being fully over, all would return to the summer village. This was the beginning of the exodus. Every day one or more families departed to join the Last Stone and as their deserted cabins were immediately seized for firewood, in a short time the size of the camp was perceptibly diminished and our circle of visitors had fallen off wonderfully.

There was little or no trading going on. The snow melted rapidly (although there was still plenty on the prairie) and the inspiriting sound of the Indian drum was heard only at intervals. The numerous vacant places, with perhaps a chimney standing where a cabin had been, looked desolate enough, making one regret the bustling, lively times in the early winter. More families continued to leave until there was not more than half the original camp remaining. The soldiers did not move, and the headquarters were here as long as they stayed.

An Indian arrived one day from the lower camp and reported that ten horses had been stolen by the enemy the night before. This news caused much alarm among the Indians, and nothing would do but all must retreat to the lower camp and join forces. The soldiers held a council and harangued that none should move away, under penalty of having their property cut to pieces and perhaps their horses killed. This effectually put a stop to any further stampeding and the horse-guards exercised redoubled vigilance.

Fresh meat began to get scarce again, and the Indians were loth to break in upon their dried stores. Another hunt was therefore arranged, comprising all the able-bodied warriors and leaving no one behind but the women, children, and superannuated men.

Now was a time of great tribulation. Suppose the camp should be attacked while its defenders were away? The people were in constant terror. My spyglass would be borrowed a dozen times a day by somebody who imagined he had seen something, and there were certainly few who slept at night without having at least one eye and ear open. This delectable state of affairs was much increased by the arrival in the night of a couple of messengers from the Riccarees, who came in hot haste to say that the Tobacco, a Mandan, while quietly going from one camp to the other, a distance of perhaps two or three hundred yards, was shot down by a war-party of Sioux who, with a yell of defiance, made good their escape.

The camp was instantly aroused and a party mounted and took the trail. When the messengers left they had not returned, and strong hopes were indulged that they had been successful in overtaking their hated foe and inflicting terrible vengeance.

This startling news created a profound sensation and comments were freely exchanged among young and old. The daring of the Sioux was beyond all precedent, to attack and kill in the very heart, as it were, of their enemy's camp, within sight and hearing of hundreds of their mortal foes. What would they do next? Every one asked this question of himself.

After this there was no running from lodge to lodge. When darkness came all kept within doors, though not without a strong feeling of apprehension. The squaws barricaded the entrances with firewood and lumber to prevent their being rudely opened, for a feeling of insecurity was ever present in the minds of all. No one ventured far from the encampment, and further intelligence from the Rees was eagerly awaited.

We afterwards learned that the pursuing party followed the Sioux beyond the forks of Knife River when a snow-storm set in, blinding the tracks, and compelled them to give up the chase after travelling nearly twenty hours. At one time they were so near that they could see the buffaloes dividing on either side as the Sioux made their way through them. So hot was the pursuit that the Sioux had not made a single halt from the moment they commenced their retreat. There were but two of them, and this very fact contributed to their escape.

The Rees returned in moody temper and breathing vows of vengeance, with their horses badly used up. Another large party immediately started out, determined not to come back until they had accomplished something.

Among them was a young Riccaree squaw whose husband had been killed some time since in battle. This heroine announced her intention of going on the war-path and marrying the first of the party who should strike or kill a foe. The Tobacco was a very quiet Indian and a universal favorite among his companions. He very rarely came around the whites unless he had something to trade. His skin was much fairer than the generality of Indians and his hair had a yellowish tinge. Many said he was a half-breed, and he certainly looked like one. As is generally the case, the quiet and inoffensive Indians are picked off and the rascals live on and flourish.

More pleasant, spring-like weather prevailed and the Indians began to be uneasy again lest the river should suddenly break its icy fetters and overflow their camp. Removing was a subject of constant discussion and everything pertaining to the chase was totally lost sight of. The band of soldiers decided not to join the lower camp, but to move out to the hills, where they would have the same advantages of pasturage and game which they had enjoyed throughout the winter. In a few days the cabins were deserted and the skin lodges pitched on the prairie at the edge of the bluffs, about a mile distant. The squaws took advantage of the fine weather to dress as many skins as possible before returning to the summer village.

Several horses were stolen, but they belonged to Indians who had incautiously left them out all night. The snow was rapidly disappearing and it was the season when war-parties might be expected to hover around. Untiring watchfulness was therefore necessary.

Chapter XXV

Leaving the Winter Camp

IT was now the latter end of March. The buffaloes were getting poor in flesh as it was near the time to calve. The hair on their skins was becoming loose and falling off where the animals rubbed themselves, making what is known as a spotted robe, and of far less value than one killed in the depth of winter when the hair is firm and black. The horses also were well run down, and many which had been prime runners in the fall were now hardly able to catch a cow, although the speed of the latter, as might naturally be supposed, was greatly reduced. The women had a comparatively easy time, for the skin lodges did not require much fuel to make them comfortable.

We lay encamped in this manner almost four weeks. The weather was occasionally quite springlike and then again cold and stormy, with heavy falls of snow. At times there would be so much water on the ice that no Indian would venture to cross and perhaps in a few days it would be frozen seemingly as hard as in midwinter. Whenever there was an air-hole of any magnitude crowds of both sexes would resort to it for a bath, sublimely indifferent to the chilling state of the water and atmosphere. These hardy people seem perfectly insensible to cold, their constant exposure from infancy upwards rendering their bodies as callous as their faces. A Mandan, the Big Left Hand, told me that when a comparatively young man he could hunt the buffaloes on horseback in the coldest weather with no other protection than a breechcloth.

Having occasion to make another trip to the fort I started early in the morning with a voyageur of the American Fur Company who was going down to Fort Berthold. We travelled rapidly and when within a mile or so of the lower camp (though it was out of sight among the Mauvaises Terres) we dismounted to rest. We could plainly see the Indian horses feeding among the hills and when, after resuming our saddles, we came in sight of the lodges a great commotion was evident. Mounted Indians galloped to and fro gathering up their horses and hurrying them into camp, and as we drew near the warriors dashed past us in full battle array.

A few words explained everything. While we were quietly resting on the ridge a small warparty of Sioux, five in all, were stealthily approaching us under cover of a ravine and were preparing to fire, when they were discovered by the scouts from the Gros Ventre camp. The alarm was instantly signalled, resulting as we have seen in the gathering in of the horses and the starting out of the warriors. Finding themselves discovered, the Sioux, knowing that immediate pursuit would take place, retreated precipitately, while we, unconscious of our narrow escape, leisurely remounted our horses and continued on our way until we met the Indians hurrying forth.

We remained in camp all night to learn the result of the pursuit. The following forenoon the warriors returned, having followed the tracks a long distance, until they feared from the direction that they might fall into an ambuscade and concluded to abandon the chase. We then proceeded on our journey and arrived at the fort without further adventure.

Upon my return to camp I found that the soldiers, after a consultation, had harangued to move in three days and every one was busy with preparations. The teams had been sent from the fort to move down all the goods, peltries, and other plunder remaining on hand, and now that uncertainty as to their future movements was at an end a better feeling prevailed among the Indians.

On the day appointed to move camp the squaws were early astir, horses were driven up and saddled, and all awaited the order to pull down the lodges. One by one started off and took

up the line of march, which was headed by the
Poor Wolf, who carried the pipe on this occasion. Soon all were in motion, pressing forward
with glee amid the incidents peculiar to an Indian camp on the march.

The gay young *bannerêts* caracoled about on
their fancy horses and seemed to enjoy greatly
this opportunity of displaying themselves. Sometimes the load of a pack-horse would become disarranged, when off he would go, plunging and
kicking, followed by two or three squaws whose
shrill exclamations of anger were ill calculated to
quiet him. Then again would occur a mêlée, in
which fifty or a hundred dogs harnessed to their
travées participated, to the great detriment of
their loads but very little to their own, the harness
and *travées* protecting them. These combats
would be as suddenly ended by the squaws rushing in among them and dealing their blows right
and left, changing the fierce snarls to a succession of deprecatory yells and cries.

Our second day's march led us through a rolling prairie and along the ridge, almost within
sight of the winter-quarters formerly occupied by
a portion of the camp. But no horses were feeding
among the hills, no smoke curling up from the
lodges floated softly in the air. The camp was deserted and its occupants had gone to the summer
village, where we were soon to join them. We

camped that evening on a little creek, called by the Indians, Blue Water. Fuel was plenty and the pasturage so luxuriant that our horses did not wander off a hundred yards.

A spark from one of the fires, wafted by the air, kindled the dry grass into a flame, and fanned by the wind it blazed furiously on every side. Quick as thought the alarm was given, and everyone rushed forth to fight the fire with whatever happened to be at hand. One picked up a robe, another a blanket, a third an apishamore. Others trampled it out with their feet, while several squaws used large pieces of dry meat, which they were preparing for the kettles, with excellent effect. The flames were soon extinguished by these combined and vigorous exertions. In a few seconds more the fire would have spread beyond control and the whole camp would have been laid in ashes. The grass was as dry and inflammable as tinder, and when once under headway would have burnt furiously. This excitement having subsided, quiet reigned once more, but the night was not suffered to pass without further alarms.

The whole camp was thrown into sudden commotion by the rapid discharge of two or three guns, followed by an attempted stampede of the horses. Several broke from their fastenings and rushed through the camp, but were luckily stopped and secured. The women and dogs added the music of their voices to the general clamor and for a short time the confusion was indescribable. When quiet was restored it was ascertained that nothing was missing although one of the young men who fired the alarm confidently declared that he had seen something creeping through a cooley towards some horses.

No reconnoissance was attempted, for it would have been madness, if not impracticable, and a posture of defense was maintained until daylight, when hostile footprints were discovered crossing the bed of the creek. No enemy being in sight, however, the horses were released from their fastenings and the camp fell into its regular routine.

While descending the slope leading into the timbered bottom below the village a bull was discovered and successfully run by nearly one-half the mounted men, who appeared to enter into the fun with all their hearts. As we entered the trail through the timber each one seemed animated by a desire to press forward as quickly as possible, and as a natural consequence collisions and jars in the dense thickets were of constant occurrence.

Soon the gay cavalcade emerged from the forest glades and crossed the broad sand-bar left bare by the receding waters of the previous autumn, and climbing up the steep bluff upon which their village was built, were once again at home in their favorite summer haunt. The dull monotony that had ruled since their departure in the fall was at an end. Droves of horses scattered forth on the prairies and the rival forts were thronged with crowds of visitors, each one intent on getting a cup of coffee in the Indian room, according to the usual custom when they returned from winter-quarters.

The busy squaws were hard at work, putting the large, round dirt lodges in habitable order, carrying firewood, and cooking. Their lords and masters, after watering and driving the horses out upon the prairie, sauntered from one fort to the other and from lodge to lodge, eating their fill and spending their time in royal ease. The winter hunt was at an end.

Chapter XXVI

Springtime and Hostile Raids

SPRING had come. The Indians had made an excellent hunt and we expected to have in consequence a very good trade. But the squaws were so busy repairing their dirt lodges, in addition to their ordinary domestic duties, that they had as yet dressed but few robes except those which they traded to supply immediate wants. But upon the strength of what they would do when their robes were dressed the men lounged between the two forts, begging all they could from one company and threatening in case of refusal to give their patronage to the other.

Every Indian who had any robes at his disposal was therefore courted and treated with the greatest consideration. Each morning a large camp-kettle, full of well-boiled coffee, liberally sweetened, was set out in the Indian room, with an accompanying pan of small biscuits each about the size of a Spanish dollar. To each one that came in was given a biscuit and a tin-cup full of the beverage, and if desirable to pay special attention he was invited into the Bourgeois' room, where his cup of coffee was infinitely more worthy of the name and the biscuit considerably larger.

This daily morning reception took place at both posts, and as may well be imagined was extensively attended by the notabilities of the Minnetaree camp. The sum and substance of their conversation was "mahts-ee-quoah" (sugar) and how many cups of it they could get for a robe.

The first thing I heard after the gates were opened was the inquiry if the "mahts-ee-quoah" was ready, and the last thing before closing them for the night was "mahts-ee-quoah." McBride lost all patience at this state of affairs. "D——— these Indians," he would say, "it's setoh-minne mahts-ee-quoah" (sugar all the time with them).

The weather was cold and the river still frozen, although there was plenty of water on the ice. But the wild fowl commencing to fly northward gave assurance that spring was at hand, and on all the lakes and creeks around the shooting was capital.

We were busy for several days in making packs, *i.e.*, tying up our robes and peltries into bales for shipment to the States. Ten buffalo robes are put into a pack and securely tied with cords cut out of a raw hide. Wolf, fox, elk, deer, and beaver skins are also tied into packs containing various numbers according to size. We were also occupied in salting and curing the remainder of the buffalo tongues on hand and packing them up into barrels.

The Indians gambled as vigorously as ever and many robes and guns, and sometimes horses, changed hands in the course of the day. The various bands or societies had also their season of dances. That galaxy of beauty, the Wild Goose band, was the first to indulge in a *fête champêtre*, which example was quickly followed by the others.

Some of the dances were wild and very picturesque, that of the Lance Band in particular, being composed of warriors in the prime of life, splendidly arrayed, with bonnets or head-dresses of war-eagle feathers and bearing lances decorated with plumes and pennons of scarlet and blue cloth. They of course paid us a visit and danced in the fort, singing and firing off their fusees in the air. A present was given them after the dance was finished, as is the custom.

The Strong Hearts also took an opportunity to display themselves. Conspicuous among them was my friend, Doctor E-ten-ah-pen-ah, who, dressed and painted in a style indescribably grotesque, enacted his part as if the whole burden of success rested upon his shoulders. He wore a number of small wood shavings stained with vermilion in his hair, each the symbol of a wound received.

Every time a dance came off in the fort a present was given or thrown to the participants, whereupon they danced more vigorously and re-doubled their shouts and yells, and as these fes-tivities were of daily occurrence our liberality was heavily taxed.

Horse-racing in the evenings became again the popular amusement. On one occasion a difficulty arose as to the allotment of the stakes, and from words they came to blows, until finally one of the disputants put an arrow through the heart of the winning horse. This act made a great talk in the village, but as the aggressor belonged to a power-ful clan the insult was suffered to pass by without further notice. The next day not a vestige of the horse remained, the dogs having enjoyed a grand feast during the night.

As if by magic, one morning the vast expanse of prairie on the opposite side of the river was discovered to be, as the Indians expressed it, "black everywhere with a terrible plenty of buf-faloes." Some of the herds came down to the very edge of the timber and every one rejoiced at the sight. The soldiers harangued in the village to stop all unnecessary noise and get ready for the surround.

The houses in the fort were patronized by the idlers, who discussed the appearance of the buf-faloes and speculated upon it in their own delib-erate way. It was not policy to object to this wholesale invasion of our quarters for they re-

garded the traders simply in the light of a convenience, eagerly seeking for the very articles
which these lords of the forest and prairie had no
use for. They could not wear all the skins their
women dressed nor could they eat them. If the
traders were not here to buy them, giving in exchange blankets and cloth and other desirable
luxuries, they would have to leave them on the
prairie, and by sitting around the huge blazing
fires in the houses of the whites they saved fuel
in their own lodges and spared the squaws the
labor of carrying so much firewood. Moreover the
pipes of chash-hash-ash they so freely indulged
in cost them nothing. Therefore, entertaining
these ideas, it was hardly a matter of surprise that
they looked upon the fort as greatly honored by
their presence.

The Indian room was particularly favored, and
as the interpreter in charge was exceedingly
averse to this state of affairs and was at no pains
to conceal his dislike, the young bucks especially
found great delight in purposely tormenting him.
My room was the headquarters of many of the
principal men. Old Raising Heart, the Bobtail
Wolf, Snake-skin, the Hawk, and Doctor E-ten-
ah-pen-ah were regular in attendance.

My comrade, the Bobtail Wolf, continued his
lessons in the language, repeating over and over
words and phrases until I had got them correctly

and written them down, to his intense satisfaction and the astonishment of the rest of my redskinned friends. After an animated conversation (almost always enlivened by a cup of coffee) the cotêrie would disperse to attend to their horses or some public business in the village. The Bobtail Wolf usually remained behind to enjoy a quiet sleep, and should I have occasion to leave my house, sometimes for hours, the old gentleman would always stay to do the honors to any visitors dropping in. The greatest treat I could give my friend was a large pan of bouillon, or broth in which fresh meat had been boiled, well seasoned with salt and pepper, to which latter condiment he was especially partial.

I had decorated the log walls of my room with several colored prints representing buffalo hunts, which were a source of great interest to my visitors. Everything was carefully and truthfully criticised. Any defect in attitude or shape, any error of costume or weapons, all these little minutiae were regularly and accurately commented on.

Often was I importuned to sell these pictures, but I objected, for they seemed a connecting link between the refinements of civilization and the roughness of savage life. When the buffaloes made their appearance, as before related, in such prodigious numbers I said that I knew they were coming, that my pictures were strong medicine, and so long as I kept them on the walls buffaloes would be close and plenty. This announcement made quite a sensation among my hearers and the virtues of my pictures were at once admitted.

The surround was made, the Indians crossing over on the ice, which was still strong enough to bear them except at the banks, where an open strip of a few yards often caused a great deal of trouble. The heavily laden pack-horses would struggle fearfully and sometimes have to be unloaded before they could be extricated. The buffaloes remained for several weeks, apparently as plenty as ever, but after a few surrounds the crossing became so bad that many hunters would not risk their horses and a regularly organized system was accordingly abandoned, all being at liberty to hunt as they pleased.

Many crossed over, and "approached" with great success. One of these small parties returned early in the morning in hot haste and recrossed with the utmost celerity. They reported having discovered a party of Sioux making their way towards the timber, evidently with the intention of laying in ambush for some one of the many hunters that were constantly straggling through the forest. Avoiding them by a détour, they arrived first at the river, and crossing, gave the alarm. In an instant the excitement in the village was terrible and the warriors were soon armed and on the ice, disappearing in a dense body through the timber.

A short interval of anxious suspense ensued, when the silence was broken by the rattling of arms and all the yells and cries that accompany an Indian battle. Expectation was raised to the highest pitch, when suddenly the warriors appeared on the bar, escorting a small party of men in white blanket capotes. Almost everybody rushed down to the landing-place to receive them, and as they drew near they proved to be a portion of a large Assiniboine war-party against the Onc-pa-pas and Blackfeet.

They had been detached from the main body to bring to the Gros Ventre village one of their number who had been taken sick and was unfit for continuing on the war-path. The firing, &c., was therefore intended merely as a salute to the strangers, who were invited into the lodges and treated with all possible hospitality. They said that over three hundred lodges of Assiniboines, Crees, and a few Chippewas were coming down to the Gros Ventres when the green grass came to unite with them in making the great Sun Medicine. The Sioux had been harassing their camp (just below the mouth of the Yellowstone) all winter and had recently made an attack by which they had lost seven of their warriors and had a number severely wounded, but still able to make their escape.

The excitement that attended the arrival of these warriors was not suffered to die out, for the next afternoon two more of the party who had gone on arrived in great glee, with three horses and a colt they had stolen. They reported that the number of Sioux lodges in the bad lands of Heart River was terrible—all the horses tied close at night, and every precaution taken to avoid surprise. Just as they were about to give up their attempt in despair they came upon three lodges a little apart from the main body and were fortunate enough to steal the horses. The rest of the party (from whom they had separated) had not been seen, and they could not afford to lose any time in hunting them up. The prairie had been set on fire by the Sioux, and the fate of their comrades was very uncertain. The Assiniboines made a very short stay and hurried on to their camp, now supposed to be on White River.

Two others arrived before night without any spoils or any tidings of their companions, but early the following day the three remaining Assiniboines appeared in great triumph, driving before them eleven fine horses in excellent condition. There were now only two more of the party to be accounted for and there seemed hardly a possibility of their escape.

The successful partisan of this foray was quite a young, handsome fellow, dressed, as is the usual custom when going to war, in a white blanket capote and capeshaw. As he proudly ascended the bank, his horses led and weapons carried by officious friends, gazed at admiringly by all the young squaws, envy was rife in the breasts of the Minnetaree warriors, who now burned to distinguish themselves on the war-path. War was indeed in every one's head and nothing but war-parties was thought of or talked about. Pierre Garreau, who had been unceasingly urging upon the young men to avenge his sons' death and wipe out the insult offered to their people, and had got no satisfaction but promises, now found the tide of public feeling turned on war with a force and fury he had little anticipated. After giving a couple of their horses to the Gros Ventres the successful warriors started for their camp, but it seemed that the blaze which was now burning fiercely would suffer no diminution.

The same evening a party of thirty-eight Assiniboines arrived, with proposals that the Gros Ventres should unite with them in a general war against the Sioux. Hardly had they told their tale ere the remaining two who had been given up for lost came in, completely jaded and worn-out. They also had been fortunate in stealing five horses the night after the eleven were taken, when the Sioux were exercising their utmost vigilance. But so sharp was the pursuit that they were compelled to abandon their spoils, and so close upon them were the Sioux at one time that they could hear them calling from one to another, "Where are the dogs that eat dirt?" They secreted themselves in a hole and remained there all that night and the next day, but succeeded the following evening in eluding their foes and effecting their escape.

While the buffaloes were so near, the hunters determined upon having one more surround before the breaking up of the river. They crossed in the afternoon, intending to bivouac on the other side and have their horses fresh for the hunt in the morning. The next day there was an alarm of Sioux, and for a short time the usual confusion prevailed, but the matter was partially explained when the hunters made their appearance on the bar and prepared to recross, having abandoned the idea of hunting.

Two Sioux from the Onc-pa-pa camp were with them. It seems that a son of the Crow's Breast, while taking his horses to pasture, found a couple of Indians sleeping. The tramp of hoofs aroused them and they sprang to their feet and called out to him. But he, mortally scared, ran back, whooping and yelling, to the hunters, who, rushing forward, discovered their error. They came to the

Gros Ventres from their own camp at the forks of Knife River to ascertain where the camp of the Assiniboines who had stolen their horses was. Finding a fat cow the afternoon previous, badly wounded with an arrow, they killed her for meat. This detained them so late that they slept in the timber, not caring about entering the village at night.

The Sioux were received, belonging as they did to the Onc-pa-pas, who were on friendly terms, with all hospitality. The Gros Ventres showed their appreciation of the rights of neutrals by preventing any demonstration by either Sioux or Assiniboines, who scowled at each other when they met but attempted no violence. The Onc-pa-pas, however, gave the Assiniboines to understand that a large war-party, consisting of nearly all the fighting-men, would take the field immediately on their return and that they would rub out the whole Assiniboine camp. This put the latter in an immense excitement and they were in the utmost hurry to get back as soon as possible and give the alarm, that they could retrace their steps to the heart of their own country for safety.

Taking advantage of the excitement in the village, a war-party of eight Gros Ventres under the Round Man as partisan stole off in the dead of night, against the orders of the soldier band.

The two Sioux remained a day and then returned to their own camp, saying that a large party might be expected in to trade after the river broke, which from the quantity of water on the ice and the general thaw that had set in could not be far off.

The wild fowl in immense numbers began to fly north, a sure sign that the icy grasp of winter would soon be loosed. The next day the river commenced rising with great rapidity, and there was so much water now on the ice that it was impossible to cross. In the afternoon of the second day the ice commenced breaking up and moved down several hundred yards, when it formed a gorge and stuck fast, but the river, rising rapidly, bade fair to start it again in a few hours.

Everybody had been watching for its first movement and when the dull, crushing sound that accompanied it struck the ear the excitement and joy were universal. The men in the fort dropped their work and rushed to the river's brink, along with hundreds of Indians, while the tops of the lodges were crowded with eager, excited groups, and the dogs, of course, testified their entire approbation by prolonged and vigorous howls.

By nightfall the gorge broke and the ice rushed by, whirling, crushing, and grinding in huge cakes and masses intermixed with floating tree-tops and logs of all shapes and sizes. Through the night the sullen noise, as of distant thunder, continued, and morning revealed the river full from bank to bank and running by with impetuous current.

It was a strange and interesting sight and one could spend hours along the bank watching the rush of waters, the floating cakes of ice, and the whirling logs, carried off from sand-bars where they had been snugly reposing since the fall of the flood in the previous summer, now for hundreds of miles to be bruised by constant contact with the ice until, battered and almost shapeless, they would be borne upon distant waters. The graceful regularity with which the vast floating fields of ice followed the bends of the river and the glittering of the sun's rays upon their surface were well worth watching.

Young Indians, out of bravado, just before the river finally gave way sprang on the moving masses of ice and leaped from one to another until they gained the shore. Others plunged into the chilling water where an eddy was comparatively free, while others again fired their guns and joined in the general outcry.

CHAPTER XXVII

Warfare and the Calumet Dance

THE arrival of Major Clark from his post
among the Blackfoot Indians with the company's Express for St. Louis was the next event
after the breaking up of the river. He had a comfortable, covered Mackinaw boat forty feet in
length with a crew of ten men and was running
day and night. The Major remained with us only
long enough to get the news at the post and ex-
amine into the state of the trade with a view
to making up the outfit for the ensuing year,
to be brought up on the annual steamboat. The
principal chiefs of the Blackfeet sent an invitation through him to the Gros Ventres to meet
them in friendly council at the mouth of Milk
River.

After staying a little over an hour Major Clark
continued his voyage, his stout oarsmen plying
their long sweeps vigorously and running their
frail barge through the ice at the rate of fully
fifteen miles an hour. By the next day the river
had fallen several feet and was comparatively
free from ice. Drowned buffaloes floated by and
two young men swam out after one and succeeded in landing it upon a point of the sand-bar
fully a mile below the village, where they pro-

ceeded to butcher it, without appearing in the least inconvenienced by their chilling swim.

The early spring weather was exceedingly disagreeable. With an occasional clear, calm day, for over six weeks storms prevailed. The wind usually commenced blowing at sunrise and only lulled at nightfall, filling the air with fine particles from the extensive sand-bars opposite the village. All day the wind beat against the pickets of the fort with such tremendous force as to incline them considerably from the perpendicular. Often would the sand be driven in such clouds that it was impossible to see a dozen yards. At such times no work could be accomplished and everybody stayed within doors, even the Indians keeping close to their lodges.

It was during a storm of this kind that a very large war-party of Yanc-toh-wah Sioux ran off a band of nearly two hundred horses from the Rees, embracing many of the very finest in the village, and thus struck a blow which crippled them seriously for a long time. I was in the camp a few days after their loss and it was pitiable to see the straits to which many were reduced for food. Those who had horses shared the proceeds of their hunt with those who had none. Some families had but one or two remaining out of a large band and with all their exertions a surround barely furnished a full meal to each dweller in the camp. I was with them three days and felt quite satisfied to get one scanty meal per diem.

Out on the prairie a couple of miles from the river the wind was as strong as elsewhere, but without the annoyance of sand. It was far pleasanter to remain there among the horse-guards than to stay within doors, for the sand drove through the gaping chinks of the logs and covered everything with a thick, substantial coating of dust which put any approach to personal comfort out of the question.

After the usual amount of preparation two parties, comprising in all about sixty warriors, were ready for the war-path. The largest one, under the leadership of the Red Tail, intended to cross the river and strike through the Sioux country until they reached Fort Pierre, where they had hopes of cutting off some of the lodges of Sioux always encamped in that vicinity. The other, under the First Feather, was to keep on this side of the river on the lookout for the camps of Yanc-toh-wahs generally to be found there in the summer.

Trade went on very briskly. The squaws were dressing and bartering their robes as fast as possible and the men were supplying themselves with everything necessary to fit them for war. White blankets (to make capotes) were in the greatest demand and so unusual was the rush for them that we began to fear we would not have enough left for the Sioux trade, their fancy also running on white, which is the favorite color for war-parties. Hitherto scarlet and blue blankets had been the rage, but they were now not even looked at.

Guns and ammunition were of course in request, and instead of the usual listless idling around or the evening promenade and equestrian exercises of the young bucks, nothing was heard but the trumpet-cry of war. Those who were too old to go exerted themselves to fan the martial spirit of the young men and one and all seemed fully imbued with the prevailing excitement. Party after party started off and there was a very perceptible diminution of men in the village, to be still further reduced when the principal expedition of the season should take the field. This was to comprise the very flower of the village, men who had often and successfully trodden the war-path, and the fact of the Four Bears intending to accompany it inspired those who were a little doubtful with fresh courage.

It now became a serious question whether there would be fighting-men enough left in camp to

guard it, and the old Dry Pumpkin was already
going about haranguing not to leave the women
and children unprotected. So thoroughly was
everybody imbued with the fighting mania that
even the Gambler, whose life was perfectly blame-
less of any attempt to take human blood, declared his intention of going, an announcement
that caused more surprise and remark than any
yet made. A scarred and war-worn veteran, the
Wolf's Eye, was to be the partisan. He carried
the pipe and no matter what member of the party
stole a horse or counted a coup the partisan received the credit, for it was through his Medicine
that the deed was done.

An interval of comparative quiet followed.
Much was to be done in the coming moon. The
Onc-pa-pas and Blackfeet would be in to trade and
returning war-parties might be looked for at any
moment. We were very busy between building a
boat to cross the trading-parties of Sioux when
they should come in, erecting a bastion for the
defense of our post, and clearing up the rubbish
that had necessarily accumulated during the
winter. The snow had entirely disappeared except in a few sheltered places among the hills,
and the Indian women were gathering willows to
repair the fences around their corn-fields, pre-
paratory to breaking the ground for the coming
crop.

The camp was still abundantly supplied with meat, so there was no necessity (and very little inclination, if the truth were known) for the hunters to go out. Every bright sunny day groups of women were scattered over the prairie close to the pickets of the village, with their children playing near them and their dogs of course lying around, dressing and preparing their robes, either for domestic use or trade. Those for themselves were dressed as soft and white as possible, while very little pains was taken with the skins intended for the traders. So keen was the rivalry between the American Fur Company and the Opposition that anything with hair on, from an apishamore up, was eagerly taken, and helped to swell the number of packs.

There is a great deal of work to be done before a buffalo robe is fit for use. When it is in a green (or raw) state it is stretched on a frame of poles, roughly but strongly lashed together in a corner of the lodge, and the flesh adhering is carefully scraped off. It is then left to dry, when it is taken down and put away until wanted, for during the busy hunting-season it is as much as a squaw can do to flesh the robes without finishing them. When the hide is to be dressed it is laid upon the ground and scratched with a sharpened piece of hoop-iron, tied to an elkhorn for a handle. This leaves it in a condition to be brained, *i.e.*, sprin-

kled with water and then well smeared over with
buffalo brains and grease. After being thoroughly
dried it is rubbed on a cord of twisted sinew, which
makes it soft and pliable. The two sides are then
sewed together with sinew and the robe is ready
to be traded. From every robe, before sewing it,
the squaws cut a strip down each half, the
length of the skin and about twelve inches wide.
When a sufficient number accumulates these
pieces are sewed together and used for beds,
apishamores, etc., of course reducing the size of
the skin very considerably.

The camp was thrown into a great state of excitement by the unexpected arrival of a small
boat from Fort Union bringing the White Calf
that Disappears, chief of the Blood Indians, a
band of the Blackfeet. He was splendidly dressed
and had a magnificent bonnet of war-eagle feathers, falling to his feet, and was accompanied by
his squaw, a fine-looking woman.

He had intended to await at Fort Union the
arrival of the American Fur Company's steamboat and greet his brother-in-law, the well-known
Major Culbertson,[57] but Mr. Kipp, the Bourgeois,

[57] Alexander Culbertson was born at Chambersburg,
Pa., in May, 1809. At seventeen years of age he was
employed as a clerk by his uncle, who held the appoint-
ment of sutler to the First U.S. Infantry Regiment. In
the course of this employment the youth visited various
posts around the Gulf of Mexico. He subsequently visited

fearing trouble from the Crows encamped close by, sent his distinguished guest to Fort Berthold, where he would be comparatively safe. The bustle attending his arrival was not suffered to subside, for that night fourteen horses were stolen and the next, twenty-three more, showing conclusively that if their war-parties had gone forth the Sioux were not a whit behind, and great was the panic. The camp was harangued to have the pickets strengthened and filled up and the Poor

Jefferson Barracks near St. Louis and Fort Snelling near St. Paul. In 1831 he entered the employ of the American Fur Company, becoming in course of time one of the foremost figures in the Upper Missouri fur trade, second only in prominence to Kenneth Mackenzie. He built Fort Benton and other fur-trade stations, and had charge at various times of Fort Union and other trading posts. Like Malcolm Clark he acquired a Blackfoot wife. In 1861 he retired from the Company and established his home on a fine 300-acre farm six miles west of Peoria, Illinois, subsequently removing to an imposing residence on a bluff overlooking the city, one mile from Peoria. Here (or earlier) he became addicted to drink and this, combined with the misconduct of an agent who had been employed to manage his business, led to his ruin. He died at Kearney, Nebraska, in the early seventies. Na-to-wis-ta, his Blackfoot wife, is reported to have returned to her people in the Indian country. Members of the Culbertson family were residing at Fort Benton in recent years. Data adapted from sketches in *Montana Hist. Soc. Contributions*, IX, 341–42; R. G. Thwaites (Ed.), *Early Western Travels*, XXIII, 38; Culbertson's own story in *Montana Hist. Soc. Contributions*, II, 201–87; letters in Boller Papers, North Dak. Hist. Soc Library.

Wolf, as head of the soldier band, going his rounds to see that these orders were obeyed, knocked down with his tomahawk several women who did not seem disposed to heed them.

The dry rushes in the prairie bottom had been set on fire and were burning steadily, threatening to spread far and wide. This was a fresh cause of alarm, for by the destruction of their pasturage the Indians would be compelled to drive their horses to a great distance, thereby increasing the risk of their capture. The fire burned on, sometimes feebly struggling for existence in the short, crisp grass of the prairie, but blazing furiously in the dry rushes around the lakes and streams.

In the course of two or three days the whole country seemed wrapped in flames on both sides of the river and its appearance at night, viewed from the bastion, was beautiful in the extreme. A high wind prevailed and the flames climbed over the buttes and rushed through the long grass bottoms with lightning speed, leaving behind them in the black and smoking prairie a sad scene of desolation. The whole atmosphere was filled with smoke, at times so dense that it was impossible to see any distance, although the fire was by that time many miles away.

While the prairies were burning close to us I rode out to look up a couple of horses that had strayed off from the band and in the course of my hunt was obliged to cross the line of fire. Fortunately the grass on the hills was short and burned slowly and after several unsuccessful attempts to force my horse over I threw my blanket over his head and covering my powder-horn with the skirt of my hunting-shirt, crossed the flames.

The burning would facilitate the sprouting of the green grass, and had the excellent effect of causing several copious showers. After each of these, while it was clearing, some of the young men would start off on a foot-race, naked to the clout, amid yells and firing of guns.

Notwithstanding all the wars and rumors of wars the Indians did not neglect making important Medicines. The Bobtail Wolf and his father-in-law, old Missouri, danced around the village, the old man wearing a robe and mask to represent a buffalo. In whatever lodge they danced it was expected that something would be thrown or given to the Medicine, and whoever did this received in return from the bull a pan of toro or pemmican. This Medicine was for the purpose of bringing buffaloes, by which the old Missouri's family would be immediately benefited.

The Long Hair was also preparing to dance the Calumet or Pipe of Peace to the Red Cow. The whole camp talked about it. The Long Hair bustled around, buying ribbons and beads to garnish the stem of the Pipe of Peace and making every possible preparation to give éclat to the ceremony. The Red Cow remained within his lodge, assisting his meditations by smoking abundance of kinne-kinick. The young men watched the proceedings attentively and the young squaws put an extra touch of vermilion on their cheeks, while the principal men made Medicine to decide the auspicious time for this most important ceremony.

Finally the day was chosen. About noon the Bad Brave and Joint appeared on the roof of the Long Hair's lodge, dressed and painted with the strictest regard for the occasion. Chanting an invocation to the Great Spirit and shaking their medicine-rattles, they waved the calumets with their sky-blue stems beautifully garnished, and war-eagle feathers fluttering from them. They made their Medicine first to the rising, and then to the setting sun, after which they descended from the lodge and went inside.

At the farthest extremity of the spacious earth-covered lodge four of the principal men in the village, the Poor Wolf, Crow's Breast, Bear Hunter, and Little Fox, were singing and drumming with untiring vigor. Before each were placed some medicine-sticks. The Bad Brave and Joint danced, waving the calumets and shaking the rattles. The Long Hair sat by the fire in the center, over which a kettle of buffalo meat was cooking, smoking and as the fragrant smoke of the kinne-kinik was blown in clouds from his mouth and nostrils he expressed his complete satisfaction with everything by the simple monosyllable, "How!" At stated intervals the invocation from the top of the lodge was repeated. These ceremonies continued four days.

On the afternoon of the fifth day the important finale took place. After the invocation from the top of the lodge and the dance inside, all adjourned to the prairie, carrying two buffalo-skulls painted with vermilion. Seating themselves in a row, the musicians sang and drummed and the pipe was passed around.

When it was smoked out the party repaired to the lodge of the Little Left Hand. It was crowded with as many as could be accommodated without infringing on the space required for dancing. The oldest man and the oldest woman in the camp were there, as well as children in arms. There was no crowding, no ugly bonnets or huge fans getting continually in the line of vision. All respected the place, all were perfectly quiet, save when some young and pretty squaw happened to be squeezed a little in passing through the crowd of plumed and painted braves around the door.

By the politeness of the Little Left Hand I had a luxurious seat on a pile of robes in the midst of the principal men, close by the musicians, with the Long Hair on my right. After an introductory song and dance a deputation, including the musicians, went to conduct the Red Cow to the lodge. In a short time they returned and the procession marched several times around the fireplace in the following order: the Long Hair; the two dancers, each carrying a Calumet; Red Cow, looking fully conscious of the honor paid him, yet trying to maintain a proper expression of countenance, supported on either side by the Four Times and the Bobtail Wolf. Next came his family and relations. The musicians brought up the rear.

After they were seated at the head of the lodge the music commenced. The Bad Brave sprang to his feet shaking his rattle and waving his Calumet, and danced with a peculiar jarring step. The Snake-skin stood up and harangued, calling upon the by-standers to throw to the Medicine. They responded by coming forward one at a time and giving guns, blankets, calico, scarlet and blue cloth, &c. When all the presents had been given the dancing stopped and the crowd dispersed, while the Long Hair began to distribute the presents he had received among the Big Dog Band.

This is probably one of the most important of all the dances and medicine feasts among the North American Indians. It is, in fact, a kind of baptism, the person thus honored being distinguished ever after. The Great Spirit is supposed to take special care of him. He will count many coups and take many scalps in battle, will be successful in stealing numerous fine horses from his enemies, and will always enjoy abundance of buffaloes.

Chapter XXVIII
Military Defeat and Sioux Visitors

A SMALL party of Sioux arrived from the Onc-pa-pa camp. The leading men among them were the Four Horns, Hawk With a Loud Voice, Yellow Thunder, Iron Wing, War Eagle that Flies in the Air, and Heart of Fire. They left their camp of many lodges on the forks of Knife River, about a day's journey, and said they were so loaded down with meat that they could hardly travel. Much excitement and a great deal of angry talk prevailed in their camp at Pierre Garreau's pushing the Gros Ventres to war against the Yanc-toh-wahs, "for," said they, "it is the same as going to war against us, for we are all one people." The Sioux said their large war-party against the Assiniboines had been deferred until they should make their trade, and the camp moved off to the Black Hills, where, far removed from the din of war, in the fastness of their own country, the women and children could dwell in safety while the warriors sought the foe.

"The Assiniboines are dogs," they said. "We will hunt them until we find them, for they cannot hide in the ground like a snake, nor in the water like a fish, nor fly in the air like a bird. They must be on the prairie, and we will find them."

A large party was coming in a few days to talk about the trade, and the Gros Ventres in the village worked themselves up into a perfect fever of alarm lest the Sioux should take advantage of the absence of nearly all the fighting-men to wipe out old scores. They were as anxious for their warriors to return as they had been for them to go to war, but it was now too late if hostilities were designed by the Sioux.

This begging party remained two days. On the morning of the third they departed, promising that the camp would be in to trade in five or six days, which of course meant not until they were ready, and probably as many weeks would elapse.

A party of Indians on foot was discovered a few days succeeding the above events, coming up the sand-bar quietly as if they wished to attract as little attention as possible, but the anxious inhabitants soon divined the cause. It was one of the war-parties that had started off not long since, eager and confident that victory would attend their arms. But they returned in mourning, having lost their partisan, the First Feather. They had long been on the lookout for the enemy when one day they saw at a distance three buffaloes running. Halting his party, the First Feather went ahead to reconnoiter. He had been gone but a short time when firing was heard and his warriors rushed forward—to find their leader dead and the gun of a Sioux lying near him. They judged by the tracks that the attacking party was about thirteen or fourteen strong. Disheartened by this unlooked-for reverse, they returned in mourning to the village.

The same evening an alarm was given that people were coming. A forlorn and straggling party was seen approaching the village. At the head walked with feeble step and evident difficulty the Round Man. All were in a most forlorn plight, no blankets or moccasins, in fact, nothing but their weapons and breechcloths. The whole village turned out to meet them and as they came up their wives and female relatives rushed to kiss them, while the friends of the slain warrior set up the mournful Indian wail of woe and despair.

Their tale was soon told. They had penetrated the Sioux country as far as Horsehead Point, near Long Lake, below the Cannonball River, where they discovered a large camp of Yanc-toh-wahs. Around it they hovered, lying concealed by day and prowling about in the dead of night. The inhabitants of the camp were busily engaged around a circle of fires dancing a scalp which they had just taken, probably the First Feather's. With infinite daring the Gros Ventre warriors stole in among the lodges and cut loose nine horses and five mules, with which they commenced their retreat. But one of the horses, a white one, escaped and ran back to camp. This gave the alarm, resulting in a hot pursuit. The Gros Ventres retreated in a northeasterly direction as if they were making for the Red River, thereby hoping to deceive the enemy into the belief that they were either Chippewas or half-breeds. Being hard pressed they abandoned their horses, keeping only one apiece to ride, and threw away everything except their weapons.

In the midst of their retreat they unexpectedly encountered a party of Sioux returning from an expedition against the Assiniboines. Their horses began to give out and one of their number was shot and scalped. Nearly all were now more or less disabled. The Round Man was shot in the mouth and wounded in three other places, and fearing he could not hold out, told his comrades to leave him to his fate and bear witness that he died like a man. But his warriors were true and stood by him and one by one the Sioux gave up the chase, as their horses were completely ridden down and they had secured a scalp without any loss. Stripped of horses, blankets, and provisions, their ammunition and arrows all expended during the running fight, and crippled by wounds, the survivors kept on with true Indian fortitude, and eking out a scanty subsistence on roots and berries arrived at last in forlorn plight at their village.

The friends and relations of the dead sat by the medicine poles on the prairie, cutting and gashing themselves and crying to the Great Spirit. The Bobtail Wolf told me that the First Feather had been making medicine and crying to the Great Spirit all winter, even promising to give a robe in the event of success in war. He made two cardinal errors, my informant said: first, in promising the robe after crying all winter and secondly, in not giving it before he started.

These unexpected reverses cast quite a gloom over the village. The warriors stalked moodily about with downcast glances and the chiefs held solemn conclave in the council-lodge. Meanwhile every day or so there would be arrivals from the Sioux. The camp itself came in sight one afternoon, numbering several hundred lodges, and pitched in the prairie bottom, just beyond the timber. Very little trade of course was done the first day, which was one of general visiting. As several of the Sioux were to dance the Calumet to the Gros Ventres, it of course engrossed a great deal of their attention.

The Sioux came over early and traded actively until they were stopped by the soldiers from bringing any more robes, hoping thus to induce the traders to cross the river with a view to robbing them. They found, however, that this artifice would not succeed, and allowed matters to go on as before. The traffic over, they departed to join the other division, trading with the Rees. They proposed to rendezvous at the forks of Knife River and then move out to the Thin Hills. In spite of their threatening talk the Sioux traded comparatively little ammunition.

Beyond all doubt, had we crossed the river we would have been robbed, to say the least, for at the Ree post they behaved outrageously. Moise Arcan came up thence with dispatches and said that during a residence of over thirty years in the Indian country, chiefly among the Sioux, he had never known them to act so bad. More than two-thirds were in favor of hostilities and several of the chiefs advised all the old traders to leave the country soon, as war would inevitably break out. They said they did not want to kill those who had lived so long with them and had become in a measure identified with themselves.

When making their trade with us the Sioux reported that all through their country towards the Platte, the elk, deer, buffaloes, bears, and wolves were dying in great numbers from some sickness among them, caused by the Medicine of the whites.

A couple of logs lashed together to form a raft, such as a war-party might use to cross the river, floated down and was caught, causing much speculation and anxiety among the Gros Ventres. Some Crows also arrived from their camp at the Elkhorn Prairie in search of a child which the Spotted Horse (a Crow living with the Gros Ventres) had redeemed from the Sioux three summers before. The Sioux, in an attack upon one of the Crow camps, among other spoils took this child prisoner. The Spotted Horse succeeded in redeeming him for a very liberal ransom and now his relatives, having heard of it, were anxious to recover him, which they did, after giving six fine horses, robes, and goods. They said that when the next moon was dead a large party of Crows might be expected down to visit their relations, the Gros Ventres.

Chapter XXIX

The Revenge of Pierre Garreau

IT was now almost the middle of May and the Indian women were busy hoeing their cornfields, and planting. Grass was springing up everywhere and the burnt prairie was covered with a beautiful carpet of velvet-green. All the trees and bushes were clothed in the bright, fresh hues of early summer and the balmy air was filled with the cheerful notes of birds. The glorious golden sun shone with a brilliancy and vigor which we had vainly longed for in the short, dark days of the dreary winter. The young May moon brought clear and calm skies and a few weeks of active work completed Fort Atkinson.

On the Sunday following I had the honor of hoisting for the first time on the bastion flagstaff our national flag with its Stars and Stripes, amid the cheers and congratulations of the men. Little did we think as we watched it proudly floating over forest and prairie that in scarcely a year from that time that glorious banner would be trailed in the dust by the leaders of the most infamous rebellion the world ever saw.

The war-spirit was burning as fiercely as ever, despite the reverses that had befallen the Gros Ventres. The Round Man had recovered from his wounds and in a dream saw scalps close to the Ree village. He thereupon declared he was going to war again and told his friends to black their faces.

The old Wolf's Head said he thought his Medicine would fool him again, for he had not cut his hair after losing one of his warriors, as is the duty of a leader. In a few days this redoubtable party started, intending to go as far as the Dog Buttes, in the vicinity of which they expected successfully to encounter their foe if their partisan's Medicine was good for anything.

Shots were suddenly heard on the prairie and every one rushed forth, gun in hand, to see what they meant. Over the plain careered at full speed a band of warriors with blackened faces, whooping and yelling and firing their guns. The excitement in the village was intense. It was the grand war-party returning in triumph, bearing four scalps on the points of their lances. All the inhabitants rushed forth to greet them, the squaws singing and dancing in the exuberance of their joy. The victors formed into line and rode in a close body up to the village, where they halted to receive the praises and congratulations to which they were entitled. The leaders, in the intoxication of success, gave away horses and guns. A pole with hair attached was quickly set up over the spot where the relatives of First Feather and

Wolf's Eye's brother had bewailed them. The drum was sounded and the scalp-dance commenced in the village, while joy and gladness reigned supreme.

Only the evening before they had discovered a small party of ten near the Dog Buttes, coming towards them with their arms slung, evidently not expecting to meet enemies. The Gros Ventres rushed on them and the Gambler, having a long lance, struck the first coup in his life. Three of the Sioux were instantly killed and one badly wounded. But four scalps were taken. They could have dispatched all, but the Wolf's Eye, fearing that some of his own warriors might be lost and spoil the dancing when they returned to the village, called out to stop and then hurried back to celebrate the victory.

All that night and the next day the rejoicings continued and the scalp-dancers flourished around the village. Headed by the Wolf's Eye, the men in a dense group sounded their rattles, singing and drumming, while the squaws shuffled in a circle around them with three scalps on poles (the fourth having been sent down to the Rees, in order that they too might participate in the rejoicings) screaming in shrill tones the scalp-song. The faces of all were blackened and they looked like fiends of darkness let loose.

Pierre Garreau's sons were avenged.

In the evening the Round Man's party returned, straggling in a few at a time. Had they gone only a short distance farther they would have seen the enemy, but all agreed that their partisan's Medicine was very strong and good.

CHAPTER XXX

Indian Chatter and Friendly Crows

THE leafy month of June had come and the prairie was clothed in a beautiful dark-green. The thickets of service-berries were loaded with fruit and the wild roses shed a delicious perfume on the summer air. The Indian horses, luxuriating in a respite after the incessant toil of the winter hunt, were beginning to show by their sleek and glossy appearance that the herbage of the plains was most grateful to them.

The Missouri commenced to feel the melting of the snows in its mountain tributaries and its swollen and turbid waters rushed and foamed wildly around the base of the lofty promontory upon which the village was built. Great quantities of drift-wood and floating trees were caught in the whirling eddy below the fort, and gave constant employment to the women and girls, who put out in their bull-boats and thus secured plenty of fuel. In a short time the road leading down to the water was completely blocked up with piles of wood, and the ladies were in high glee at the labor saved in having their firewood brought to their very doors, as it were.

The bank against which the water beat was rapidly undermined and falling in almost hourly with a loud crash. Corn-fields that when planted were fully fifty feet from the river were now more than half washed away, and many a squaw looked with rueful countenance on the patch of ground, where she had bestowed so much toil and expected such good results, quickly disappearing before her gaze. With high water the arrival of the steamboat began to be agitated, and many inquiries were constantly made in how many nights the "fire-canoe" would be here.

To the whites it was a season of ease and indolence. The houses had been washed inside and out with white clay, and the area being well cleaned and swept, the fort presented a very neat appearance. The men had now little to do, and mostly passed their time in hunting and fishing.

Our provisions were nearly exhausted, the small stock on hand being used with the utmost care to last as long as possible, until the annual boat would bring a fresh supply. Consequently the usual entertainment to the coffee-loving Indians was given up for want of means, causing a great falling off in the attendance at meal-time.

The Four Bears called occasionally, but was not at all regular in his habits now that there was nothing to be made by it. But my old comrade, the Bobtail Wolf, visited me as ever and always received his pan of bouillon, well peppered and salted, which he infinitely preferred. Doctor E-ten-ah-pen-ah also continued to make my house his headquarters and as the days grew longer and longer, till it often seemed that darkness would never come, I derived great amusement in listening to the conversation of these worthies, and occasionally taking part. They were discussing the causes which led to the defeat of several of the war-parties that had gone out in the spring.

The Wolf said to the Doctor, "My brother, your Medicine is strong. It is very strong. All the He-rae-an-seh acknowledge it to be so. I beg you not to throw any of it on the Gros Ventres and thereby cause defeat and losses of various kinds in war and hunting. I am a chief. When I talk to the Gros Ventres what I say goes straight to their ears. My speech is always straight, not forked or travelling in two ways. Heed what I say and I will exert my influence among the Gros Ventres in your behalf."

The Doctor listened to this earnest harangue with becoming gravity, but when I caught his eye there was a certain sly twinkle in its corner that showed the old rascal was fully aware of his power and intended to improve it. I sometimes amused myself by the exhibition of a few trifling sleight-of-hand tricks, which greatly excited the wonder of my spectators. That which had the strongest medicinal effect consisted simply in putting three wafers on one side of a knife and causing them to appear and disappear at will. This performance never failed to create the utmost astonishment in my friends, and the Doctor was especially anxious to add it to his list of Medicines.

The Grindstone, an old Onc-pa-pa Sioux, who with his family resided among the Gros Ventres, frequently talked about a white hermit in the pines among the Black Hills. He had a hut on the summit of some towering rocks. No one had seen him, but they knew him to be a very tall man because they (the Sioux) found a deer which he had killed and hung up in the top of a lofty pine tree. He is the person, they think, who poisoned all the creeks and streams, causing such distress among the wild animals. There had been no thunder this spring, and it was currently believed that he had killed the thunder-bird.

The previous summer when on a visit to the Crows the Wolf painted a young Crow warrior and said he gave him half his Medicine. He was a chief, and he gave him the same chance to become one. The young man took the name of the Black Cloud and painted half his shield black. He then went to war and stole two horses, when he sent word down that they were for the Wolf. His Medicine was good and he wanted his shield black all over.

The Mandans began to agitate the question of returning to their old village, close by the Riccarees, to plant corn in the same fields they had tilled years ago when their nation was strong and powerful and the terror of its arms extended far and wide. Some thirty families prepared to move away. The squaws loaded their effects in bull-boats and started off by water, while the men drove the horses across the country.

One afternoon the Round Man came to propose going on a wolf-hunt, saying that he had found close by a cave in which a she-wolf was suckling her pups. As there was no inducement to do anything else I assented, and shouldering my gun we started off. Crossing a wide strip of prairie, we came to the hills and after a much longer walk than I had any reason to expect descended the steep sides of a ravine, at the base of which the Round Man pointed out a hole in the ground which he said was the entrance to the wolf's den.

We stopped, like prudent hunters, to thoroughly survey our ground before commencing operations, and a pipe was smoked to propitiate the Wolf Spirit in our behalf. The Round Man threw in stones while I stood with my gun ready to shoot the wolf as soon as she made her appearance. The stones rolled one after another to the bottom of the den with a dull, heavy sound, without provoking any response. Next a long pole was thrust down and vigorously poked about, but without producing any better result. At last, as there was no other alternative, we commenced cutting away the bushes at the entrance to widen it, keeping a sharp lookout all the while lest Madam should unexpectedly make her appearance.

After expending some labor we made the hole wide enough to admit of the passage of the Round Man, who, stripping himself to the clout, crawled in head foremost with his knife in one hand and his tomahawk in the other. I listened anxiously for the startled growl, but none came and directly my friend backed out of the den, reporting that the wolves had left their lair, and that but recently. We hunted all the rest of the afternoon, but were unsuccessful in finding them. A few days earlier, before the pups were able to run about, our enterprise would undoubtedly have resulted differently.

The scouts on the hills signalled the approach of mounted Indians, men and women, from above. Directly a motley crowd went forth to meet and escort the visitors (supposed to be Crows) to the village, while the squaws hurried to fill their kettles and made every preparation to feast their guests. Soon the wild procession came in sight on the crest of a hill, and descending into the plain halted to smoke with the dashing blades of the

Gros Ventres. The latter rode around their visitors in high feather, while the Crows, with their strongly-marked aquiline features and profusely garnished skin dresses, burnt and blackened by exposure to wind and weather, looked Indians all over.

The men were tall and powerful and all were finely mounted. Fully one-half of the party were women, who took charge of the extra horses, and in point of numbers the cavalcade presented a goodly appearance. The squaws were very large and coarse, with long, tangled, black hair, which, falling free and unconfined over their shoulders, did not add to their attractions in the least.

No sooner had they disappeared within the enclosure of the village than I went straightway to my quarters and put all my possessions under lock and key, as the Crows' ideas of *meum* and *tuum*, unlike my Gros Ventre friends, were strangely confused and I had conscientious scruples about placing temptation in their way.

Of course, after going through a round of feasting the next places to visit were the trading-posts, and until the gates were closed they peered into every nook and corner with a pertinacity that was not to be bluffed off, and which only a Crow can equal. The women were especially annoying, and in spite of our vigilance quite a number of knives and other small articles were stolen,

chiefly from the men's quarters, who anathe-
matized "Injins" in general, but the Crows in
particular. Like all prairie Indians, who visit a
trading-post only at long intervals, everything is
strange and new and in satisfying their very
strong curiosity they often become exceedingly
troublesome.

The band of horses belonging to the post had
been for some time under the care of an Indian
who usually performed his duties as guard with
great fidelity. In common, however, with the rest
of his comrades he rode off to greet the Crows
and on returning where he had left the horses
quietly feeding, but two only could be seen. This
was unlucky, should we not succeed in finding
them on the morrow, as there were a number of
very fine animals belonging to individuals con-
nected with the post.

Early the next morning Malnouri and myself
mounted the two remaining horses and started
off determined to recover them if they had only
strayed, and not been stolen by a war-party of
Sioux, who were nearly always lurking in the
neighborhood. We each took a different trail,
appointing a place to rendezvous in the event of
either one being successful. Noon came and saw
us refreshing ourselves at a cool spring which
gurgled through the hills. Both had ridden over
a wide expanse of prairie without discovering

the slightest trace of our missing caballada, nor had anything been seen by the scouts of the village. After a short halt we renewed our search, taking as before a different circuit. I struck into an old buffalo-path, which led me through the ravines and over the hills for miles until it was lost on a high, sloping prairie, whose vast expanse swept far away to the northward.

Here I halted, and dismounting, took a careful survey of the prairie with my glass and was just able to distinguish a group of some kind a long distance off. It might be either Indians, buffaloes, or the missing band. I proceeded cautiously until I was able to distinguish clearly that they were horses. It was our band, crowded close together, with dishevelled manes and raised tails, surrounded by a large gang of gray wolves who were induced to fall back a little on my approach by the discharge of a pistol. Right glad was I to see old Mac again, and starting the band off at a gallop I had the satisfaction of reaching the fort just after Malnouri had arrived with rueful countenance, which was quickly cheered by the trampling hoofs as the horses, his two favorite runners among them, dashed into the corral, the gate of which, securely fastened, precluded all possibility of a further stampede that night.

After spending a couple of weeks and thoroughly wearing out their welcome, so far as the whites were concerned, the Crow horde took their departure for the camp of their tribe on the Yellowstone, in great tribulation lest they should meet with a party of either of their deadly foes, the Sioux or Blackfeet, which we most devoutly wished they might. They feared also lest their camp, finding the Yellowstone country too hot for them, would move off to a more secure hunting-ground in the Wind River Mountains, and thus their small body would be compelled to traverse a long and very dangerous road.

CHAPTER XXXI

A Musician and a Ride for Life

THE old adage, music hath charms to soothe the savage breast, was not exemplified in the case of the Crane, a Gros Ventre Indian of exceedingly tall stature—hence his name. A violin belonging to me attracted his fancy and nothing would do until he obtained possession, giving far more than its value in fine, painted robes, and stalked off with his prize in triumph to his lodge. I felicitated myself on the capital trade I had made and imagined the Crane entertaining his guests with dulcet strains from his fiddle. Several days elapsed, and I saw one morning the tall form of the Crane approaching, with lowering brow and measured tread.

"Borraquoi" (my friend) said he, "my squaw's heart is bad towards me. She calls me a fool and says the robes she dressed were to be traded for blankets, and she can't sleep because of the noise I make. Take your fiddle and give me back my robes."

I could not help sympathizing with his squaw in the annoyance his attempts to extract music at all hours of the day and night must have caused, but declined trading back on any terms. The Crane, after sitting a while, got up without another word and retired to the village, but the end was not yet. In a short time I saw his squaw coming toward the fort, carrying the luckless violin on her back after the usual fashion of Indian women. I quickly fastened the door of my room and watched her through the window. She laid the cause of her unhappiness at my door and retired around the corner, where I allowed her to wait until despairing of my appearance she picked up her treasure, with every manifestation of anger, and departed.

I went back to my room, and influenced by one of those impulses which cannot always be controlled and are often unaccountable, took down my revolver and double-barrelled gun and proceeded to place fresh caps upon them.

While thus engaged the door was opened and in marched the Crane, evidently carrying the violin under his robe. He halted upon seeing the nature of my occupation and ejaculated "How!" I replied, inviting him to sit down, which he did, with a black cloud upon his brow. My pistol was by this time capped and carelessly throwing my gun into the hollow of my arm I dropped the muzzle as if merely by accident full upon the Crane, who sat at the opposite side of the room. "Click, click," went the lock of one barrel; "click, click," the lock of the other. The Crane's countenance changed expression and he slightly moved his seat. I picked up a piece of buckskin to polish the mountings and in doing so, as if by chance brought the muzzle again to bear upon the Crane. This had now continued several minutes and I began to be concerned as to how it would end when his countenance brightened, as if his mind was made up and greatly relieved thereat.

With the simple remark that "women are fools," with which laudation of the sex I thought proper to coincide, he gathered up his robe and left in very good humor, and from that day to the day of his death some two years after, neither he nor his squaw ever alluded to the subject again. How they compromised matters I know not—whether the Crane pursued his musical studies in peace or whether he abandoned them altogether out of regard for the comfort and domestic tranquillity of his family. I was very glad it ended as it did, for neither of us wished to push matters to extremities.

It was now about the time when the annual steamboat might be daily looked for, and expecting it almost hourly, as it were, the days seemed interminable, and we were fairly at our wit's end to devise means to pass away the time. Not a white cloud appeared in the direction from which the chimneys of the approaching steamer would first show themselves that was not mistaken for the steam from the escape-pipes, giving rise to the very natural excitement consequent upon the announcement that the "Mahti-shee-sheesh" was coming. To sleep all the time was impossible, and from the slender amount of provisions on hand our mess-table was by no means attractive, corn coffee being, in the estimation of a mountaineer, a forlorn substitute for the genuine beverage.

This being the state of affairs I gladly availed myself of the opportunity presented to join a party of Gros Ventres going down to the Rees. William Fisher, one of our men, increased our strength to seventeen, all mounted on picked horses. Our trip was accomplished without any incident, and after spending a couple of days very pleasantly at the Ree village we started on our return. At the upper crossing of Little Knife River the Indians stopped to smoke and let their horses graze.

But the halt was destined to be of short duration. A large band of Sioux suddenly appeared on the hills not more than two miles off and dashed towards us, evidently with the intention of cutting our trail. The instant they were discovered we rushed for our horses, and mounting made for the broken land on the Missouri. A warrior named the Wood was our leader and we strung out in Indian file, each one's place being regulated simply by the speed of his horse, who was kept at his fastest pace with but the one thought, to get away from the pursuers. For the first few miles the race was closely contested, neither party getting the advantage, but when our foaming horses gained the broken land our leader's superior skill was evident.

Never before had I been so forcibly impressed with the instinctive, unerring sagacity of the Indian. Knowing every foot of the country, without slackening speed he carefully avoided the ridges, following up the ravines and completely concealing us from our pursuers. The hard, sun-baked soil of the prairie gave not the faintest hoof-print, and we now had greatly the advantage, since the chances of the Sioux finding us in those innumerable ravines were materially lessened. At one time we were almost within gunshot, and halting suddenly, scarcely breathed until they had ridden past.

The race had continued some ten miles and we were near the Red Springs when the Wood halted us to "discover." Crawling cautiously to the top of the nearest knoll, we could see the Sioux riding about in a confused group as if they had lost us and were trying to come upon the trail again. Our spirits rose greatly and the Wood announced his intention of going to some deserted winter-lodges not far off, where we could intrench ourselves, adding that if we were dis-

covered before we reached them our only re-
source was to make for the Missouri, and trust
to its waters.

Swiftly and cautiously we hurried on until the
friendly shelter of the forest near the Red Springs
was gained. A couple of large, round lodges in a
tolerable state of preservation were selected, close
to the river. Into one of these we secured our
horses and after fortifying the other with a breastwork of logs kept a sleepless watch all night, the
Indians listening anxiously for the slightest
sounds.

Morning broke at last, but no traces of our
pursuers were visible. All that day we laid close
in our retreat, and at nightfall resumed our saddles. The Wood, leaving the usual trail across the
prairie, followed the river, keeping under cover
of the broken land as much as possible, and
morning found us on the sand-bar waiting for
the bull-boats to take us over. Even now we
dreaded lest the Sioux, having anticipated our
destination, should make a sudden onslaught,
but our fears were fortunately without foundation.

Neither our horses nor ourselves had eaten
anything since leaving the Ree village nearly
three days before. The poor animals had suffered severely, and it was pleasant to see them
feeding on the rich grass and indemnifying
themselves for past hardships.

Chapter XXXII
Arrival of the Steamboats

A FEW nights after this adventure we were roused by a violent pounding at the gate and voices shouting for the whites to get up, the steamboat was coming! Without loss of time every one was out, and eager inquiries passed around. It seems that an Indian had arrived on the other side, calling for a bull-boat, whereupon several of our friends hurried at once to the fort, telling us that he had news of the steamboat.

The squaws were afraid to cross over in their bull-boats, fearing it might be a trick of the Sioux to lure them into an ambuscade, but some of our men in their eagerness went over in the skiff and when they returned quite a large crowd gathered around the new-comer to hear what he had to say. He had heard nothing, seen nothing, it was merely a ruse to get him crossed, as none of the squaws would venture. A very quiet and subdued party of white men returned to their fort and slept soundly the remainder of the night.

But our disappointment was not doomed to be of long duration for the very next afternoon an unusual outcry was heard in the camp and every one rushed out, expecting to see nothing less than an immense war-party of Yanc-toh-wahs

340

debouching from the hills on horseback to give the Gros Ventres battle. But soon the word was "Fire-canoe," and sure enough, against the bluffs that lined the southern shore of the river was seen what at first appeared to be a faint white cloud floating on the summer air, but by the regular puffs we knew must be the escape from a steamboat.

All was now bustle and commotion. The Stars and Stripes were run up on the flag-staff, and each man made the most careful toilet his limited wardrobe would admit of. The Indians, too, shared the general excitement and the *bannerêts* made their appearance, painted and decked out in all the colors of the rainbow.

The tops of the tall black chimneys now became visible above the elm-point, and soon after the boat itself came into full view, slowly but steadily breasting the strong current. Which boat was it, ours or the American Fur Company's, was anxiously questioned. She turned the bend not more than a mile off and was now coming directly towards us. Nearer and nearer she steamed. The paddle-wheels could be distinctly heard. Then a white wreath of smoke enveloped her bows, and directly the report of a cannon was borne on the air. The salute was promptly returned, and continued until she lay at the landing within a stone's throw of the post. All doubt was at an end. The boat was our own, direct from St. Louis with a full equipment for the ensuing year.

It seemed strange to see civilization, as typified by the steamboat, in the heart of the wilderness. The Indians, grouped on the brow of the bluff, were interested spectators of the scene. There were yet many among them who remembered the first steamboat that ever ploughed the waters of the Upper Missouri and the dreadful scourge that soon after broke out in their midst and has proved so signally fatal to the race.

Mountaineers greeted acquaintances and hurried away with mysterious black bottles secreted about their persons. The deck-hands unloaded the freight, and all was bustle and excitement. The teams were soon busily engaged in hauling up the supplies to the fort, and after staying only long enough to put off the freight intended for us the steamer continued her voyage.

It was midnight before the last wagon-load was stored away, and then, securely locking the gates, we left the new hands to be initiated into the mysteries of mountain life by the old ones. I opened with hesitating eagerness the large package of letters and papers to learn of all that had happened during the past year in the civilized world, and the tidings from the loved ones in their far-off home.

The following day was one of continued bustle. Indians thronged the store, bringing furs which they had reserved to trade until the boats should arrive with fresh goods. Packages were hastily opened, and anything wanted was sure to be found at the bottom. For two days we had the monopoly of the trade, but on the third day the boat of the American Fur Company arrived, having the Indian agent and annuities on board.

The Agent held the usual council, gave the usual stereotyped advice to love their Great Father and their enemies, to which they responded with the usual grunt, and the council broke up, without the Indians having a very exalted opinion of the Agent, or his ability. The annuities were landed and, compared with the preceding year, the pile was beautifully less, so insignificant in fact that the Indians considered it rather an insult than otherwise. The government appropriations are supposed to be liberal, but it so happens that by the time they reach their destination they have, and not mysteriously either, dwindled down into a paltry present.

During the time that the boats were up the river the new voyageurs, *mangeurs du lard* (pork-eaters) as they were termed the first year of their novitiate, were becoming fully initiated into the charms of mountain life, and the old hands, whose time had expired and who were going down to the settlements, were busy taking farewell of their Indian sweethearts and loading their trunks with moccasins and trash generally. Whiskey smuggled by the deck hands was not wanting, and the carousal was at its height.

In less than ten days after leaving us our steamboat returned from Fort Stuart, eighty miles above the mouth of the Yellowstone, and after shipping the packs of robes and peltries took her departure for St. Louis. In the changes that were made I was placed in charge of the post until the arrival of one of the partners of the Company from the lower country, which would not be until late in the fall.

In a few days the American Fur Company's boat also returned, and it was with a feeling of relief that we saw her smoke-stacks disappearing behind the forest as she pursued her way down the river. The annual carnival was at an end—the reign of Minne-bae-tah (fire-water) was over for another year—and in our voluntary seclusion we would be undisturbed by the throbs and throes of the civilized world.

The Gros Ventres returned in due time from their visit to the Crows, having obtained from them a supply of horses, of which the Crows possess immense numbers. Our friends, the

Sioux, paid us occasional visits, doing no damage beyond stealing a few horses and keeping us constantly on the *qui vive*.

In the fall the Reverend Father De Smet, the celebrated Apostle of the Indians, arrived from the Blackfeet in a small boat with four men. The Reverend Father was one of our passengers on the *Twilight* as far as Fort Leavenworth, where he left to join the Utah Expedition. He had crossed the Rocky Mountains and visited the missions on the Columbia River among the Flatheads, Nez Percés, and other tribes, and having completed his tour was now on his way to St. Louis. Father De Smet is universally revered by all the Indian nations, and known far and wide. Among the rude mountaineers he commands the utmost respect by his gentle, winning manners and the practical, common-sense view he takes of the errors in their mode of life. Many strange and true stories are told of his wonderful adventures among hostile tribes, and the almost supernatural awe in which they hold him. The whole of a long life has been devoted to the welfare of the Indians and they have no truer or abler advocate.

Father De Smet remained with us over night and baptized five or six half-breeds, children of some of the retainers of the post, as well as a number of Indian children in the Four Bears' lodge, to all of whom he gave a medal. The morning sun saw the Father on his voyage, with his stores replenished to the best of our ability and the heartfelt good wishes of all.[58]

[58]Father Pierre-Jean De Smet, famous Catholic missionary to the western Indians, was a native of Belgium who came to America as a young man in July, 1821. A member of the Jesuit Order, he was engaged in various priestly and educational duties until 1838, when his career as a missionary to the Indians began, to continue for a quarter of a century. After accompanying the army to Utah in 1858 in the capacity of chaplain, he returned to New York where he sailed for the Pacific Coast, returning thence overland to St. Louis in 1859. See sketch in *Dict. Am. Biog.;* H. M. Chittenden and Alfred T. Richardson (Eds.), *Life, Letters and Travels of Father Pierre-Jean de Smet,* S. J. 1801–73 (New York, 1905), III, 762–76.

CHAPTER XXXIII

A Quarrel Over Prices

THE beautiful Indian summer had come again, with its delightful weather and hazy skies. Vast flocks of wild fowl were flying south and Nature's signs admonished the Indians that it would soon be time to seek their winter-quarters. Preparations were rife throughout the camp, skin lodges were put in order, and a day appointed to move.

The Poor Wolf and Crow's Breast, of the soldier band, came to me and said that it had been decided not to allow traders in camp unless they increased the price of a buffalo robe to ten cups of sugar, and other goods in proportion, asking a considerable advance over present rates, which were already uncommonly high.

Deeming it politic to keep them in good humor pending the arrival of the new Bourgeois, Mr. Wickham, I held a council and gave a feast to the Gros Ventres, to ascertain exactly their views about the coming trade. The Four Bears, Crow's Breast, and Snake-skin were the principal speakers. They unanimously declared that if one Company went the other should go too, but in no case should either go unless they agreed to give the increased price demanded. In

347

expectation of Mr. Wickham's speedy arrival I deferred an answer for the present and the council broke up in the best of humor, but with the understanding that, as matters stood, there would be no traders allowed in camp that winter.

So the Gros Ventres went away to their winter-quarters, but hardly were the last of them out of sight ere a party of Rees rode up and reported their camp also on the way to winter-quarters, which were to be established in a fine point of timber about ten miles below us.

The agreeable prospect therefore presented itself of daily arrivals from the camp of these undesirable neighbors, coming ostensibly to trade, but in reality to beg and steal. Like the Gros Ventres, they, too, determined to exact the highest rates for their robes and were likely to leave no means untried to compass their ends.

Such was the position of affairs when Mr. Wickham arrived with a couple of teams from Fort Pierre. As soon as the Rees learned that he had come a messenger was sent to tell him that a large party would be up in two days to hold a grand talk and establish the prices for the ensuing season. From the threatening tone of the message and the excited feelings of the Indians there was every indication of trouble, perhaps bloodshed, if their requests were not complied with.

After deliberating upon the subject, Wickham vowed he would not be browbeaten by a party of beggarly Indians and even contemplated reducing the present rates. Every preparation was made for the council. Huge kettles of coffee, barrels of hard bread, with blankets, scarlet cloth, calico, knives, ammunition, and tobacco— a goodly pile.

At last an Indian is seen riding up at a gallop. He proves to be the White Face Bear, one of the greatest rascals among the Riccarees. The White Face Bear grasps each one of us cordially by the hand and says his people are in sight and will be here shortly; that they have very few women with them, and are for peace, or war if their "reasonable demands" are not complied with. He further declares that he loves the whites and has loaded his fusee with nine balls, intending to fight for us if it comes to the worst.

Matters began to assume a most threatening aspect. The Rees were now in sight, each band by itself, painted and armed to signify that the choice, peace or war, lay with us. Nearer and nearer they came, halting frequently to smoke and deliberate among themselves. It was almost determined at one time to close the gates and defy them to their utmost but on reflection this course was abandoned, as it was our policy to conciliate the savages instead of exasperating them.

I stepped into my room a moment, and turning to go out met the White Face Bear, who said he was going to remain there and keep out all intruders. There were but few small articles lying around and I had no time to object, so leaving him there, hurried to the gate. The Rees were now within a few hundred yards, advancing in close order. Wickham, anxious and uncertain as to the result of the council, with his interpreter, seated himself in front of the Indian room. To begin by showing distrust would provoke and hasten hostilities; to meet them as friends might mollify and quiet them. The latter course was finally resolved upon.

The Indians had halted about fifty yards from the gates, upon which I advanced to meet them with the pipe, always an emblem of peace. I had got to within twenty paces of them when they came on with fierce and startling whoops and yells, brandishing their weapons with menacing gestures. Guns were discharged in every direction, bullets flew around me and buried themselves in the ground close to my feet, and arrows whizzed by in uncomfortable proximity to my head.

A warrior raised his tomahawk to strike me, but his arm was arrested by the Son of the Starry Robe, who, halting in front of me, looked me full in the eye. I met him with a gaze as steady, and the White Parflesh coming up, placed himself by my side and simply remarked, "Your heart is strong." The Indians divided on either side and passed through the gates into the fort. My protectors brought up the rear and we entered the yard together.

Human forms, closely muffled in robes and blankets, were seated forming a hollow square. Sullen looks and fierce scowls greeted the men who brought in the heavy kettles of steaming coffee and placed them before the Bourgeois. The feast and liberal presents accompanying it elicited not the slightest token of interest, much less the usual grunt of approbation. A pause followed. The silence was profound and full of boding. Never did Nature look more radiantly lovely than on this bright day in the golden autumn.

The nerves of all were strung to their highest tension, when the painful silence was broken by the White Parflesh rising to address the assemblage. He said they had all come to greet the Yellow Beard (Wickham) and get him "to make a road for them," *i.e.*, give them advice, which they promised to follow. The White Parflesh had known the traders for many snows and felt drawn towards them. He loved them, and would like to wrap them up in his robe. Would not the Yellow Beard take pity upon his sincere friends, the Rees, and trade easier with them?—give them life, pay a little more for their robes, which their women dressed with so much toil—ten cups of sugar, just for one day only?

Wickham replied that the traders were giving all they could and a further advance in price was impossible, and in Indian fashion begged in his turn that the Rees would take pity upon him and let him travel in the road that his predecessors had made. The Star Robe followed, and continued at length in a similar strain. Other speeches were made to the same effect and a number of handsome robes were thrown or given as evidences of good feeling on the part of the Indians. The Yellow Beard remained inflexible and the Rees changed their tone to one of anger and threatening.

Several hours had thus been consumed, during which we remained sitting in the open air. Wickham, feeling chilly, stepped into the Indian room close at hand to warm himself for a few minutes while the Bear's Ear, an Indian totally destitute of any good qualities, was speaking.

No sooner had he gone in than the Star Robe followed and told him to return and listen to the speeches. He at once resumed his place, when the Pointed Horns commenced a harangue in a most excited manner, gesticulating energetically all the while. At length he paused for a reply, amid a general shout of approbation from his people, when the interpreter, a most contemptible creature named Elien, whose Indian sobriquet of the Jaw fully illustrated his character, took upon himself to tell them (as we subsequently learned) that it was no use talking any longer, that the Yellow Beard's heart was with the Sioux, with whom he had always lived, that he did not like the Rees, and that was why he would not "look at them."

This foolish remark was at once taken up. The Rees, always ripe for mischief when the whites were concerned, became inflamed in an instant and before any one had the slightest suspicion the Bear's Ear sprang to his feet and discharged his fusee into the barrel of bread, blowing it to pieces. In a moment a crowd rushed up, guns were discharged, and the kettles of coffee were overturned and pounded out of all shape. The blankets and cloth were torn into shreds and a couple of our dogs, who unfortunately happened to come in the way, were killed.

Their blood was fully aroused and moments seemed ages of anxious suspense, when several of the chiefs interfered, and aided by the soldiers, with much trouble drove the Indians out. They retired doggedly and halted once, as if they intended to return and finish their work. No sooner was the last one out than the gates were securely shut and barred and we felt relieved from the danger that had threatened.

Wickham was an entire stranger to these Indians. He had been a number of years among the Sioux at Fort Pierre, however, and was well acquainted with Indian character, but unfortunately his interpreter on this occasion was culpably inefficient, or else the difficulty might have been altogether avoided. It was only owing to the fact of dissensions springing up among themselves at the very time they should have been united that prevented the massacre at Fort Atkinson.

The Rees did not visit the American Fur Company's post, and Wickham always insisted—and subsequent events proved him correct—that they were pushed to extreme measures by a renegade white man living among them.

The following day some half dozen Rees made their appearance, riding at full speed toward the fort. As they drew near we recognized the White Parflesh and Iron Bear, and speculation was rife as to the reason of their coming so soon after the difficulty of the day before. Their lowering brows and sullen demeanor soon showed that "their hearts still felt bad towards us," and the question at once asked by them did not help to clear up matters in the least.

The delegation had come up expressly to know why I had given the White Face Bear a bottle of wolf medicine (strychnine) to make all the Indians sick? After some trouble I learned that the Indian in question had returned to the Ree Camp and exhibited a bottle which he said contained wolf medicine, and proclaimed his intention of poisoning all who made themselves obnoxious to him.

At length it occurred to me that my homeopathic medicine-chest was standing on the table in my room when the White Face Bear came in the day before to extend his protection in anticipation of the difficulty which was soon after raised, and I began to suspect the true state of affairs. My suspicions were confirmed when upon examining my medicine-chest I found one of the vials missing.

Everything was then easily explained. I took a portion of the contents of several vials to prove their utter harmlessness and the delegation, after waiting a sufficient time to see what effect it would have upon me, returned to camp relieved of great anxiety, and myself of what might have been a very serious affair attributed to my agency, and how it might have terminated is difficult to say.

The Indians were aware of the appearance and deadly properties of strychnine from its being of late years so extensively used by the trappers to take wolves, almost superseding the old-fashioned trap.[59] It has, nevertheless, to be used stealthily and with exceeding great care as the Indians, with the superstitious notions to which they are prone, and the ravages of the small-pox and cholera brought among them by the white men fresh in their minds, entertain great fears of a general taint and sickness arising from the poisoned carcasses.

Thus happily ended our misunderstanding with the Rees, which at one time bade fair to lead to a most serious, if not disastrous termination, and which beyond doubt was instigated by an unprincipled white man to gratify a personal feeling.

[59] The method employed in poisoning wolves is described by Yellowstone Kelly in his *Memoirs*, 61 and 120–21. The strychnine was placed within the frozen carcass of a buffalo, and from ten to fifty wolves might be found dead around it when the hunter revisited the spot. If the carcass was not frozen, the catch would be smaller, since a small number of wolves would quickly devour it. When frozen, more time was required to chew the meat, and opportunity was thus offered for a larger number to partake of the feast.

INDEX

American Fur Company, rivalry with "Opposition" traders, 10, 168, 171–76; history, 4–6; trading activities, 8–10; retirement, 10, 421; voyage of annual supply boat, 12–47, 341–43; promotes early steamboat travel, 7–10; establishes Fort Berthold, 245–46

Antoine, hunts buffaloes, 211

Arcan, Moise, reports misconduct of Sioux, 318

Arikara (Ree, Riccaree) Indians, history, 25–26; living habits, 26–27; described, 29; removal to Fort Berthold, 33; on Fort Berthold Reservation, 34; raise corn, 122–25; visits, 215; thievish habits, 243; pottery makers, 262; horses stolen, 300–301; Gros Ventres visit, 337–39; quarrel over prices, 348–54

Ash Hollow, battle, 175–76

Ashley, William H., trading activities, 6, 12; defeated by Arikaras, 26

Assiniboine, voyage, 9

Assiniboine Indians, poverty, 35; history, 38; trading visit to, 125–51; lodges, 136, 139; smallpox ravages, 247; visit to Gros Ventres planned, 292; hostilities with Sioux, 292–96, 313

Astor, John J., founds American Fur Company, 4–6

Bad Brave, role in Calumet Dance, 309–12

Baths, Indians take, 54, 63, 240, 278–79

Beans, Indians raise, 125

Bear Hunter, wives, 201; role in Medicine rites, 222–23, 309

Bear-in-the-water, gives feast, 181

Bear's Ear, in council over prices, 352–53